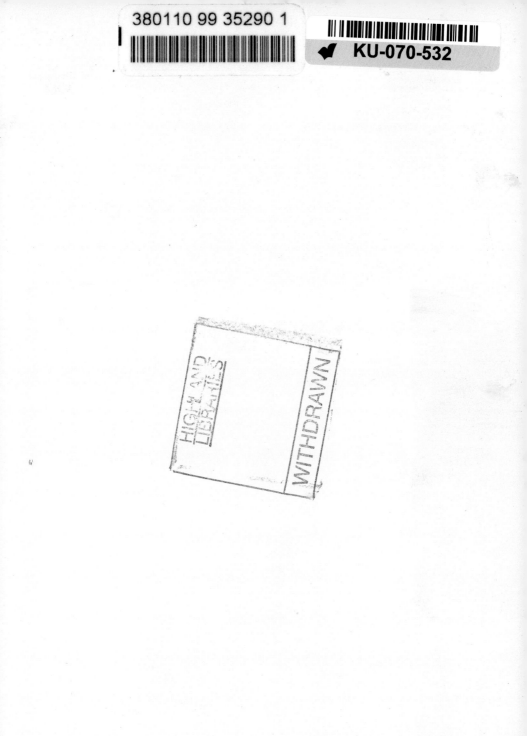

RIKKI FULTON
IS IT THAT TIME ALREADY?

The older one grows,
It has to be said
(And that with a deal of misgiving),
That one actually knows
Rather more people dead
Than are presently actually living.

RKF

RIKKI FULTON

Is it that time already?

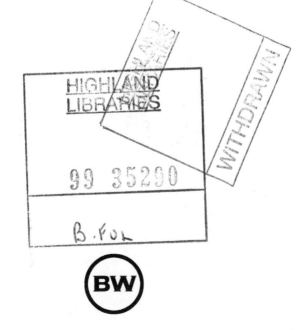

BW

First published 1999
by Black & White Publishing Ltd,
a B&W Publishing imprint
ISBN 1 902927 02 8
Copyright © Rikki Fulton 1999

British Library Cataloguing in Publication Data:
A catalogue record for this book is available
from the British Library.

Cover Picture: *Rikki Fulton* by Thomas Kluge
courtesy of The Scottish National Portrait Gallery

Photographs of Francie & Josie, Rev. I. M. Jolly
courtesy of The Herald and Evening Times Picture Archive

Photograph of Rikki Fulton with Kate and Jake
courtesy of the *Sunday Post*
© D. C. Thomson & Co. Ltd.

Cover design: Winfortune & Associates

Printed by WSOY

CONTENTS

ACKNOWLEDGEMENTS

MY GRATEFUL THANKS to BBC Scotland and London for giving me permission, and the opportunity, to plough through my personal files, so diligently preserved over my fifty years with them.

My thanks and my love to Joyce G. Moffett OBE, my English teacher at Whitehill Secondary School in Dennistoun, for her inspirational teaching, her love of life and words, her enduring friendship, and her encouragement for the writing of this book.

My sincere gratitude to a brilliant young computer consultant called John MacKinnon, who recovered the work I had lost, and thereby enabled me to finish this book.

And most of all my deepest gratitude to my wonderful wife Katie, who has been, is, and always will be, the great and unsurpassed love of my life.

1

IN THE BEGINNING . . .

I WAS BORN on 15th April 1924 on the dot of half-past twelve—I remember that day so well! The district nurse took me from my mother and smacked me on the bum. I didn't cry. I just belted her one.

I was raised in a room-and-kitchen in a tenement at No. 46 Appin Road, Dennistoun, Glasgow E1. When I say I was raised, I mean that we lived on the top landing.

I did my first turn of the stairs when I was only two. It wasn't a success. You know when people have been washing the stairs, they throw out the water: I threw mine through a neighbour's letterbox and nearly drowned her cat. I was never asked to do the stairs again.

When we moved to Riddrie, my primary school was just at the top of the street. Which is why I was always late. Then I went to Whitehill Secondary. I was a member of the local tennis club and played reasonably well—in fact a lot of the members said I should be in Wimbledon, but I didn't fancy the commuting.

Somebody asked what my father did for a living. Answer: he lived with my mother! Actually he was a newsagent and stationer, and he was a brilliant locksmith, except he was always forgetting his keys. There were two other boys there as well, a wee bit older than me. But I never got to know them very well. They were my brothers! To be honest I wasn't sure if I'd come to the right house.

I'm sorry, that can't be right. Would you mind if I started again?

JOHN AND MARGARET

IN THE BEGINNING there were John and Margaret—my Mum and Dad.

John's early life had not been exactly happy. His mother had died when he was a young teenager. His father, perhaps unable to cope with the loss of his wife, took to the bottle and became an irredeemable drunkard.

One dark evening he was relieved of his money and his pain by a footpad on the banks of the Clyde, who bludgeoned him to death and threw his body into the water. So, as the eldest, young John had to take on the task of bringing up his younger brothers Bob and Andrew, and his sister Lizzie who, sadly, looked more like a fourth brother.

John left school at thirteen and was apprenticed to an expert locksmith, and became as highly skilled as his mentor. Later, when he had his own business, he was able to boast that there wasn't a door or a safe he couldn't crack.

There seemed to be some mystery about Margaret MacMillan Moffat's antecedents, for she was never heard even to mention her father or mother at any time throughout her life. She talked about her sisters Lily, Kate and Minnie. Kate and Minnie lived in Lytham St. Anne's near Blackpool, where Kate and her husband Charlie ran a small guest house.

Whatever the mystery of Margaret's background, if mystery there was, the fact remained that she was brought up by her eldest sister Lily, who lived in Bridgeton, not far from John, with her husband Andrew and their only child, also called Andrew. Although young Andrew was technically her nephew, they were more or less of an age, and were brought up together, so she referred to him as her cousin.

Lily was a buxom, seriously corseted lady some years Margaret's senior with vermilion hair which John shrewdly suspected was dyed, and breath that was 97% proof. (I always enjoyed being embraced by her when, as a small boy, my mother took me to visit. Aunt Lily's kisses instilled in me a love of port which I have never lost.)

John was well known and well liked by Lily and her husband, a rather stern and unemotional gentleman who was also John's uncle. John's occasional visits to their home brought him into contact with Margaret, whom he greatly admired, and who eventually lit the candle of his desire to have her as his beloved wife. The complications of their family relationship, however, gave John a constant headache trying to work out exactly what that relationship would be if ever he and Margaret should wed, as he was planning. Margaret was already John's uncle Andrew's sister-in-law! If she and John should marry it would make his wife's sister, Lily—already his aunt—his sister-in-law as well, and perhaps himself not only Margaret's husband, but also her nephew!

It was this strange interrelationship which probably accounted for Margaret's life-long dread of consanguinity. (There was a huge stushie many years later when she discovered that I had taken 'cousin' Andrew's exceedingly dishy daughter to the jiggin'.)

John, however, having failed completely to solve the familial equation, decided to be pragmatic about it. If Margaret showed any interest, and Lily and her husband offered no objection to their friendship, then he would proceed.

But he was aware that it was essential to carry out his approach in a properly traditional manner. Having come to a decision—which was out of character for him—he threw caution to the winds and requested permission to walk out with Margaret.

Aunt Lily and Uncle Andrew were very supportive—they seemed to think it would be good to keep things in the family!

John and Margaret walked out one Sunday afternoon, strolling along the lush swards of Glasgow Green, and down on to the banks of the Clyde.

It was a quiet, charming, entirely proper occasion.

When John delivered his fair companion to her door, well within the time limits of propriety, they assured each other that they had enjoyed their assignation, bade each other a fond, if antiseptic, farewell, and parted.

The following Sunday evening found John waiting somewhat impatiently at the entrance to Margaret's close. Autumn had reached out a tentative finger, the night had turned chilly, and a fog was thickening.

He was nervous, even apprehensive. In fact he had been nervous and apprehensive for nearly six hours now.

For the umpteenth time he conjured his father's gold watch from his waistcoat pocket and peered at it. It was obvious that time was deliberately dragging its feet as he stood at the closemouth chilled and stiff, and wondering why his arrangements had gone so terribly awry. Perhaps she was unwell. Perhaps Aunt Lily and Uncle Andrew had withdrawn their permission for them to walk out together. Perhaps she had misunderstood their 'arrangement'. Perhaps . . . ? Perhaps she had just forgotten!

It was nearly half-past nine by his watch, and he was becoming increasingly concerned. He sighed and watched his breath turn to a vaporous wraith. Three times he had headed up the stairs to her door, knuckles raised, only to have his courage desert him.

He went over the arrangements in his mind for the hundredth time.

Sunday, three-thirty, at the closemooth. She couldn't have misunderstood. Especially when they had had what could only be called a practice-run the previous Sunday. Well, there was no mistake on *his* part. He had been there on the dot, and here it was. Sunday, closemooth, half-past *nine*, b'Jeez! (His favourite outburst when he was exasperated.) What could possibly have happened?

Suddenly through the swirling fog he could just make out a couple walking arm-in-arm up the tenemented street towards him.

He strained his eyes, trying to pierce the murk, and as the couple came under the cold, unnatural gaslight of the street-lamp, the lantern of his jaw dropped almost below his pristine, starched white collar as he found himself facing a nightmare scenario.

It was *she*! The lovely Margaret. No one could mistake that tiny, doll-like figure, the sweet face framed in its auburn halo.

But who was the monster at her side who clutched her arm, his head bent intimately towards her? John was only some five feet five inches in height, while the man with Margaret bore a worrying resemblance to the Irish giant, Finn MacCoul.

With scant regard for possible injury to his person, he confronted them as they arrived at the closemouth. After all, he thought, if the worst came to the worst, he could offer him money.

'Whaur wis ye?' he demanded, aggrieved. 'Ah've been waitin' fur ye fur gaun on fower hoors.'

Margaret gaped at him in surprise.

'Waiting for *me*? Why on earth were you waiting for me?'

Finn MacCoul tensed into combat mode. 'Will Ah thump 'im, Maggie?' he enquired.

'Don't be ridiculous, Albert,' she chided. Men! She could eat them for breakfast. 'I asked you a question, John,' she demanded. 'Why should you be waiting for me?'

John, an inarticulate man at the best of times, was not equal to the task of pleading his case.

'Well,' he quavered. 'Ah thought we hud a—a—*arrangement!*'

6

Margaret shook her head in bewilderment. 'Arrangement?' she queried. 'What arrangement?'

'Well,' said John, all wounded reasonableness, 'were we no' oot thegether last Sunday?'

'We were,' she replied icily. 'How could I forget? We walked round and round Glasgow Green for two hours, and you never even asked me if I would like a wee refreshment.' (A complaint that would be repeated throughout their married life.)

John was hurt by her unreasonableness. 'Well,' he said, spreading his hands, 'ye only hud tae say!'

'It's not the lady's place to say,' she pointed out.

Finn McCoul was puzzled by the exchange and was becoming restless.

'Are ye sure ye don't want me tae thump 'im, Maggie?' he asked.

Margaret ignored him. 'What is this arrangement you keep talking about?' she asked John. 'You can't be talking about tonight. You didn't ask me to go out with you tonight.'

John knew in his heart that there was one last chance to put forward his final argument to this jury of one. He took a deep breath.

'Aye, well, Ah know Ah didnae exactly *ask* ye, Margaret, but Ah thought that—well—seein' we were oot thegether *last* Sunday—ye wid huv understood that—that Ah wantit us tae go oot thegether *this* Sunday—an'—an'—an' *every* Sunday—fae noo on. . . .'

His voice fell away, and a quiver came to his lip.

Margaret looked at this honest, straightforward, emotional young man for a long time, then, turning to her escort she said: 'Goodnight, Albert. Thank you for a lovely evening. . . . *John will see me to the door.*'

My mother and father were married on Friday 27th December 1907.

3

SURPRISES IN STORE

1908 WAS AN interesting year. Edward VII was king, and the celebrated Herbert Henry Asquith was Prime Minister. The Old Age Pension came into force for everybody over seventy, the rate being five shillings per week, and seven-and-sixpence for a married couple. Winston Churchill married his beloved Clementine, and the hit songs of the day were 'Shine On Harvest Moon', and 'Oh, Oh, Antonio'.

But the most interesting event for John and Margaret by a long chalk was when Mr. and Mrs. John Fulton moved into their first home, a room-and-kitchen at No. 55 Walter Street, Dennistoun, Glasgow. Space was at a premium, but it was a start, and it was a good choice. Haghill School was just next door, and, should they have a family, their children would not have far to travel for their education, and, as it transpired, it was also convenient for handing play-pieces through the railings of the playground.

Margaret had been a clerkess in the office of a tea company, and John was employed by the monstrous Singer's Factory in Clyde-bank, which necessitated a hazardous journey between his home and his work, calling as it did for a bewildering safari by tramcar, and a need to change from one route to another. It meant rising at 5.30 each morning for both of them, but neither seemed to mind. John was used to it, and Margaret was happy to direct her tireless energy to caring for her husband and running their home.

Even at this early stage it wasn't too difficult to guess who was going to be the dominant partner, and Margaret's restless ambition had already surfaced. She had been in Walter Street for less than five minutes before she began to crave for something better. She was the prime mover in everything they did. Her 'wee brain', as she referred to it, never stopped working to think of ways to advance their lifestyle.

John on the other hand, sought only peace and quiet, his own chair, a good tea, and a newspaper.

Happily, Margaret had found someone she could really talk to. Mrs. Armstrong was a large, warm-hearted, worldly lady who owned the local dairy. She had taken an immediate liking to the young couple in Walter Street, and soon became their guide, philosopher, and very dear friend. She listened patiently, and with understanding, as Margaret spread out the stall of her hopes and aspirations. It was obvious that John couldn't expect to get very far in his job. There were no career ladders to climb at Singer's, and few respectable married women sought work—unless, of course, they were working for themselves.

Now there was a thought!

It was Mrs. Armstrong who suggested the idea of possibly taking over a small local shop, if and when something suitable became available. Margaret was enthralled by the idea. It would be hard work certainly, but with Mrs. Armstrong's help and guidance, she was sure it could work out, especially for John who would be able to say goodbye to Clydebank.

There was, of course, just one small snag—money! How could two young people, only recently married, find the necessary funding for a project like this?

John didn't even stop to consider the scheme. Even in the few years they had been together, he had learned that the easiest way to reach an accord with his wife was just to nod his head. If Margaret thought it was the furrow to plough, he would go along with it.

But there was something that demanded precedence. Margaret had discovered the explanation for her added weight.

After two years of marriage, she was five months pregnant!

As the weeks moved rapidly towards the birth of their first-born, visits from the district nurse (a calling which invoked much giggling from children, for which their mothers would chide them for indulging in 'dirty talk') became more and more frequent.

In the early hours of the morning of the first day of December 1910, as Margaret endeavoured to cope with what, to her, was the entirely disgusting task of giving birth, the nurse noted with some concern that the father-to-be was in a state of considerable anxiety. She watched him prowl restlessly between the window and the kitchen bed like a tiger on heat, and sought to reassure him.

'There, there,' she crooned. 'There's nothing at all to worry about, Mr. Fulton. It's the most natural, the most beautiful, the most wonderful thing in the world. Your wife's going to be just fine, I promise you.'

John stared at her as if she was brain-damaged.

'Aye,' he pointed out. 'It's all very well fur hur, *but who's gonnae make ma piece?*'

Young John turned out to be a fine, healthy baby, and Margaret sighed with relief that her duty had been done, her final sally directed straight at her husband. *'And you thought it was difficult getting to Clydebank!'*

Two months later the call came from Mrs. Armstrong that there was a shop for sale in Roebank Street, only a few hundred yards from where they lived. The shop, it seemed, sold practically everything from newspapers to hardware, drysaltery and stationery. A bank loan was swiftly arranged, guaranteed by Mrs. Armstrong, followed by an extraordinary decision by John and Margaret that required real courage and determination. They let out their home in Walter Street to, of all people, the young bank manager who had arranged the loan. They literally set up a temporary home in the back shop of 28 Roebank Street, furnished with only a double bed, a chair and their recently born offspring.

Margaret diligently watched over her child and attended her customers while John continued to travel to Clydebank until they could be sure the business was viable. Happily, it proved to be so. Margaret decided that the shop was prospering and it was time for her return to their home in Walter Street, and for John to take over the business and free himself at last from Clydebank. The irony was that baby John, who had spent the first two years of his life in the Roebank Street back shop, grew up and went to work in it for most of his life.

My father had a wonderfully dry sense of humour and he was popular behind the counter in Roebank Street, although we didn't hear all that much of it at home. My favourites from his stories have always included the man who came in seeking an *Illustrated Weekly* (now defunct), but asked for an 'Ulcerated Weekly', to which my father replied: 'Dae ye waant some ointment tae go wi' it?'

A woman who came into the shop regularly during the war when many household goods were in short supply, had paid daily visits to my father in a quest for toilet rolls. He was very sorry, he told her, using the shopkeeper's constant excuse: 'we're jist waitin' on them comin' in.' The poor lady howled in anguish. 'Oh, Mr. Fulton! Oh well, *Ah'll jist have to wait!*'

Much earlier in his career as a shopkeeper he served another local lady whose order was for 'A penny's worth of Epsom Salts and a *Sunday Mail*. My father dutifully passed over the two items. The lady looked at the packet of Epsom Salts in wonder. 'Oh my,' she said. 'D'ye get all that for a penny?' 'Aye,' said my father, 'D'ye waant another Mail?'

One customer seeking a Christmas card arrived in the shop dragging her female offspring who was howling: *'Ah waant a wee Jesus! Ah waant a wee Jesus!'* To which the mother, already weary of the child's yowling, surrendered with: *'Aw, fur Christ's sake gie 'er a wee Jesus!'*

*   *   *

It was another six years before the family complement increased, and for a second time John and Margaret appeared to have been taken unawares.

The new arrival in 1916 was Jim, who was honoured with a middle name, that of Moffat after his mother. He later came to be called 'Sunny Jim' because of his bright, handsome face and his uninhibited laughter.

At this point Margaret decided that the family was complete. She had already taken another upwardly mobile step by moving their home from 55 Walter Street all the way to 46 Appin Road which was just a hundred yards or so round the corner, figuring that it was better than no step at all. So, what with a sound business, a good home, two lovely boys and a compliant husband, she had to admit that progress had indeed been made and the family well and truly, and finally, established.

Eight years later, however, the members of the Fulton household were in deep shock.

Margaret was pregnant again!

The production of their children seemed to be a constant surprise to them. It was almost as if they couldn't understand who or what was causing it. Whatever, the arrival of an unanticipated, and unwanted, third child was to bring serious unhappiness for Margaret.

4

FIRST STEPS

AT TWELVE-THIRTY P.M., on Tuesday the fifteenth of April 1924, I made my very first entrance—or should I say exit-cum-entrance?—on the world stage, just in time for lunch. I found myself projected into the reluctant hands of a group of three men who were ruled by a dynamic little woman of less than sixty inches in height who cared for, dominated and guarded her tribe with the ferocity of a wildcat. It was a firmly, and finally, established family. No addition had been expected or desired.

My birthplace was the kitchen-bed with a huge, clumsy feather mattress, like a monstrous sack of potatoes, which my mother somehow managed to turn over by herself when she was making the bed. My cot was a family heirloom made of splendid mahogany in which both John and Jim had slept as babies. It stood against the wall between the range and the kitchen bed so that John and Margaret could keep an eye on their latest, unexpected, offspring.

For a room-and-kitchen, 46 Appin Road was capacious. A scrubbed table with large leaves on either side occupied the centre of the kitchen surrounded by four kitchen chairs, and a pulley heavy with newly washed clothes swaying above it. On one side of the range was my father's chair, a strange contraption covered in brown corduroy which could be turned into an uncomfortable single bed but was never used as such, and an ancient rocking chair opposite. Probably another heirloom. A tiny sink at the kitchen window was fitted with a single swan-neck tap able only to deliver cold water. Hot water was achieved with the aid of a huge black kettle that sat steaming permanently on the range. Above the range two gas mantles hissed as they produced their eerie, depressing, sickly greenish-yellow light when daylight had gone.

A decent-sized square hallway accessed a long narrow bathroom with 'all mod cons' including a bath of some size, which, alas, many of our neighbours mistakenly assumed was for the purpose of storing coal. The 'Good Room', as the parlour was referred to, was spacious enough to house a large suite—a three-seater settee and two armchairs upholstered with green cut moquette—and a monstrous aspidistra at the window, its colour matching the slatted venetian blinds. The room was kept dust-free and constantly polished in expectation of visitors but, otherwise, never used apart from the cupboard bed where my brothers slept.

My first visitors were my father and brothers. John was now fourteen and Jim was eight. They crouched over me, and stared with disbelief as if I was a parcel that had been sent to the wrong address. Having come to a decision about what it was they were looking at, they then stared equally intensely at my mother, almost accusingly, wondering perhaps if she had obtained some secret potion from a gypsy woman at the door.

My father, in particular, was in shock. He had been in shock from the moment he had been told of Margaret's unexpected condition. I got the impression that he had begun to wonder about the virgin birth.

Later, when I was old enough to think about it, I had a sneaking suspicion that I had not been planned.

But I hadn't taken long to find an answer. With the front side of my beautiful mahogany cot down, it made a splendid podium, and I made full use of the facility.

The dance routines were totally improvisational as were the songs, which I sang in a language that only I could understand. My first and only composition carried a rather unusual lyric which went something like: 'I BEN TOOOOOOOOOO SWEP!' It was a short song! I also fell down rather a lot which they seemed to enjoy, and I unintentionally performed my Big Finish with a pratfall that caused the demise of my father's top hat. My audience, particularly my father, did not react as warmly as I had hoped, so I instinctively did what all clowns do—which was to move on very quickly to the next joke. This time I smashed one of the most popular records of the time called 'Yes, We Have No Bananas!' A deafening silence had followed the destruction of these items but at least I had caught the attention of my audience, even if their reaction was only to glare at me and pick up what was left of my props.

Of them all, however, it was my mother who had been most shaken by this glitch in her carefully planned life. It had taken her sixteen years to reach the present desirable status for herself and her family, and had presumed that 'That Sort of Thing' was well and truly behind her. Now, it seemed, her plans for the creation of a properly established family were in serious disarray.

Her answer to the problem was to have a nervous breakdown.

By this time my mother was forty and deeply concerned about having a child so late in life. She was convinced that at such an age most decent men and women would have long since cast aside such disgusting practices. Once word had got out, her neighbours and friends would shun her, and bear witness to her wantonness. Henceforward she would be regarded with pity and loathing. Already she was sure people were talking about her, staring and pointing a finger at her in the street.

Within some months of my arrival my mother took to her bed, unable to eat, unable to cope with everyday life. Even now I can see the vision of the tiny woman, once a bundle of energy and initiative, standing upright on the kitchen-bed in a red dressing-gown, staring at me with bleak, hostile eyes.

It took many months for her to return to something resembling normality, but the scar had been left and, although I wasn't aware of it at the time, I was the cause and the effect of her suffering. As a child, I became confused by her erratic mood swings; at times I would be crushed to her bosom, hearing her declare fiercely: 'I love you! I just *love* you!'; on other occasions, all hell would break loose. It was as if the trauma of my arrival had made her wish her newly born child harm, hoping that it would be taken from her in some way, so destroying the evidence of her profligacy.

5

ALMOND STREET

I remember another garden,
    A sea of grass and weeds waving in the wind,
    The lawn an untidy haircut
    With a wooden edge to keep it in its place.
Herein my mother trod,
    Her tiny form reaching heavenward
    To weave her magic spell of rope,
    And hang her dripping wet signal to her Mondays.

An apple tree,
    Struggling in a corner,
    Unaware of its humble origins or unexpected planting,
    Yet growing anyway.
A fence, once resolute and proud,
    Now weary, wondering which way to lean.
    Things of green, unmarked, unnamed,
    Tended with hope in the constant absence of bloom.

Oddfellow stones,
    Gathered in gregarious clusters without pattern or design,
    Marking the route of some forgotten pathway,
    Leading nowhere.
And an open kitchen window,
    Through which redolent fragrances danced in the air
    To the enthusiastic tympani of pots and pans
    And the applause of chattering eggs, bacon and potato scones,
Composing their symphony to the garden
    Wherein faded the bloom of my childhood.

                                RKF.

I WAS ABOUT THREE when we moved to Riddrie.

As it happened, this was to be the final act of my mother's upward progression.

Riddrie was a quiet and pleasant place to live and had been laid out with some thought, even artistry. The Blackhill Bowling Club formed a semicircle, its straight edge abutting Cumbernauld Road with Tay Crescent its curve from which all the streets, named after rivers, fanned out. Earn Street, Almond Street, Tummel Street, Dochart Street, Tilt Street and Gala Street sweeping round in another curve at the top. Almond Street was the longest street in the scheme, cutting through Gala Street to join the banks of the Monkland Canal, and coming to a stop at the main entrance to Riddrie Primary School.

We were amazed at the amount of space we found in our new home compared to Appin Road. It was a four-apartment house. No. 5 Almond Street, Riddrie, Glasgow E1. Even the address signalled our upward move. It had a kitchen, living room and bedroom downstairs, and a bedroom, Good Room and bathroom upstairs. I simply couldn't believe that we were actually going to live in a real house. No longer would it be necessary to descend three flights of stairs to play in a back court, or follow Jim to the great uncultivated wilderness at the bottom of Appin Road. Most of all, it seemed like paradise to have a garden back and front, although none of the family seemed to have any botanical inclination. Occasionally one of us would go out and cut the grass with a blunt pair of shears and poke disinterestedly at the soil, but Kew Gardens it certainly wasn't.

Leslie Bond lived at No. 9, the next house but one. Leslie and I were almost exactly the same age and immediately became close friends. Our relationship, however, was not exactly based on mutual respect and trust. We were just as likely to 'drop each other in it' as not, depending on the circumstances and advantages to be gained.

Riddrie Primary School was a red brick building standing at the very top of Almond Street and reaching down to the notorious Monkland canal—now the M8 motorway. Over the years there was a continuous outcry against this abandoned waterway since it had abruptly ended the lives of a number of children foolish enough to play on its banks.

Much to the alarm of our parents, it was often the stage on which Leslie and I played out our fantasies. The old towpaths became the shores of faraway places, the planks at the rusting locks were the only passages across deep ravines. With hills and valleys aplenty, the brave White Hunter and Jungle Jim held sway here when free from the eagle eye of their families.

When we were inducted into Riddrie Primary we took it as only natural that we would be placed in the same classroom. Leslie, however, was sitting directly behind me, and, at some point I turned to speak to him. For an answer he poked a friendly finger in my eye. To our dismay, my screams resulted in what the teacher saw as bad blood between the two boys and we were assigned to separate classes, a decision we considered to be an infringement of our civil liberties. We dismissed it, however, as a complete lack of understanding of our particular code of friendship.

We drove our tricycles up to the school gates, escorted by our mothers, and made for our separate classrooms. The Mums took the tricycles to and from our homes at the required times. Three o'clock was the highlight of our day and, happy to be reunited, we would hurtle, legs astride, down the precipitous slalom that is Almond Street.

*   *   *

If my mother had in fact made a wish at the time of my birth, it could be said that it had been very nearly granted. When I was about seven years old I was stricken with an illness which almost despatched me. It is possible that my mother might have seen this as God's answer to a hideous prayer, and then tried fiercely to make up for it.

Tuberculosis was the sick-bed-fellow of diphtheria and cancer in those days and was a widespread scourge regarded with dread. My mother insisted it was simply the aftermath of mumps, and, indeed there was a lump on the right side of my neck the size of a free-range egg which seemed to give credence to the explanation. Whatever the problem was she felt responsible, and was prepared to see it through. It was she who had to arrange the visits to the Royal Infirmary at regular intervals to have the poisonous lump pierced and drained by what seemed a painfully primitive process. It was she who carried out the daily dressing, staying with me when I became depressed, feeling like an outcast as I often did. I had become an unhappy, sickly child, lacking energy and interest, pulling myself up the seemingly never-ending climb to Riddrie School, with a disgusting flannel covering a gauze smeared with evil-smelling Iodex ointment.

The school holidays, however, provided the opportunity for my convalescence, and were ample reward for such a miserable time.

My mother and I were ensconced in a delightful hotel in Eaglesham where I was 'built up' on good country eggs, fresh milk, butter and milk puddings. Every day we strolled round the hotel grounds or through the delightful village, and breathed in the good clean air of the countryside while my father commuted daily from the shop.

If my mother had indeed harboured unkind thoughts about the consequences of the birth of her third child, they were gone and I was alive and well.

I never knew what the illness was until 1954 when I had turned thirty and was working with the BBC in London. I had been working very hard over a long period, coping with four series of programmes every week, three on radio (one of which I wrote with a partner) and one on television. I decided to go for a check-up in a London hospital, hoping that all was well, but in particular to find a way to get some sleep.

The doctor gave me a thorough examination in the course of which he noticed the scar on my neck, and felt the calcified gland.

'I see you've had tuberculosis,' he said casually. It was an unexpected diagnosis after all these years and made me just a little concerned. However, he declared me tired but reasonably fit, and prescribed pills which would put me to sleep and others to waken me up to face another long day. As I left he just happened to mention that there was a good side to my having had the illness. It had made me immune to the dreadful disease for life.

The memory of that period came flooding back and I recalled that William Dunn, a third member of the triumvirate formed with Leslie and me, and who lived directly opposite to me, had contracted and died of it.

Obviously I had been lucky.

*   *   *

Schooldays are remembered with either hatred, affectionate nostalgia or indifference. In my own case I have to choose indifference. I can't boast of being academically inclined; my interests were outside the school and inside my head. As is the case with so many people, my education began when I left school. From that moment I was free to seek whatever knowledge interested me, and spent quite a lot of money building up a fair reference library; something I have enjoyed doing ever since.

In some ways the teachers in Riddrie Primary were an odd group of men and women who had passed the joy of youth. It was almost as if the education authorities deliberately chose a mixture of staring eyes, long pointed noses or outsize Adam's apples. All the teachers under whose charge I was, had some or all of such characteristics and I can't recall any of them having any great warmth—except one. Miss McLaughlan. I think I liked her because she reminded me of my mother. Both wore their hair in the same popular 'ear-phone' style. My one complaint was the occasional rap over the knuckles, or, as I put it to my mother—'She gives us the belt with the pointer!'

School was fun if you had the good fortune to be given the privilege of cleaning the blackboard, or collecting the milk money, or acting as 'guardian of the classroom's sliding door'. Such a boy would be required to sit at the front seat nearest the door, no matter what his intellectual status. All other boys and girls were allocated their seating positions in strict accordance with the marks achieved at the Friday Test.

A mixed class, of course, brought a natural interest in the different genders. The young beaux had their dreams. The libidos, like the Kraken, were waking. And it was often the brightest girls— those who occupied the sacred seats at the back of the class—who were regarded with awe and seen to be the most attractive, causing the young stags yearning and heartbreak. But as the seven-year stint passed, it was curious, and sad sometimes, to have to watch our dream-girl slowly turn into a scrum-half.

One surprising upturn in a later primary class had to do with physical violence of all things. This I abhorred, mainly because I was very afraid of being hurt.

We had a dangerous bully in our class called Machen. There were two brothers who hailed from Peterhead, and the smaller— and he was very small—of the two was a bundle of terrifying aggression known as 'Puggy' because he sported a completely flat nose. It was assumed that his nose had been flattened in one of his many fights.

The two boys wore boots of soft leather and little suits of heather-coloured material which we used to think of as the 'orphan's uniform'.

Puggy had held the class in a grip of terror from the moment he entered the school, and this was forever being translated into bloody noses and black eyes for whoever dared to incur his displeasure any time a teacher left the class.

For some reason I had never had a confrontation with him. Probably because I made a point of keeping out of his way. But one day I found myself beside him and another boy who was getting the rough edge of Puggy's tongue as a prelude to yet another punch-up. He must have mistaken my expression of surprised horror for one of threatening anger, and to everyone's amazement *he backed off*, hands outspread in supplication, pleading with me not to engage.

There was silence from the entire class as I rose from my seat. I was twice as tall as he was and more. Puggy virtually walked backwards, his hands still in surrender mode.

I didn't really know what to do next. I had never been in a fight, and had no idea how to hit anyone. I scowled a lot as he backed further and further towards the window. Someone thoughtfully shut the classroom door. There was no way he could escape. His brother stood in amazed silence in a corner with his mouth open.

I warned him what I would do if I saw him hurt any one of 'my friends' ever again.

I was as astonished as everyone else as he nodded his head and crossed his heart and went to his desk. From that moment there was peace in our classroom, and any boy (or girl come to that— Puggy wasn't sexist) had only to call my name and Puggy would be in Peterhead before I had taken a step.

I did not understand what had happened or how, but I had no time to try to work it out. I went to the lavatory, shaking and perspiring, and was sick.

There was violence too from another source in those days. The teachers themselves.

The discipline demanded in a primary classroom was positively mediaeval. The classroom of some forty boys and girls had to sit up straight and rigid in their seats with arms folded tightly across the chest. Talking was strictly forbidden.

I have an abiding memory of one of our male teachers, Mr. Anderson, calling me to the front of the class. I had no idea what I had done, but he insisted that I had been talking—a heinous crime indeed—and I had to be punished.

The punishment from a male teacher was inevitably crossed hands. There was no appeal, no evidence for the defence, out came the belt. The great thick leather tongue of torture. I had no option. I laid one hand on the other, palms up and he brought the leather down with truly painful force. He paused for a few seconds, glancing at my wrists. He would be in trouble if he scarred the tender part of the wrist.

Satisfied he was in the clear, he gave me the second one. I put my hands behind my back. He signalled to me to offer my cupped hands for a third. I refused and kept my hands behind my back.

'I think I've had enough, sir,' I said bravely.

His eyebrows went up and his eyes narrowed.

'Is that so?' he said. '*Hands.*'

I refused.

The teacher lost his temper completely. '*Have I to drag you to the cloakroom?*' he screamed, his voice reaching falsetto and his rather protruding Adam's apple bobbing up and down.

I wasn't at all clear as to why he felt he might have to take me to the cloakroom, so I thought it better to take the punishment and get it over.

I offered my hands already blood-red and tingling. He brought the belt down with unbelievable force, but, as he did so, I disengaged my hands. He yelled with pain as he inadvertently belted his own private parts and almost castrated himself.

He was on sick leave for almost two weeks.

I was very upset about it!

6

THE PINCHERS

LESLIE'S MOTHER was the epitome of self-assurance. She took every opportunity to declare that she was 'not bringing up children—but bringing up men'. And, indeed, the two boys were made to work for their food and board.

She was generous with soups and puddings, and with giving the neighbours the benefit of her knowledge and culinary skills. This generosity, however, was not always appreciated by the recipients. One morning she spotted the youngest of the three girls who were immediately next door.

'Did you enjoy the pudding I gave you yesterday?' she asked.

The little girl thought for a moment. 'Oh is that what it was?' she said, remembering. 'Mummy put it down the lavatory!'

From that day, Leslie's mother decided the neighbours could look after themselves.

Leslie's father had a garden shed which was our headquarters in which we made our plans for further devilment. The gang grew as boys from other streets joined us. The initiation test was to navigate the back gardens of some twenty-eight houses in total darkness. The damage done to plants, flower beds, cold frames, and manicured lawns was horrific. Leslie almost had a leg amputated when he jumped a fence into an abandoned gas boiler.

To say nothing of Blackhill Bowling Club!

One dark night, just for the sake of variety, we crept on to one of the exquisite greens and could hear the members busy at the bridge tables, happily bidding 'three-no-trump' and 'grand slams' while we were collecting the stones from the paths and carefully laying them on the green nearest the clubhouse to form three giant-sized letters.

'CLP' it shouted. No, it didn't stand for the Carntyne Labour Party. It was the acronym which identified Our Gang—the 'Clothes Line Pinchers', an active cell of the main gang whose purpose was to carry out sweeping raids throughout the scheme, rearranging the washing lines of our long-suffering neighbours who had been brave enough to leave their washing out overnight.

Ah, how many bright Tuesday mornings during the long hot summers echoed the calls of desperate housewives from their back gardens.

'Coo-oo-ee, Mrs. Dale. Hev you got mai washing?'

'No, wheh?'

'Cos Ai think Ai've got yours!'

*　　　*　　　*

Leslie, although he was always voted in as Head of the Gang, was seriously accident-prone. The Bonds' back garden had a slight rise from the path where a forest of large blackcurrant bushes had lived for some time. With the help of Leslie's brother, Arthur, we had sought to contrive our own funicular by using an old zinc bath tub with a clothes rope tied to a pipe at the bathroom window and strung through one of the handles and on to a clothes pole on the lawn.

Arthur and I were not prepared to have a go unless the thing had been tested and, as usual, Leslie was the first to do the test-run. He climbed out of the bathroom window, grasped the handle of the old bath with both hands and plunged into space. As the clothes-line snapped, Leslie dropped neatly into the middle of the

26

blackcurrants. For the umpteenth time, he was helped indoors and had to have a few days in bed to recover.

In the winter, snow and ice used to cover one of our favourite play areas. The Riddrie Knowes—now seriously built up—was where the youth of Riddrie and parents and small children would slide down a steep incline on rather doubtful terrain. The sledges were bought or home-made—Leslie and friends had to make do with home-made.

Not surprisingly, Leslie was first on the track and went down the hill at speed with only the moonlight to show the way. All we heard was a strange groan as we lost sight of our good friend. Either he had not noticed it, or he was unable to avoid it, but he landed in a deep trench and managed to crack a number of ribs.

We all had to forego the fun and games, get him home and call a doctor.

7

TOGO'S PROMISE

MY MOTHER HAD LONG SINCE come to terms with her phobia of having produced a child at the ripe old age of forty. More than anything the move to Riddrie had helped greatly to settle her. Her neighbours were delightful, friendly people. When she went out for her groceries and took me with her, they were always happy to have a gossip on the way. 'So this is your baby, eh?' they would say. 'A fine looking wee lad, and you keep him so immaculate.'

This was true. My sartorial elegance was a mark of her caring pride, and was mentioned frequently, as she meant it to be. To everyone in the street the appearance of the children indicated the status of their parents, particularly the mothers.

I can remember clearly a little summer suit of navy-blue and white striped cotton, which an admiring neighbour had said made me look 'a right wee toff'. These clothes were ever more to be referred to as my wee toffs. I was even despatched to a little friend's birthday party attired in a rather snazzy chocolate-brown flannel suit. By itself this would have been considered *haute couture*, but my mother insisted on having a swish cream-coloured, bespoke silk waistcoat with pearl buttons to go with it, specially made by Mrs. Lockhart in Gala Street, who was the local dressmaker.

When I was approaching five years of age, and had only been

at school a few months, Dr. Smith—our physician God—decreed that my tonsils were to be removed, and since my parents had forked out the handsome sum of five shillings they were not prepared to challenge his prognosis.

When we first came to Riddrie, I had slept with my Mum and Dad and dreamed peaceful dreams in this parental garrison. One of my warmest memories of childhood is of the mornings. My father had to rise early in winter and summer to open the shop at six o'clock, to serve the needs of the steady stream of men on their way to start their long shifts at the huge Blochairn steel works, and my mother would rise before him to make his porridge from the oats she had steeped overnight. I would sit up beside him in the big, cosy bed, watching as he devoured nearly all the porridge, and waiting for him to hand over the plate with only a few spoonfuls of the warm, sweet milk with creamy crumbs of porridge floating in it for me to finish. But on this occasion they hadn't told me that it was going to be an unusually special day, and that the doctor was coming to make me feel better. There was nothing to worry about, my mother assured me, sparing the gory details perhaps for later.

But I was concentrating on a project of my own.

I had inherited a strange cat made out of black velvet and stuffed with horse hair. It boasted black thread whiskers and little button eyes, but of legs, paws and tail there was none. This strange cuddly object was in partnership with an ancient teddy bear which had been handed down through heaven knows how many generations.

I loved them both very dearly, and my most secret wish at this early age was that these much loved inanimate creatures could be given the breath of life. I had never divulged this deep longing, but now I confided it to my mother. She was something of a religious pragmatist, and, without seeming to consider my request nonsensical or out of the question, she fielded my question expertly, and suggested that the way forward would be to petition my Maker.

On the night before the tonsillectomy I knelt at the side of the big bed, and made my plea to God that my strange little cat and ancient teddy bear would come alive. With the kind of conviction that only children have I was convinced that He had heard me, and my prayer would be answered.

The next day I was laid on cushions on the table in the living room and covered with blankets. In the comfort of your own home, as they say. Dr. Smith told me that he was going to show me a new way to go to sleep that only *he* could do because it was magic. He placed a helmeted frame with a towel embedded in it over my face, and told me to take deep breaths and count each one. I can still remember the sweet smell of the chloroform and watching the little red and green Christmas trees shooting up through the blackness as I wandered into the Unknown.

Recovery from the operation was in my mother and fathers' bed downstairs once again. My small stature at the time made me regard this as 'The Big Bed' although it was, in fact, an ordinary double bed with a huge stuffed mattress which my wee mother had to pound and turn each day. I have no way of knowing what a modern tonsillectomy is like, but I am witness to the fact that it was no picnic in 1929. When I came round, the pain in my throat was worse than I had ever known. In spite of my awful discomfort and difficulty in speaking, the first thing I asked was whether God had worked the miracle as arranged. Sadly, the answer was a disappointing negative, but my mother pointed out that I hadn't given God much time to make arrangements, and explained that He had a lot of people to look after and was very busy.

Some three days later the pain began to subside, and I was able to quench the awful thirst that burned in my throat. I lay in the big bed, unhappy and disappointed that God had ignored my plea, when, suddenly, the bedroom door opened and my father walked in wearing his hat and coat and a huge grin. He put his hand in his coat pocket and, as if by magic, produced the most beautiful little puppy I had ever seen. He was a little fox terrier with a jet black coat, little white spats and a brilliant white shield on his chest. My father put him on the bed and he scampered around like a thing demented, barking his happiness at becoming one of the family.

According to my mother God had indeed heard my prayer and answered it in his own inimitable way.

I had been asked to choose a name for the sixth member of the family, and the only name I knew for a dog was Rover, but the family suggested that perhaps Rover was not a name for such a tiny little handful, and John came up with the perfect name. He had read of a Japanese Admiral by the name of Count Togo Heihachiro, but, not surprisingly, we called him simply Togo.

He turned out to be a real character if ever there was one, and a randy little so-and-so. When I think of the way my wife Katie and I have protected our lovely little Westies over the years, I can't help remembering how self-reliant Togo used to be. He lived a happy, carefree existence. Confident and eminently resourceful, he took his pleasure where he would. Often he would stay away for days, happily cadging food from neighbours who had come to know him well from previous visits, then proceeding on his way to meet the girlfriends.

We took him with us on holiday to Largs one year. My mother and father had taken a self-catering holiday in a tenement block right opposite the pier. The room had a huge bed and I was still small enough to sleep between them. I loved sitting up like my father, reading *The Children's Newspaper* by gaslight, knowing that Togo and I would be off to the bakery early in the morning for the five crispy rolls which, along with hard-boiled eggs, would make our breakfast after the porridge. It is difficult enough to believe that Togo had such complete freedom at home; let out by himself whenever he felt like it, never knowing the tug of a dog-lead during the whole of his life. But I often wonder how he was so calmly allowed to follow the same routine when staying in a strange town. Togo's wish to go for a wander over the grass plots of Largs, or run after sticks thrown into the sea by total strangers, or, what was more to his taste, hunt up the local talent, were met with a confidently open door. But on this particular morning he disappeared while I was in the bakery. I couldn't find him any-where. I panicked completely and ran to tell my Mum and Dad. Breakfast was of no interest to any of us. We tried to eat but we weren't in the mood for food. All we wanted was to find Togo.

The three of us scoured the streets of Largs, and I knew Largs like the back of my hand, but of Togo there was no sign.

Lunchtime passed, but I couldn't eat anything. I was devastated, crying my eyes out especially when my Mum and Dad suggested that I would have to be brave, and accept that something might have happened to him. Darkness fell and the illuminations and street lighting cast a melancholy signal. I wanted to go out again and continue the search, but my Mum and Dad, who were as upset as I was, insisted we tried to get some rest, hoping that someone might have seen him and put him in the hands of the police.

I couldn't, or didn't want to, go to sleep. I was in pieces at being separated from the little creature that I loved more than anything in the world. I couldn't believe I was never to see him again.

Some time in the early morning while it was still dark, I had drifted into a troubled sleep and was in the middle of a nightmare when I was wakened by a sound at the door. It was a bark that I knew well. It could only be Togo. I jumped out of bed and opened the door and in walked His Lordship, hungry, happy to see us, looking for his evening meal and hoping that we had had as good a day as he had.

He must have fathered God knows how many pups in his eleven years. If perchance you see a black mongrel fox terrier with white spats on his front paws and a white shield on his breast, you will know at once he is a descendant of Togo.

I have been crazy about dogs from the moment I had Togo. I loved him with a passion I had never known before, and he returned that love in the wonderful way dogs have. But even at that age I seemed to be aware of the fragility and brevity of life—especially of dogs—so one day when I was about seven I had a quiet word with Togo. Personal and private. I told him how much I loved him, and asked him to do me a very special favour about something very important. I asked him to make sure that when the time came for us to part, he would try and wait for me so that we could be together for the last time. He looked up at me with those incredible brown eyes and wagged his little docked tail.

It still astonishes me that my beloved little dog remembered. I was sixteen when the time came. I had left school and was working in an office in the centre of town. I arrived home to an empty house, sat down at the piano as I often did, and started to play. Togo was lying under the table behind me and started to make sounds as if he had been hurt. I went down on to the floor beside him and took him in my arms. He stopped making any sound, and with a last look up to me from that dear face—he died in my arms.

Togo had kept his promise.

8

LIFE BOY

HOLIDAYS WERE great adventures for me. John and Jim went their different ways. John was given a tour of Europe for his 21st birthday, plus the obligatory gold signet ring, and returned to the bosom of his family speaking a strange patois which he insisted was French. Each time a meal had ended he would declare, with suitably expressive hand, '*Je suis fini*' ('I am finished') suggesting to us that he was about to kick the bucket, rather than the correct '*J'ai fini*' ('I have finished'). When Mum and Dad went on holiday, John and Jim were left to look after the two shops, and a roomful of crumpled brown and white paper would provide the evidence of hundreds of fish suppers. John would be in charge of the Roebank Street shop, while Jim would run Cumbernauld Road. The shop girls would arrive a couple of hours after they did, allowing them to get home for breakfast and some sleep after their early rise.

On these occasions I would willingly be dumped in Prestwick under the watchful eye of a stern seaside landlady called Mrs. Wilson, who ran a delightful B&B called Craigard, only a few minutes from the beach. I stayed there many times, and was a devoted patron of the Prestwick Pavilion, not to mention a faithful daily customer of Connell's Café. The ice-cream was unbelievably mouth-watering. It was necessary to go round the back of the café, and Mr. Connell himself would spend the whole day scooping out tuppenny pokyhats in halfpenny pokes which made the amount of ice-cream seem even larger.

Another favourite was the fish-and-chip shop which had no main street front. There was a long passageway which had to be negotiated from the main street down to the service window, and somehow that made the adventure even more exciting.

On balance, though, I think I preferred Largs. I still get a buzz when I remember the sheer pleasure of the solitude I found in that place. I came to know it so well that I could draw a detailed map of the town from memory. It was my way of enjoying the antici-pation of the holiday there. I had established many a secret place that no one knew about. And there were many ongoing projects to be attended to. I was determined to trace the source of the Gogo Burn, and having failed, I would attempt to dam its pathetic little outlet to the Firth just under the bridge at the putting green.

I used to sail my toy yacht in the boating pond close by, and one year when Jim was there, he found me sitting on the edge of the pond watching everything except the yacht, and when I looked it had been stolen.

The 'mountain' in Douglas Park was topped by a little wooden café—The Bonnie Blink—where visitors would pause for refresh-ment. Then there was the Fairy Glen, a wooded area with the trees carrying twinkling coloured lights, which provided a pleasant walk for holidaymakers. When the weather deteriorated most peo-ple set off for the picture house, which was down an alley and widely known as The Fleapit. But we went all the same.

I had a regular job in Largs every year I went to the town, a job that required a great deal of knowledge and experience. I was a young boy in short trousers, but I was well qualified. An expert. It was my job to hand out the numbered tickets to tourists for the street photographer who would then produce a trio of prints; three separate strides as they approached the bridge. Those who wanted a memento of their holiday would collect the pictures at a shop on the Main Street the next day. As far as I was concerned I was well paid in ice-cream.

During another holiday, this time in Prestwick, I wandered down to the beach to look at the layout of what was to be the Prestwick open-air pool, and the huge girders marking out the shape and size.

I came upon the mountains of sand and mortar which were shipped in bogeys on a track that ran a fair length along the higher ground close to the golf course. It must have been a dinner break or a non-working day because—for safety reasons, I supposed— the bogeys had been turned on their sides. To me, though, it was a miniature railway line. A life-size Hornby train. I was excited by the possibilities, and started straining to put one of the bogeys on the track when I was approached by three boys who asked me what I was doing. I explained rather earnestly what I had in mind, that I wanted to get a bogey on the track and play at trains. They tested the weight of the nearest bogey and announced that it couldn't be done.

'You'll never do it,' said their leader.

'Why?' I asked.

'Cos it's too f*****' heavy,' he said, and all three walked away.

I had never heard the word before, and wasn't sure what it meant, but I thought it seemed very expressive. When I was preparing for bed that night, I related the day's events to my mother, describing how I had wanted to play at trains with the bogeys down at the pool site with some friends, but we had to give up because the bogey was too f*****' heavy.

With a look of startled horror, my mother was left open-mouthed and speechless. Could she have heard correctly? she wondered. Had she inadvertently taken a total stranger in off the street?

Swiftly I was thrust down on to my knees at the bedside where I spent the night babbling my apologies to God, and asking His forgiveness without knowing what awful sin I had committed.

On a later occasion my tongue got me into more trouble, but this time I had committed no sin, used no foul language.

The church officer of St. Enoch's Hogganfield church was a mean, surly sour-faced man of uncertain temper who disliked young boys. His name was Mitchell and he must have known most of the boys who were, or had been, in the Life Boys as well as the more senior Boys' Brigade.

I have never managed to forgive him for what he did. I still bear the scars of the manner in which he punctured my fourteen-year-old dignity.

Somehow I had heard that the Church Dramatic Club, although not active, still existed and had an account at the local bank a few yards up from the church. The account was still in funds, and I decided to have a word with the minister with a view to its revival.

I hastened to the church at vestry hour, excited at the prospect of restarting the drama group. Unfortunately I had to pass the four-eyed monster who guarded the ecclesiastical cave and ask to speak to the minister. He looked at me suspiciously and asked what I wanted to speak to the minister about, and I was stupid enough to tell him. He told me I was wasting my own and the minister's time, but I insisted on having a word.

The Reverend Robert Morrison asked what my problem was, his mind on another plane entirely.

He considered it for almost fifty seconds and judged that he could not possibly hand over the running of the Drama Group to a fourteen-year-old boy. I was deeply disappointed as I left the vestry, and Mitchell was there waiting to hear what the outcome had been.

I gave him a lop-sided grin and said wryly, 'You were right. You must be psychic!'

At that, for some reason I couldn't fathom, he went purple with rage. Mrs. Brown, the session clerk's wife, was standing watching wondering what was going on. She was a strange little creature who always dressed in black skirt, black dress, black cape, black hat and long-laced black boots. She was more like some little Victorian Granny.

'What did you call me?' Mitchell was shouting.

'I didn't call you anything,' I said. 'I said you must be psychic.'

He grabbed me by the scruff of my collar and started to drag me to the door. 'By God, Ah'll give ye psychic,' he screamed. 'Ye neednae come in here wi' yer dirty American talk.' I called out to Mrs. Brown to help me. 'Tell him what the word means,' I pleaded. 'Please Mrs. Brown, explain to him that I wasn't using foul language.' But Mrs. Brown just rolled her eyes, bit her lip and shook her head. It was clear she had no idea what 'psychic' meant either.

'Never you mind Mrs. Brown,' yelled Mitchell. 'You're gettin' oota here. An' don't let me see you in here again!'—and he threw me bodily out into the street.

One day years later when I was living in Byres Road, I was taking my black poodle, Friday, for a walk and suddenly noticed that Mrs. Brown was waving to me from the other side of the road. I hadn't seen her since I was ejected from the church hall, and I had never forgiven her for not standing up for a young boy against a monster like Mitchell.

She was visiting one of her daughters in Dowanhill, she said. I had Friday on a lead and he was intrigued by Mrs. Brown's curious laced boots as we talked. We chatted for a few minutes and I took care not to remind her of the time I was thrown out of the church. We wished each other a cheery goodbye and parted and I continued my walk with Friday—with a wide grin on my face.

Friday had peed all over her black boots and she didn't know about that either!

All of the chums had joined the Life Boys and advanced to the Boys' Brigade. The captain was one Kenny Ross, or Wee Kenny as he was called, although not affectionately. He had obviously taken as his role model Dickens' Yorkshire schoolmaster, Mr. Wackford Squeers, and every Friday, grim-faced and arrogant, he added to our disaffection. Nevertheless, we learned a great deal from the Boys' Brigade. Many of us became fairly skilled at Morse code and semaphore, which proved to be helpful later on.

But the highlight of the evening was the scramble to be first in the queue at the Lomax fish-and-chip shop for a tuppenny fish or one of Mrs. Mackinnon's home-made fishcakes.

These were good days, exciting and carefree days. School, the BB, the tennis club, great and everlasting love affairs—which lasted for anything up to three weeks—and the Elite Café, where we downed a relentless diet of 'ninety-nines'.

On Saturdays we went to the Rex Cinema or the Riddrie Cinema with everything prearranged. 'See you inside' was the Friday night call to the 'steadies', and there we would find them, in the back row on the right hand side. We greeted each other as if it was pure coincidence that we had all come to see the same film. A row of five girls had become a row of five boys alongside five girls, and within seconds became a row of alternate sexes. Then with meaningful glances between them, the boys placed their right arms around the shoulders of the current girlfriends, who adjusted their seating arrangements to accommodate. We stayed absolutely still for fear of breaking the spell thus far created, and left the cinema in a happy bunch, making sure we walked home on the other side of the road so that we could use our *left* arm and rest the now benumbed right one.

The same arrangement took place every Sunday. Any sightseers visiting Hogganfield Loch in the summer would see the young virile males marching in groups round the loch in a clockwise direction, with an equal number of young females wandering round in an anticlockwise direction, and before a full circuit could be made, the two groups had split into couples.

Style, of course, was everything then. The hair carefully combed into a 'shed', plastered with water or Brylcreem. And the over-coats . . . ! Ah, new overcoats of a particular style were as important as shoes. Each winter we paraded in the latest belted overcoats of our choice. All important was the collar which had to stand at a specified distance above the ears, followed closely by the essential belt, and, finally, the design of the cloth. With the school muffler tied at the throat and tucked into the chest, we were ready for anything or anybody. Stylish, trendy and happy with ourselves, we made our way towards the local fleshpots.

But how ridiculous we must have looked with our warm coats covering our upper bodies, and our long bare legs open to the chill winds of winter.

9

PLAYING BY EAR

MY MOTHER'S MUCH LOVED PIANO had been transported to Almond Street. It was an ancient walnut instrument with brass candlesticks on the breast and what sounded to me to be wooden strings, but my mother was a splendid pianist. She played by ear and could play anything she was asked, drawing on a limitless repertoire, and the ability to reproduce instantaneously a tune or song she had heard only once.

'Hum it over to me and I'll get it,' she would say, and always did.

At some four years of age, in an effort to copy her, I hauled myself up on to the piano stool and banged energetically up and down the keyboard producing such discordance as would have earned Shostakovich a standing ovation. But then, one day, much to my surprise, and totally by accident, I hit a sequence of notes with one finger which sounded familiar. Could it be, I asked myself. Had I actually produced a tune? I tried it again, and again, playing it over and over with one finger until I was sure I could repeat it at will, then went to seek out my mother.

'I've made up a tune,' I announced to her, covering my options. 'It's a wee bit like "Goodnight, Sweetheart", but it isn't—I made it up myself!'

I spent days and hours at the piano, trying to reproduce the melodies I had heard my mother play, and slowly, but surely, it became obvious that I was playing by ear. My mother's musical gene had implanted itself in me, a gift which was to be of immense value in later years.

John and Jim had also inherited my mother's love of music, but neither had the ability to play by ear, and youthful distractions had probably made the music lessons a nagging chore rather than a pleasure. In later life, John's greatest joy was to sit proudly at his grand piano and interpret the works of Chopin—although not necessarily the way Chopin had composed them—regretting, perhaps, that he had not practised more assiduously when he had had the opportunity. However, he made up for it when he sold the business and retired.

My parents had provided a violin of some quality for Jim and placed their budding Menuhin with a local music teacher. Jim, like the rest of us, adored good music but after some two or three lessons, both he and his teacher agreed that, in his case, a gramophone was the preferred instrument with which to create it. Jim's gift to me was an introduction to classical music.

Sadly, my parents were not to be caught a third time, and music lessons for me were unequivocally ruled out.

'It might have spoiled your ear, dear,' my mother knowingly explained.

This decision brought its own 'reward' to my parents, particularly to my father who was not, himself, an aficionado. My constant practice—which brought forth both an unusual style and sound— took place within a few feet of him when he was trying to read his paper. The problem was that I could play melody and chords with my right hand, but could do no more than make Charlie-Kunz-like motions up and down the bass keys with my left, banging out 'chords' known among the trade as 'a bunch of grapes'. The dissonance thus created actually produced the few occasions when he spoke to me at all.

'Heh, sur. Wull ye stoap that THUMP, THUMP, THUMP.'

Having gained some experience of performing (?) in my cot in Appin Road, I had progressed to a larger podium in Almond Street by placing my blackboard, which was taller than I was, across the arms of my father's chair. From here I presented my 'one man show'. There was no audience other than the Teddy and Cat, but I babbled on anyway, and even if anyone had been watching they wouldn't have understood what I was talking about. I most certainly didn't!

It was another step up the ladder when Leslie, his brother Arthur and I decided to hold a concert in the back garden of No. 5. We created the stage with bed sheets pegged to a clothes line strung up into a geometrical nightmare. The shortage of pegs decided the prices for our young audience. In view of the fact that we had only managed to create the front tabs we would charge an ordinary safety pin for entrance to the 'auditorium', and our audience had to hand in their safety pins and wait until the rest of our 'theatre' had been created. We also charged a halfpenny for a glass of lemonade at the interval. We realised that, there being only one tumbler, it would take some time to refresh our audience.

But it was a success. Arthur had remembered every sketch he had ever heard at the Alexandra Park concert pavilion. And we were given a standing ovation from the very small children, which was understandable since there were no seats.

But we weren't inclined to continue.

My mother often took me to the Alexandra Park pavilion, and I loved the concert parties and, more especially, I loved the pierrots. Then there was the Christmas panto. My Mum and Dad loved George West and his 'feed', Jack E. Raymond. George West dressed and made up more like a clown than a straightforward comedian. He was a very funny man who worked extremely hard. The pantos opened in October or November, and sometimes went on through till April.

My Mum and Dad and I were all very fond of Largs and holidayed there often. It was almost like groupies following their favourite performers when we went on holiday and immediately booked our seats to see George West all over again. When his long-running panto was over he rested and prepared for the move to the Barrfields Pavilion in Largs for the summer.

What really puzzled my parents when they took me to the theatre was that when the final curtain came down, I used to cry. The simple truth was that not only did I not want to go home, but I wanted to be on the other side of the curtain. They simply couldn't understand. But I did—I wanted to go on the stage, though I had no idea what I was going to do 'on the stage', if I ever got there.

But that was solved for me much later—after the war.

Other memorable performances (!) to be recorded in the CV included solo interludes on a pink and mauve 'moothie' for the school concerts. I felt very special seeing my name printed on the programme. At a district-wide competition that was to be held in the Kelvin Hall, I memorised and practised—for what seemed ages—a Burns poem, not to mention having performed a number of previews for my classmates. But tragedy struck—when the Great Day arrived I fell ill with 'flu and couldn't participate. It's strange, but any time I thought of that poem I was sure it was a lengthy piece, but it has only two short verses.

> Oh why the deuce should I repine,
> And be an ill foreboder?
> I'm twenty-three and five feet nine,
> Ah'll go and be a sodger.
>
> I gat some gear wi' meikle care,
> I held it weel thegither.
> But now it's gane—and something mair:
> Ah'll go and be a sodger.

However, when the Christmas holidays came along and the discipline was let up I showed a talent for 'writing' and 'directing'—or at least that was what I thought. I approached the teacher with a play hot off the school desk. On receiving permission to proceed, I had, of course, to cast it. I chose a number of chums to follow me across to the playground shelter to rehearse. It was really just a scam to get out of the classroom.

The parts were not too difficult. It was a play from a story I had read about an elderly gentleman who had an aversion to lampposts, and whose daily exercise was to walk along the street belting the lampposts with his walking stick, for which heinous crime he was eventually arrested.

My dramatised version, having no props or scenery, called for a number of chums to stand in line and portray the parts of lampposts, while I, playing the star part of the old man, and having no stick, improvised and took the liberty of conveying my objection to the lampposts by kicking them.

Unfortunately, since the entire work was presented in mime, the storyline of this deep and meaningful piece of theatre never seemed to become clear to the children who had been favoured with its first ever performance. However, in my mind the play had been a success, although we had left behind us a hoard of dazed and deeply disturbed children, and not a few thoughtful teachers.

10

BIRD'S EYE VIEW

TO QUALIFY FOR SECONDARY SCHOOL, there was, of course, the general examination—'The Qually'—plus a paper on Bible study, which I imagine has long since been cancelled. I did well enough to find myself in Whitehill Secondary School, class 1A.

Proud though I was, I was embarrassed at having to wear a blue blazer that could have covered two of me, and a pair of flannels that were too short. These were my brother John's hand-me-downs, and that was the custom of the time. It didn't pay to dress a young man in new, tailored clothes, and I was growing fast.

The grading was nothing compared to the significance of the lady who came with it. This was Joyce Moffett, who held more than my twelve-year-old-self enthralled. She was to be our register/English teacher. She was a young, warm, immensely attractive Irish lady, with an exquisite speaking voice that I could have listened to forever.

She was, it has to be said, a dish! The sixth form boys would have died for her. All her pupils adored her. She was an inspirational teacher of English—which was my favourite subject and which took me through my exams. She it was who gave us our love of books and language, and somehow managed to impart to us certain ideals and philosophies which must have stood all the boys in 1A in great good stead for most of our lives.

In later years I often wondered where I could find her. I spoke of her, and quoted her so often, that Katie became intrigued and wished we could meet. It was a wish that was granted. We were surprised and delighted when, chatting with Una McLean one day, we discovered that Joyce lived only a few minutes from us in the West End of Glasgow. We were overjoyed to have found her, but regretted so much that we had not been able to do so much earlier.

The celebratory dinner we had together was wonderful. Joyce was lively and interested in everything. The questions were endless. We smiled when we remembered the occasion when Joyce had designated Charles Kingsley's magical book *The Heroes* as required reading. As she was to discover, it was my favourite book; one that I knew backwards. My Mum and Dad had given me a wonderful box of eight cloth-bound books for Christmas one year just before I went to Whitehill: *Gulliver's Travels, Swiss Family Robinson, Arabian Nights, Alice in Wonderland/Through the Looking Glass, Andersen's Fairy Tales, Treasure Island, Grimm's Fairy Tales,* and *The Heroes*.

I was more than happy to have to read *The Heroes* again. And when it came to the day when questions were being asked, a large number of the boys were floundering more than a little. Joyce was quick to notice the arrogant creature who was so relaxed and sitting at the back of the class with a supercilious grin on his face. 'Very well Fulton,' she said. 'Let's hear from you!'

Joyce asked question after question all of which were answered with speed and confidence. She was forced to admit that I had obviously read the book as required.

Little did she know the number of times I had read it.

Perhaps it was the amount of reading, and the reading of those particular books, that have made me wish sometimes that I had never grown up. The Peter Pan syndrome. I have always hated change, always regretted the day that Father Christmas/Santa Claus went out of my life; that the little elves and fairies had departed from the bottom of the garden; that the world was, alas, devoid of magic; and that the great adventures of Gulliver and the Robinson family, Jim Hawkins and even Alice—all of which I had thought of as real—were only stories. I was sad when the magic was taken away from me as a young boy, with nothing to take its place but harsh reality. No point, then, in wishing or praying any more, I thought. If all the magic was unreal, then probably God was, too.

It was Joyce, also, who introduced us to the classic plays, one of which was Shakespeare's *Twelfth Night*, not that I was over-fond of that English gentleman who created such a travesty of the history of the life of one of Scotland's greatest kings.

Joyce decided that we should perform a scene from the play for the school concert to be held in St. Andrew's Halls. I was cast as Sir Toby Belch. The rehearsal was the lesson, and I was Sir Toby Belch clad in anything but a 16/17th century costume, acting in front of an audience for the first time in my life.

I had had some trouble understanding the line 'a plague o' these herrings.' 'Perhaps a little digestive problem,' she prompted. I was pleased. When we came to perform it, the rift that preceded that line could be heard in Edinburgh.

Another opening, another show, as they say. The CV was getting longer. Mrs. McKinlay who lived in Gala Street was the lady who produced the *Kinderspiels*. Mr. Milne was a splendid pianist who played for the children's plays that were presented in the Large Hall of St. Enoch's Hogganfield church. Mr. Milne's son, Gordon, was another pal and he, Leslie and I were cast, with a large number of others, in a *Kinderspiel* called *The Bells of Beaulieu*. (I have never known how to spell that name!) I loved every minute of it, and so did Leslie. But it wasn't so much the play he was enjoying. It was the girls who were in the cast who interested him.

*   *   *

A couple of years later I became so intrigued about what went on backstage in a real, live, professional theatre that I suddenly realised that if I played my cards right I could have an entrée.

Brother Jim was going out with a very attractive blonde called Nancy at this time, and her aunt was in charge of the bar in Glasgow's Pavilion Theatre. I asked Nancy if she could persuade her aunt to arrange for me to go backstage during a performance, as I was writing a novel about a murder which takes place in a theatre and I desperately needed to do some research.

Whether anyone believed such precocious twaddle is doubtful, but the visit was arranged, and I was ensconced with the electrician on his bridge at the prompt side (on the left from the audience's viewpoint in the Pavilion) where I could have a bird's eye view.

The modern, computerised lighting systems we have nowadays are a world away from the old-fashioned platforms some feet above stage-level, close to the stage manager's corner. The electricians ran along and around the gantry, their eyes never leaving the handwritten lighting plot, as they manipulated a bewildering array of heavy switches, wheels, giant fuses and dials. The chief electrician was interested to hear how I came to be on the board with him. Here I had to tell the white lie again. 'I am writing a novel and need to research the back stage,' I told him. He was struck by the unexpected answer from a fourteen-year-old boy. 'Is that right?' he said. 'Ah've never met an author before.' I didn't like to tell him that I hadn't either.

The electricians had a clear view of the stage from the footlights (which are rarely used nowadays) up to the lighting bars, and they would be able to see the actors about to enter the stage, as they had to pass underneath the electrician's bridge to enter on the prompt side. The Pavilion had practically no space behind the cyclorama (the back-cloth of the stage, often used to represent the sky) in those days, so if the actors had to enter from the O.P. side (opposite prompt), they would have to go underneath the stage and up a small stairway to make their entrance.

From my vantage point I watched Jack Anthony, the man who could make a cat laugh, in *Aladdin and his Wonderful Lamp*.

I nearly fell off the lighting bridge when a great, evil roar of laughter suddenly erupted, and the huge, bearded, turbaned figure of Abanazer appeared right underneath me and strode on to the stage snarling at everyone. Hisses, boos and cries of 'Gerrof' greeted him, but he was completely dauntless, and snarled back at his audience, goading them to further frenzy with a few well chosen insults.

I was terribly impressed. I had never been this close to an evil magician before, and I held my breath to see what he would do next, keeping a wary eye on the electrician, just in case this villainous creature should climb up beside us. Alas, having mouthed a dire warning or two, he turned with grand contempt and marched off to further thunderous, and increasingly high-pitched jeering. As he walked off the stage nonchalantly underneath me, he paused for a moment then produced a rather mucky handkerchief from his sleeve and *blew his nose!* I was very disappointed. He wasn't very frightening at all, except for the fact that the sound he made when he blew his nose would have wakened a dead elephant.

The magic that had been was totally destroyed, but it returned when Jack Anthony, the star, invited me to his dressing-room below the stage. Jack was a delightfully warm, good man. I was introduced to his wife, Carrie, whom he referred to as 'his good lady.' He asked me how I came to be on the lighting gantry. I was beginning to feel more than a little guilt about the white lie, but there was no option, I had to tell it.

He wasn't remotely taken aback. He seemed to think it was quite normal that a boy of fourteen could be an author.

The *Sunday Post* was running a general knowledge quiz and the question was about the origin of the word 'humour'. As it happened I knew the answer to that and sent it in. I was really chuffed when I saw it in print. (For those who may be interested, the origin of the word humour, according to mediaeval physiology of the time, was that the character of a person was based on the dominance of one of the four 'humours', the four chief fluids of the body: blood, phlegm, choler and melancholy. Just thought I'd mention it.)

Anyway, I had another go with the *Sunday Post* and wrote a review of the panto 'as seen from the electrician's gantry.' The editor's reply was very kind and pointed out that the panto had been running for some time, and had been reviewed on the opening night.

When I had done my last broadcast with the BBC Showband in October 1955 and returned to my beloved Glasgow (I hated London), Jack Anthony and I met again performing for one of the many Sunday charity shows at the Alhambra theatre. Jack enjoyed these Sunday concerts enormously, having retired some years before, as they gave him the opportunity to meet so many friends again, and hear the laughter that he had so expertly produced in the past. He was gob-smacked when I told him that I was the fourteen-year-old boy who had watched him from the lighting bridge, and lied about being a writer.

I also pointed out that the experience of seeing the inside and out of a 'real, live professional theatre' as a youngster was the litmus that finally made me decide to go on the stage.

There were many hurdles on the way, but I'll come to that.

11

DISHONOUR AMONG THIEVES

IN 1938, and for some reason that I can no longer remember, Leslie and I were recruited to join a concert party run by a university student some years our senior, to raise money for the Red Cross.

I had already done a stint or two for Archie McCulloch by playing piano for the troops in some of the barracks. But this was real acting stuff! Included in the company was a young boy called Billy Ettles, a good-looking lad with a splendid voice who, because of his small frame and charm, we reckoned would be a very popular act. Our university student organiser obviously had an eye for talent. We had an excellent accordionist whose father was a fireman (not that that made him a star), a couple of girl dancers and a young lady called Essie Richardson who could play the piano in more than one key. Her father was the hall-keeper at St. Andrew's parish church in Alexandra Parade—and therein lies a story.

Leslie and I were given a short two-handed drama entitled *Dishonour Among Thieves*. The plot involved a burglar who breaks into a house and attempts to crack the safe. Suddenly the lights come blazing on. Enter the householder resplendent in silk dressing-gown, revolver in hand. Householder reveals that he is in the business of manufacturing home safes, and is the inventor of the safe the burglar is endeavouring to open. It is, says House-holder, absolutely burglar-proof, and he challenges Burglar to open it within fifteen seconds. If he succeeds he will go free. If he fails the police will be called.

Great drama then ensues as Burglar sweats to find the combination (much massaging of hands and blowing on fingers), while Householder counts off the seconds.

Comes the end when, almost at the last second, Burglar triumphantly throws open the door of the safe. Householder then shoots burglar dead, takes off dressing-gown to reveal outdoor clothes and pockets contents of safe.

Householder exits cackling evilly.

So far as I can remember, Leslie and I had done all that was necessary within our remit. On top of our dramatic piece we were entrusted with some 'cross-overs'—an esoteric phrase that only actors like myself and Leslie could know!

M.C. IS ABOUT TO MAKE ANNOUNCEMENT.
ENTER MAN WITH CUP who interrupts him.
MAN: (TO M.C.) Here, taste that. Go on taste it.
M.C. DRINKS FROM CUP AND SPITS IT OUT.
M.C.: That's foul.
MAN: No, it's cat.
MAN INTERRUPTS AGAIN, NOW CARRYING A COAT HANGER.
M.C.: (TO MAN) Here, where d'you think you're going with that?
MAN: What d'you think? I'm going to put the aeroplane away!

Whatever the standard of the performances, the concerts—which we presented mostly in local church halls—were well supported, and the money raised was gratefully accepted by the Red Cross. It was also a tremendously enjoyable pastime for our little gang of troupers, so it was with heavy hearts that we had to say 'goodbye' to our maestro who had to quit and concentrate on his studies.

Leslie and I called on him and pleaded with him to continue, but he was adamant and we understood. Then he suggested that Leslie and I should take over the concert party ourselves.

And why not, we thought—with *our* experience!

This added extra zest to the enterprise. Not only did we have to create our own material as well as performing—now we saw ourselves as writers, producers and directors, and we would also be organising venues for the shows, deciding on running-orders, and rehearsing. Heady stuff.

Fortunately we were still in touch with the friends who had performed in the shows previously. We were organised in no time, but I'm not at all sure I remember why we changed our names to Bob and Harry. Well, lots of stars have changed their names, for heaven's sake!

Our first venture took place in the Large Hall of St. Enoch's Hogganfield—to the frustration and chagrin of Cerberus Mitchell. That gave me tremendous satisfaction. With staggering original-ity, we called the concert *Eggs, Beans and Crumpets*, without even a glance in the direction of P. G. Wodehouse. Mrs. Morris, the minister's wife, a large, good-humoured lady, chortled encourag-ingly when I showed her the title on the printed tickets.

Unfortunately, Essie, our regular pianist, couldn't be with us that evening, so we enlisted the help of Billy Hill, a very tall young man a few years older than we were, a great friend and brilliant pianist, who also played by ear and taught me so much about piano-playing.

All was going splendidly until Leslie announced young Billy Ettles's spot. I suppose we had always suspected he was a bit older than he looked. Obviously he didn't realise his falsetto voice was about to disappear—and it had to happen on the night of Our Very First Bloody Show! Big Billy couldn't begin to accompany our Boy Soprano as he went up and down scales we could never have imagined. The audience became a little restless and our troupe became more and more nervous. Big Billy had done his best, but with unexpected changes in the keys and pitch, and long embarrassing pauses as wee Billy strove to control himself and his ruptured voice, it was all too much and our orchestra of one made a panic-stricken exit to find the directors hiding behind the curtains, wondering how they could get out of this tragedy. Perhaps sneak out of the hall, or maybe just leave Riddrie.

After what seemed like an eternity, poor little Billy was left standing in front of the audience with no idea what to do while Big Billy and Leslie and I argued about what should be done. Then little Billy turned and left the stage, tears running down his cheeks, crying in a newly found tenor voice.

I had to hand it to Leslie. He walked on to the stage with great aplomb and, with what sounded like an admonishment, told the audience: 'Sorry about that, ladies and gentlemen, but you'll have to excuse young Billy. After all he couldn't help it, his voice is breaking and he didn't know. And now we would like to do a little drama for you entitled *Dishonour Among Thieves*. Thank you.'

My father had mocked up a little safe for us which was the only prop we had. The stage was absolutely empty. There was nothing, absolutely *nothing* in this 'room' other than that little safe. I had sneaked on to put it in place at the back of the stage while Leslie was making his announcement, and I had a feeling that a few chairs would not have been amiss.

But we had one other prop I was sure would make them gasp.

I suggested that the Householder should *stab* the Burglar instead of shooting him when Leslie (Householder) had to kill me (Burglar). But Leslie was rather keen to use the gun. So we compromised and Leslie would shoot me and stab me as well—just to make sure.

We had engineered quite a large, padded square wooden board which was strapped to my back under my jacket, and my father had made a little wooden dagger with a sharp nail on the end.

As soon as Leslie had announced 'The Drama' he exited shouting 'Lights out! Lights out! For God's sake *put the lights out!*' and he then fumbled desperately to get his dressing-gown on in the dark.

The stage went black and I entered waving a torch around, searching for the safe and, amazingly, finding it—though it must have struck a few people that it couldn't have been difficult to find the safe since it was the only thing in this strange room. Leslie made his entrance with his dressing-gown round his neck and one shoulder. There was a certain lack of dignity about his character. However, we pressed on with the dialogue, such as it was—we seemed to be having some difficulty in remembering the original sketch, and were forced to make up the text ourselves.

We may have had one or two problems, but we thought the scene had been going well enough. Now there remained only the dramatic climax. As soon as Burglar (me) had managed to crack the safe, Householder (Leslie) whipped out his gun and shot Burglar, then followed it up with the dagger. It was a great effect, we thought, though it was spoiled just a bit because I had fallen on to my side and had this strange hump on my back, and the dagger kept falling out. Leslie had to stab me quite a few times before the dagger stuck, only to fall out again with a very wooden 'clunk' when I finally rolled over dead.

And there was worse to come.

Essie Richardson had talked her father and mother into inviting us to perform our concert in St. Andrew's parish church. The stage we had to work on was typical of the platforms of most other church halls. They had put up a framework to carry the curtains and added an extension to the front of the stage to give it extra depth. An upright piano stood stage right facing the audience, at the back of which was a pile of little primary chairs, which were used by the young children during Sunday school.

Getting on to the stage was like tackling an assault course. There was a four-step tread on the right side of the stage, which was all but blocked by that vast number of primary chairs. And it wasn't possible to get from stage right to left because there was no passageway between the back curtain and the wall (just like at the Glasgow Pavilion). If anyone had to exit and then get to the other side they would have to make their way across the front of the stage and the audience or wait till the curtains were closed.

I had to make my first entrance from the right, just behind the piano, to join Leslie for what we called 'the warm-up'. Leslie had to greet our audience and tell them how delighted we were to be here in St. Andrew's parish church hall etc., and I was supposed to make a number of extremely witty comments. It was a well-filled hall, perhaps because of the high profile of the Red Cross, and because the local people were hoping for some entertainment to help them stop thinking about the threatening war clouds.

Our audience was very receptive, which may have been why I felt unusually confident, and perhaps just a tad over-enthusiastic. Wearing a pair of my father's over-large boots I clumped onto the tread, banging my boots heavily as I came up and stopped in front of the piano.

I was enjoying myself thoroughly. Every time I had something to say I did a little heavy-footed dance, banging the boots more and more heavily on the stage, with the strong conviction that it would get a laugh. But on the contrary it was the unexpected silence that warned me there was something amiss, though I had no idea what it was. The atmosphere had become incredibly tense. Leslie's mouth had fallen open and his eyes had widened to their extreme as he stared over my shoulder absolutely transfixed.

There was a slight gap between the stage and the extension, and the piano had begun to graduate towards this gap with every beat of my father's boots. I turned my head and followed Leslie's gaze just in time to see the piano's rear castor reach the gap in the platform. In slow motion, it did a graceful back somersault as if it was in its death throes—which sadly it was. The sound of the crash was awesome. It could have been heard in Alexandra Park as the big upright fell backwards and reduced the primary chairs to firewood.

As I said to Leslie afterwards, 'It was a good job I was on the stage when that happened!' I thought he was going to hit me with the piano.

We struggled on without any musical accompaniment until the interval when we could get the piano upright and push it out into the hall in front of the audience to assess the damage. It was a nightmare.

I had put right the innards of one or two pianos with elastic bands and fuse-wire in my time, but this was one upright kettle of fish. Broken hammers, strings, hitch pins and most of the action out of alignment. I did what I could in front of the audience who watched with interest as I tried to squeeze it back into shape. But I had a feeling it was never going to be the same.

My ad lib about 'Anyone wanna buy a slightly used piano?' didn't go down too well. The concert was over and a bewildered audience found themselves in the street puzzling over the unusual finale.

*   *   *

Leslie's parents were staunch members of the Bowling Club at the foot of Almond Street. They played bowls in the summer and bridge during the winter evenings, and on Saturday nights there would be some form of entertainment. Mrs. Bond was rightly proud of our public performances and the resultant input to charity. So when it fell to her to arrange the 'Saturday Night Live' bit, she naturally asked us to provide it. We agreed we would do only our double act since the venue could not support the whole company.

It turned out to be less straightforward than I thought.

Leslie had decided to sing.

We had always had a difference of opinion about his singing. When young Billy Ettles had been our Boy Soprano life had been easier, since the order of the day was 'one singer, one song', but since his departure, Leslie had pressed more and more to take over the singing spot. We often fell out about it, but it was natural on this occasion that since he had been given the mandate to put on The Blackhill Bowling Club Show by his mother, he would dictate the running order—which would be our double act, and his singing. Neither Billy Hill nor Essie Richardson would be available to play the piano, so Leslie's father—who at some point in his life had taught himself to read music—agreed to stand in. Mr. Bond wasn't actually a great pianist, and it was just unfortunate that the song Leslie had chosen to sing was the beautiful ballad composed by Jerome Kern, 'All the Things You Are', a devil of a piece to play with its changing keys and frighteningly difficult chords.

The act had gone reasonably well up to this point, but as the song began Mr. Bond's eyes could be seen darting wildly up and down between the sheet music and the piano keys, his head nodding frantically as he searched for the right key and the correct chord.

It looked as if trouble was brewing.

The opening bars gave a rough indication of where the key lay, and at a nod from his father, Leslie jumped in with his vocal chords firing on all cylinders. Father and son staggered drunkenly along the musical maze of the verse, and unsteadily approached the dangerous crossroads of Kern's brilliant modulation when, alas, Leslie took a hitherto uncharted route as his father ploughed grimly along another pathway altogether.

Bravely they struggled on to some sort of finish, but did not manage to meet again, and Leslie, beetroot-red and perspiring freely, vowed never to sing again—at least not in public.

To his great credit, Mr. Bond, a kind and amiable man, turned from the piano stool and patted Leslie on the head. 'Well done, son,' he said.

12

MEET THE FAMILY

BLACKHILL BOWLING CLUB produced another surprise, particularly for the Fulton family.

From our windows we could see the bowlers on the green as they played during the long light of warm summer evenings. I had noticed my mother and father one evening taking turns to gaze through a pair of binoculars. There was an excited air about them.

'Aye, Ah'm sure it's him,' I heard my father say.

My mother agreed. 'Oh yes,' she said. 'I'd know him anywhere.'

I was intrigued. I could sense the excitement they were feeling. It didn't take a genius to work out that they had spotted someone very important to them.

'It's your Uncle Andrew,' my mother told me. 'Daddy's brother.'

This was a great moment for me. I didn't seem to have many relatives and I was so happy at the thought that I could even add just one to their number. But neither my father or mother seemed over-enthusiastic. They explained that there had been a quarrel between my father and his brother not long after Andrew had returned from the 1914-18 war and the two had not spoken since.

Better to let sleeping dogs lie, they said, and packed away the binoculars.

But I was intrigued by the situation and decided that the dog had slept long enough.

Down I went to the Bowling Club and stood at the edge of the green wondering how I would be able to recognise my new found uncle. But, Lord knows, it wasn't difficult: suddenly I was confronted by the face of my father! With the exception of the nose, perhaps, this man seemed to me to be like his twin. There could be no doubt about it. This was my father's brother.

'Hello,' I said to him.

He looked up from his task of arranging the bowls, then responded with the warm smile of someone who was used to dealing with children.

'Hello,' he said. 'What are you doing here?'

'I came to see you.'

'Me? And why do you want to see me?'

'Cos you're my Uncle Andrew!'

'Am I? And d'you live here?'

'Yes,' I told him. 'Just two houses up. Will you come and see my Mum and Dad?' But he wasn't too sure about that.

Obviously he had no idea that someone he knew, far less a close relative, lived so close to his club. But, with a bit of persuasion, he agreed. I took him up to the house and the two brothers shook hands and resumed a relationship that had foundered some sixteen years before.

This was a great moment in my life. So far as I knew I only had one cousin, Helen, daughter of my Aunt Agnes and Uncle Bob who was the caretaker of Quarrier's Homes in Bridge of Weir. But I had augmented the number of known relatives by five. Uncle Andrew, Aunt Mary, cousins Margaret, Douglas and Andrew. It also brought forth a creature called Lizzie, who looked more like my father than my father did. She was a spinster lady, and I wasn't surprised. She lived with an old crone we came to know as Aunt Jinnet, my father's great aunt, who could have played any one of the witches in *Macbeth* without make-up or change of costume. She was forever scuttling about searching for her hankie, essential for mopping up a recurring dreep at her nose, and always too late she would discover she had been sitting on it. She and Lizzie, like many of my antecedents, came from Bridgeton. They were not what I would call prepossessing. Lizzie looked like my father in drag, and Great Aunt Jinnet like Old Mother Riley after a really bad night.

Lizzie was a very quiet lady with practically nothing to say beyond asking where the lavatory was. She worked for McFarlane Langs and her annual contribution to whoever was the host of the current Christmas do, was a large chocolate and walnut cake, while Great Aunt Jinnet, who was rumoured to have a bank account, was known to hand over ten-bob notes to the children. Moved by nothing so much as self-interest, I agitated to have our household join in the Christmas tradition and host the dinner for our relations. I can still see Aunt Jinnet's surprise—nay, fright— when I wished her 'a Happy Christmas' and kissed her on the cheek. Prone to sitting on her handkerchief and forever thinking it had been stolen, she searched for and found it in the usual place, and wiped her cheek where I had kissed her.

I was rewarded with the treasured ten-shilling note, and decided that it had been a reasonable day's work.

13

MAKING A SPLASH

MANY A PANTOMIME could have been seen at No. 5 had it not been private. Our family managed to include a mixed bag of pantomime, drama, French farce and black comedy all at once, usually generated by my mother and father.

My mother called him 'Daddy', and if he wanted to call her, he would address her as 'Aaaaaaay—ur ye therr.' When speaking to me of her, he and John would refer to her as 'Your Mother'. These idiosyncratic references made it seem that they had forgotten her name, and that she was only *my* mother. I never once heard my mother or father use each other's name.

My mother was indeed a remarkable little thing. She had the stamina, energy and drive of ten of us. So in awe of her were we, that if one of us crossed her, however unwittingly, and found ourselves the object of her displeasure, the other three would quickly form a frantic supportive chorus to her argument, each grateful that we were not the poor wretch in the dock.

Imagine, then, the panic one Saturday morning in September when we realised that the anniversary of her birth had come and almost gone without its being marked. Here we stood in a trembling assembly—sans birthday card, sans prezzy, sans hope of reprieve, sans everything.

What to do?

My father, with a rare show of decisive leadership, positively shot into town to return soon afterwards laden with goodies which he quickly thrust into our nervous hands at a hastily reconvened meeting.

We stood wide-eyed and shivering in the living-room, listening to the enormous banging and thumping which emanated from the sitting-room upstairs where, it seemed, she had repaired to vent her wrath on wardrobes, bed-settees, armchairs and any other object large or small which dared defy her avenging washing-clout.

My father approached the foot of the stairs like a sergeant about to lead his men over the top at the Battle of the Somme.

'Aaaaaaaaaaaaaaaaaaay,' he quavered tentatively.

The bumping and thumping ceased abruptly leaving an eerie, nail-biting silence.

My father cleared a dry throat and bravely ventured on.

'Would ye—aaaaaay—come doon a wee minute.'

The use of the diminutive was telling. It made his call an invitation, a supplication even, certainly not a command.

He withdrew and rejoined his sons to await developments. We squared our shoulders and braced ourselves for what was to come. Whatever was to come it certainly took its time coming. The silence persisted for a good three minutes while the four of us stood and sweated in anticipation. As, indeed, we were meant to.

And then we heard it. The first soft fall of a size three on the top step of the stairs, followed by a measured series of others as She descended like some pinnied Peruvian Goddess from Her carbolic throne.

Suddenly She was there. Straight-backed and proud, Her eyes black as coal, stretched to Her full height of four-feet-eleven-and-a-half-inches, Her hair awry, face ruddy and glistening from Her exertions, with a piece of soapy-wet flannel cloth dangling from one hand, and the other on Her hip. She glared at us with a glare that Medusa would have envied.

My father seized the initiative once again. (He was surpassing himself!)

'Aaaaaaaaaaaaay,' he stammered ingratiatingly. 'We—aaaaay—jist wantit tae say that—aaaaay—it's yer birthday, and—'

But he got no further.

Her eyes, glittering and remorseless, swept the tide of her off-spring and flooded us with such scorn as she turned away that we could only hang our heads and cover our faces.

We heard the size threes remount the stairs and clip clop across the room above. Within seconds the banging and thumping resumed with renewed ferocity.

We silently commiserated with one another, aware that we were in for a long period of unrelenting weather.

Surprisingly the thaw came much sooner than expected. When the family foregathered for what we had assumed would be a decidedly gloomy tea, my mother was in fine fettle and chattered happily as if nothing had ever ruffled her pretty feathers.

The other strange thing was that all the presents—the pathetic bundle of gaily wrapped and beribboned parcels previously refused with such disdain—*had gone!*

Gratefully and unquestioningly, we accepted the return of the status quo.

My mother's vanity, too, could provide amusement, and even danger. When she washed her hair and had her bath she regarded it as a secret rite to be witnessed by no other living creature. I had seen it all before when I was tiny, but the ritual was always carried out when the family were out of the house and doors locked. She would have her bath and wash her hair, dry it at the fire and assault any sign of grey or white with an eyebrow pencil.

Her refusal to wear glasses at all resulted in several accidents. One day Jim and I were with her in the centre of the city. Time was getting on, but she decided that it was necessary to cross the road to Saxone's at the corner of Renfield Street and Gordon Street. The shop was obviously in the process of closing. A very bald-headed man had already started to lay out the long iron bars that waited to be slotted into their security positions. He had just laid out the bottom one when mother arrived on the pavement and made to enter the shop. The bottom bar—and the poor gentleman who was preparing the security gate—were invisible to her. And, like a blind general, she charged at the entrance, tripped over the bottom bar and falling headlong into the shop, bringing the bars and the man—who turned out to be the manager—to the floor.

Mother was furious of course. Jim and I helped her to her feet, but this poor man was still lying on the floor, trying unsuccessfully to staunch the flow of blood coming from his head, as she approached him. He was then forced to listen to this irate woman berating him and demanding to know why he had so carelessly left his iron bars all over the floor.

'That could be dangerous,' she warned, and walked out of the shop in high dudgeon—in quite the wrong direction!

Probably my mother's greatest performance was when she and my father took a break in the excellent hotel in Shrewsbury which was under the auspices of the Newsagents' Federation.

The hotel sported a splendidly decorated pond where the visitors could float leisurely in a punt and let the whole world go by. But, true to form, my parents' efforts to enjoy the amenities ended in disaster.

It was never really talked about, but the picture became clear bit by bit. For reasons quite unknown, my father and mother had decided to do something they had never done before. But, had the rest of the family been there we would have known at once that our mother was about to do something which she had done *many* times before!

In spite of their complete lack of experience, and my mother's propensity for swiftly achieving the horizontal, my parents hired a punt, and my father, ever courteous, took my mother's hand and bade her get in ahead of him, promising she would come to no harm. 'There's no danger,' he told her.

There *was* danger!

Even the security of her husband's arm when walking in the street was not sufficient to ensure her staying upright.

The minute she put one tiny foot on the untethered punt, it moved discreetly out of the way. Margaret had some difficulty placing a second foot on the end of the punt and seemed to think that the first one would look after itself. My father tried to get hold of her hand, but the punt had decided it was due elsewhere. Margaret's legs were stretched to the limit as she presented a near perfect arabesque, worthy of any ballerina.

There is a term in ballet called a 'fish dive' which is described as 'a move in which the ballerina dives to be caught by her partner, with her head and shoulders just clear of the floor'. This describes perfectly the way my mother arrived, puntless, in the pond. What was supposed to be an unusual and exciting experience had become more like a sketch in a pantomime. My mother could be heard throughout the hotel. She was outraged. She had never been so embarrassed.

'You said there would be no danger,' she screamed, the waters of the Severn dripping copiously from her best frock and hair. *'You should have saved me.'* Followed by my father's aggrieved *'B'Jeez, ye nearly hud me in alang wi' ye!'*

14

WOMEN'S HOUR

LIKE SO MANY women of her generation, my mother's great and abiding hobby/taboo was 'The Bowels'. She shared John's adherence to the Intestinal God, although they never openly discussed it. In fact discussion was never a part of their marital agenda. Margaret asked questions and accepted or rejected the answers she was given. She alone issued the Orders of the Day, and disallowed all appeals to a Higher Court, for the simple reason that there wasn't one.

Her passion for internal regularity, which used to be known as 'a good cleaning out', and is now known as 'colonic irrigation', was constantly on her mind.

How great must have been her approbation of my father, who sat quietly each morning after his porridge, waiting patiently with the conviction that nature would take its course. There he would sit in his chair neither reading nor, it appeared, thinking. He sat with the confidence of the unquestioning mind until a signal from his left colon indicated that the time was nigh. My mother was undoubtedly an avid devotee of this all-important waste-disposal unit, and would be prepared to discuss the subject with anyone who was remotely interested, especially if they had something interesting to offer.

Mrs. Smith, whom my mother had followed from Appin Road

(the Jones in her life with whom she was determined to keep up), and Mrs. Paterson who lived in Knightswood, held an afternoon cup-of-tea chat each Wednesday in turn. There, the conversation would range over a number of highly academic subjects such as metaphysics, ethics, or even Einstein's theory of relativity. However, as Mrs. Paterson said, she didn't think it was good manners to talk about one's in-laws. Other major topics included what sort of day Willie (Mrs. Smith's husband) had had. In fact, while Mrs. Smith was still present, the subjects suggested by Mrs. Smith rarely included anything other than Willie's advance in the business community. He was a high flyer in his firm, Lorimer & Moyes in Albion Street, which specialised in hairdressers' accoutrements. Willie had recently been invited onto the board of directors, so that would be the subject selected—unopposed. Fortunately Mrs. Smith always had another engagement which required her urgent attendance, and she would, therefore, be unable to stay for a second cup.

Having seen Mrs. Smith off to her home some twenty yards away, my mother and Mrs. Paterson would make themselves comfortable with a fresh teapot, and settle down to discuss the only truly important issue.

I can remember being present during an intense debate on the subject. Although on this occasion it was Mrs. Paterson's turn to be teacher and my mother the pupil. Even now I can almost hear Mrs. Paterson's voice as she presented her startling revelations, and my mother sitting enthralled, lips pouted and eyes narrowed, determined not to miss a syllable.

'The thing is, Mrs. F . . .' (first names were often not politically correct in those days, even among long-time acquaintances), 'the thing is that . . . as I understand it . . . just to give you an exemple . . .' (West End accent)—my mother's eyes had narrowed to slits in concentration as she prepared herself for the words of wisdom, if they were ever going to arrive—'Just to give you an exemple . . .' Mrs. Paterson went on at last, 'supposing now, you make a deposit . . .' (such elegant, inoffensive language), 'supposing you make a deposit of four ounces . . .' (nowadays such a situation might require the postscript 'plus VAT'), 'what we don't realise . . .'—somehow my mother knew the punch-line was almost within reach—'What we don't realise is thet although we've made a deposit of four ounces—*there are still two ounces to be accounted for!'*

My mother's eyes widened at the horror of it. 'However,' Mrs. Paterson went on comfortingly, 'Therefore, a small lexetive now and again is advaysable. Efter all, what is the point of putting more coal on a fire if the ashes hevn't been cleaned out!'

My mother's eyes went heavenwards at this awesome revelation. At last she understood. She felt that she too, like Paul, had found herself on the Damascus Road—or even the lavatory. From now on, at every opportunity, in every shop, at every corner of every street, she would preach the gospel according to Mrs. Paterson.

She had been blind, but now her bowels were open.

15

STRANGE RITUALS

AFTER HER EXCITING CONVERSATION with Mrs. Paterson, my mother was aglow at what she had learned that day. She was aching to spread the startling news, starting with my father. He had one particular fault which drove my mother out of her mind. In no way could he be bothered with ashes in fires that should have been removed before fresh coal had been fed to them. When it was time to shut up shop all he wanted was to put aside the stresses of shop-keeping and luxuriate in his favourite chair at home with his evening paper and sniff the wonderful aroma of his favourite food reaching him the minute he came through the front door. There was no embrace, or kissing, when they greeted each other. It didn't seem to occur to them, although there was no doubt they loved each other dearly. My mother would call from the kitchen: 'Is that you, Daddy?' and he would make the same reply every time: 'Who were ye expectin'?'

The courtesies at an end, he would seat himself in his chair and start to read his paper. He held it high as he read, which meant that, looking from the other side of the room all you could see was his midriff and his legs. Now and again he would lean to one side, putting his weight on one buttock with the newspaper still in position, and break wind. He was a model of body control; a truly remarkable farter. If it had been an Olympic sport, he would have taken the gold. Even Togo would run under the table when my father let go, and my mother would run into the living-room screaming. 'Daddy, how often have I to tell you. I wish you wouldn't *do* that!'

'Whi-it?'

'*That!* Now please don't do it again. Especially when I'm making the tea.'

'How? Huv we goat veesitors?'

She always gave up. She would never be able to make a gentleman of him. I was always pretty sure that each time she scolded him like that she had a bit of a giggle when she got back into the kitchen.

But she had no worries about my father's innards. After all she made the magic potion for him herself every morning, so there was no point in telling him about Mrs. Paterson's latest scientific news. But she had one very particular ally with whom she could share her colonic voyage of discovery, and that was Aunt Agnes.

My father had pneumonia three times over a period of years during my growing up. Each time he took ill I was sent off to Aunt Agnes to be cared for until he recovered. Uncle Bob was the caretaker at Quarrier's Homes for orphaned children in Bridge of Weir. My cousin Helen was more or less the same age as me, and every morning without fail Aunt Agnes would demand an answer from us both when she asked: 'Have we anything for the book today?' If we were unable to give her a decided 'yes', we were faced with one of the world's most unsavoury flavours, if it could be described as a flavour. Come hell or high water, a huge spoon carrying liquid paraffin with a blob of Cascara Sagrada would be poured into our unwilling gullets. It took the rest of the day to recover!

Other than that I enjoyed my stays in Bridge of Weir. It was an idyllic place for a child, with its acres of green land and trees, and with wonderful carefree games to be played among the hedgerows and along the banks of the River Gryfe. These were special holidays for me, with no school or homework to think about, and my mother keeping us informed of my father's progress. I got to know many of the boys from the orphanage over the years and made a number of friends. Orphans they certainly were, but there were times when I wondered if they were happier than I was. My aunt, uncle and cousin didn't go to church on Sundays. There was no need—the hymns and the sermon were broadcast from the church throughout the village. Their lives were simple, tranquil and for me a sanctuary. And the fresh air and the way of life were very much to the benefit of my own health.

*   *   *

Uncle Bob and Aunt Agnes were as prudish as my own parents, but not nearly so funny. When my father was in good health, everything that could be done in preparation for his early morning rise, was done the night before. He even shaved and washed so that he wouldn't have to spend time in ablutions, and he took his clothes off in a way that allowed him to put them on in the morning quickly and simply with no rush. His jacket and waist-coat (and in winter his cardigan also) would be taken off as one garment; likewise his shirt and semmit, and finally he would remove his long-johns still housed within his trousers. With three deft movements he could be dressed in seconds, ready to leave the house to open the shop.

My father wore a natural wool semmit and long-johns in the summer, and a heavier quality in winter. This, naturally, provided my mother with an annual solution to the problem of my father's Christmas present. My mother would watch his reaction carefully as he opened the giftwrapped parcel with an expression of eager anticipation, almost as if he couldn't possibly have guessed what the present was.

'Just whit Ah wantit,' he would announce.

This life-long habit, however, created another, and more intricate procedure. As the time for holidays approached, the atmosphere in our home became electric. Anyone entering our house would have sensed the heightened tension; an almost carnival air, without remotely understanding what was taking place. . . .

This was our father's bath time!

It was another of his rituals, but this time the entire family were involved. Such activity you have never witnessed. Everyone was rushing hither and thither, totally involved in my father's ablutions. My mother could be seen scurrying up and down the stairs testing the temperature of the water. My father, unusually active, moving purposefully from room to room seeking soap, bath salts, nail scrubber and sponge. The entire family collapsed into chairs in the living room to recover from the stress and excitement.

But there was more!

After the bath nights, the routine of changing into clean gear, although complex, was carried out with the skill born of long practice. It went as follows:

1. In winter remove jacket, waistcoat and cardigan as one garment.
2. Hang over back of chair.
3. Remove shirt and semmit together.
4. Put on clean semmit.
5. Put on clean shirt.
6. Take off clean shirt and clean semmit together.
7. Put on pyjama jacket.
8. Take off trousers.
9. Take off long-johns.
10. Put on clean long-johns.
11. Put trousers back on.
12. Take off trousers and clean long-johns together.
13. Put on pyjama trousers.
14. Go to bed!

In the mornings my mother somehow managed to waken and switch off the alarm clock before it had a chance to signal the start of a new day, even Christmas Day, so that my father could be wakened gently when his porridge was brought to his bedside.

How my mother managed to get out of bed from the inside position next to the wall under a hot water tank and negotiate the assault course without waking her sleeping husband was a mystery, but as she herself said, 'Things don't always go according to plan!'

She often graphically, and hysterically, confessed to us how, having manoeuvred herself as far as the bedroom door, she would sometimes take the opportunity to seek a further contribution to the housekeeping. Making sure that her husband was still sound, she would remove some of the larger coins from his trouser pocket. On checking again that she had not disturbed his slumber, she would find that he had lain quite still watching her with staring eyes. She could never forget the fright this gave her, not knowing whether to laugh or scream, and always her ill-gotten gains would go crashing around the bedroom floor along with his trousers.

*   *   *

These were happy moments when the family were together in front of the fire listening to John laying out his vision of Fulton Brothers Incorporated, or if any of us had heard a good joke, my mother would be the one who laughed the loudest, although not necessarily immediately. The problem was that although she loved a good joke, she rarely got the hang of it. A smile would visit her mouth then fade away. Her eyes would narrow in concentration, her mouth would pout and her head would nod in a parody of understanding while we all sat waiting for the laughter that we felt sure would come in the fullness of time. After a few minutes this became funnier than the joke itself, and we would all find ourselves in hysterics, including my mother who could see the funny side of her inability to see the funny side of her inability! And the evening would end in a riot of uninhibited laughter.

But there was more.

We would all be deeply asleep when the early hours of a dark morning would be rent with great heaving, high-pitched hoots coming from the bedroom downstairs, at which point lights would be put on, dressing-gowns donned, and the family would be in session again, but now gathered round my mother and father in their bed, my mother sitting up with tears streaming from her eyes and gasping for breath, helpless in the grip of uncontrollable laughter, and in danger of losing her dentures.

She had seen the joke!

Her talent for telling jokes was of much the same calibre as her ability to understand them. Her source was the neighbours, who occasionally passed on some rather mild waggery. It had taken my mother a good forty-eight hours to work out one 'funny story' her immediate neighbour had come up with. Come to that, her familial audience had a similar problem! My mother could scarcely begin to tell her joke for laughing. It was dependent on the fact that trains at this time were still fuelled by coal, and eventually she managed to come out with:

'Why does an engine driver have a tender behind?'

We didn't know. 'Why *does* an engine driver have a tender behind?'

She giggled some more and tried to straighten her face.

'Because,' she said triumphantly. '*Constipation!*'

Now the situation had changed radically. Silence hung in the air as the family struggled to make sense of the answer they had been given.

'Oh no, wait, that's wrong,' she said, covering her mouth with her hand. 'The right answer should have been: "Because he passes telegraph poles!" '

We decided we should talk about something else.

So popular did these family sessions become that, while barely in my teens, I started producing a little magazine every month. I wrote little fictional stories and jokes about the family, and drew cartoons depicting comic aspects of our lives. The Roebank Street shop was my print-room. I wrote out the material in longhand first of all, then carefully printed my magazine on an ancient Royal typewriter using the leaves of an old jotter I had taken apart, doing my best to make the columns and margins like a professional publisher's magazine, and colouring the cartoons with crayon. Perhaps because of this little four-page magazine I found myself unanimously elected as chief (entirely unpaid) general secretary to the Fulton family, called upon to pen an appropriate response to letters received or some event that had taken place—not always with success.

The Co-op butcher had angered my mother in some way and a council of war had solemnly decided that a letter of complaint should be written to the offender, who just happened to be the charge hand.

It was a good enough letter meant to make the recipient shake in his shoes at the prospect of 'dire consequences which could result from failure to address the matter e'er another day pass without receiving an abject apology'. The phrase was a favourite of mine and was the absolute in pomposity, leading, as it did, to the following warning: 'I have to tell you that I am in a position to take this matter to a much higher authority and will not hesitate to do so unless an apology is received by return. Yours etc.'

As on many other occasions, the reply was not only unsatisfactory, but downright crushing.

It read, 'Dear Sir, You are in a position to do bugger all!'

I decided to resign and stick with the magazine.

The routines and rituals my parents had created for themselves in twenty years of marriage were funny enough for the magazine, but a law of privacy had been passed. Their bedroom downstairs was small, measuring perhaps twelve feet by nine, and strained its walls to contain a full-sized bedroom suite. The double bed took up the whole of the door wall, blocking the pathetic little token fireplace completely, and a huge hot water tank sat precariously above their heads like some grotesque piece of art. The large wardrobe in which they shared their clothes space stood up against the wall at the foot of the bed, almost touching the dressing-table standing at an angle near the window. A gents' chest of drawers with a chair next to it—where my father laid his clothes when he undressed for bed—allowed no more than a centimetre's clearance for the door. By the time the little room had accommodated all this furniture there remained only an L-shaped passageway some eighteen inches wide, which had to be negotiated sideways with care.

It is not difficult to understand why my mother and father never went to bed at quite the same hour. The space available was barely enough for one person at a time. As the coal fire began to die down and its warmth retreated, the big ugly black clock on the living room mantelpiece, which had been a retirement presentation to my grandfather, would signal the lateness of the hour and some silent, coded signal would pass between my Mum and Dad as they began their genteel, individual preparations for the night. My mother would bid us 'goodnight' and disappear (sideways) into the darkened bedroom. My father would use her undressing time to wind the clock, check and synchronise it with his father's gold watch, then stand with his back to what was left of the fire and watch the bedroom door. In due course the signal was given when the bedroom door was opened a discreet two inches, and my father would tentatively approach to give the password. 'Ur ye in?' And on receiving a shy, muffled affirmative, he would turn to anyone not yet abed and offer his benediction.

'Don't you be sittin' therr a' night, mind!' With that he would enter the still darkened room, shut the door and undress in pitch blackness (and, in winter, extreme cold). Then, his pyjamas safely on, he would slip in beside his wife and immediately go off into a deep and unworried sleep, the light of each early morning revealing his carefully laid out clothes in a bedraggled heap on the floor where he always laid them.

'B'Jeez,' he would murmur. 'Ah thought therr wis a cherr therr.'

16

A BED TOO FAR

JUST BEFORE THE WAR my brother John had been going out with a delightful girl called Maisie who lived with her grandmother in Aberfoyle Street. Not only had they been going out, but Maisie had been helping John in the Roebank Street shop. When her grandmother died Maisie was left on her own with nowhere to stay, so my mother, being all heart, invited her to stay with us in Almond Street. We were now a family of six!

The upheaval caused by these arrangements was unbelievable.

In view of the prevailing propriety Maisie would have to sleep with my mother in the downstairs bedroom, while John would have to sleep in his own bedroom with my father, and Jim and I would sleep as usual on the bed-settee in the 'Good Room'.

It wasn't long before my mother and father became tired of the living arrangements, and wished they had thought twice. Consequently, their relationship with John's intended was not all it might have been. The dialogue was exactly the same each evening when Maisie arrived home after a long hard day.

'Oh, it's *cold*!' she would say in greeting as usual.

'Well, pull yer shurt ower it,' my father would respond without looking up. A sure sign that familiarity was breeding dislike. My father's major complaint about this poor girl was that when she had finished a light snack before retiring to bed, she would wash only her own cup, saucer, plate and cutlery.

The living conditions were bringing things to a head. After a period of time it was to everyone's relief that John and Maisie decided to get married. But the game of musical beds wasn't quite over. It began to look as if the sleeping arrangements were still in place.

For whatever reason, John designated me as his representative. My brief was to go to my father and explain that things could get back to normal now. John and Maisie were married and it was only right that they should have a bedroom of their own, and father could get back to the comfort of his own bed.

His response was unexpected, and only reinforced his dislike of Maisie.

'Ach,' he said. 'He only waants tae sleep wi' 'er!'

It was difficult to understand the logic of his answer. Normally my father was a placid, quiet man, but it was possible that the problems he was facing in the shops because of the approach of the war were getting to him.

He and my mother quarrelled as never before.

At one point they were having a real set-to, and my father, unable to take any more, put his hat and coat on and went out into the darkness. Typically, my mother's anger metamorphosed into serious worry—a few minutes before seeking comfort and reassurance from her sons that everything would be all right. But she had already pictured my father jumping head first into the canal.

'You don't think he would . . .' (cue music) '. . . *do something silly . . . ?*'

I wanted to say that he might well have stopped for a pee in the canal, but it didn't seem appropriate. It really was a lousy movie. It was, as I saw it then and still see it now, a mixture of Mary Pickford at her worst and Laurel and Hardy at their best.

John became alarmed, and put on his hat and coat, and went out

82

to search for his father. After a few minutes my mother became concerned about John. By this time Jim was crying and put on his hat and coat and went out to look for John and my father. The latter returned, unaware that anyone else had left the house, and discovered that both John and Jim were 'out there somewhere'. He put his hat and coat back on again and went out to look for John and Jim.

My mother became concerned about *everybody*! She put on a warm coat and a scarf over her head and went out looking for her husband and two sons. Maisie had wisely gone to bed, and I was too young to take part in this French farce, so I had to hold the fort. Even the dog had taken the opportunity to go out and find somebody. Anybody. Anything! Especially a lamppost.

It transpired that all four of them had been within a few yards of one another as they zig-zagged up and down the dark streets, meeting neighbours walking their dogs, or just walking, and giving them a wave or a friendly 'Good evening, what a terrible night, eh?' and trying to put on a cloak of nonchalance as they scouted for each other, all too embarrassed to reveal the reason for their nocturnal wanderings.

When, eventually, they had found each other and chatted briefly to ninety per cent of the neighbours, either in the streets or at their homes, they were all too tired to remember what the problem had been—and went to bed!

The crisis was over.

17

SILVERWELLS: A DREAM

THERE WAS A KIND of nomadic quality about the family, but this was really only my mother exercising her restlessness and trying to drag the rest of us along with her. Unfortunately, we were quite the opposite—all of us, my father, my brothers and I, had always shown a reluctance to move once roots had been put down. My mother's actual goal was not very clear, but the idea of 'doing a wee bit letting' seemed to have a strange appeal for her that the rest of us couldn't quite understand. Such was my mother's personality, however, that eventually, without realising it, we found much of our free time taken up with car journeys around Scotland with a view to purchasing properties we couldn't possibly afford.

My father had had a series of cars over the years. He started with a motorcycle and sidecar, followed by a bull-nosed Morris Cowley. The one I remember most clearly was what seemed to me to be a large, square, no-nonsense Morris Oxford which could accommodate all six of us.

I looked forward to these Sunday runs. I had a little seat of my own which was slotted into the back of the driver's seat. John and Jim had made a little folding table so that my mother could prepare the picnic. We either packed thermos flasks of tea, or carried a tin kettle to boil water on a twig fire at the side of some little burn. Everything was packed in a large picnic hamper, ready for the day's mystery tour. We left early in the day and often met some of our neighbours on similar safaris. Normally, we tried not to go too far afield so that we could allow sufficient time to get home; a family business like my father's didn't allow much in the way of leisure time. As we turned to start the homeward journey it was the duty of all to keep their eyes open for a likely fish-and-chip shop, the food eaten in the car as we drove, with someone delegated to feed the driver. We became connoisseurs of the deep-fried potato and kept a note of the shops that had particularly impressed us. I always fell asleep on the road home, but never failed to waken in time to see my favourite signal of our home-coming, the Glasgow Bridge with the great coloured lights of the advertisements, some animated, all brilliant, ever new and exciting, and at the same time familiar and comforting.

There is no joy in the world quite like coming home.

*   *   *

Our greatest adventure with the car was undoubtedly our trip to Blackpool. Mother had sisters in Lytham St. Anne's, Kate and Minnie, who with brother-in-law Charlie ran a boarding house. Kate had died very recently and my mother regretted not having made contact sooner.

The journey was planned for a Sunday, the only day when some shopkeepers could take a break. Orders of the day were decided unanimously, with the exception of my small self. On the Saturday afternoon we all went to bed at five o'clock. I was put to bed on the settee which had been placed at the window, but it seemed no one slept because of the excitement. I certainly didn't. I listened and watched as the sounds and lights faded. First the buzz of the bowling green members, then the traffic, all disappearing into the peaceful silence of the witching hour.

As luck would have it, I was just dropping off when it was time to get up and prepare for the safari. Ablutions had to be in strict order since there was only one bathroom and the kitchen sink to provide for four males and two females. The car was loaded with all the gear required for the journey, including the picnic basket, and we set off.

There were a number of times when my father, who had insisted on doing the driving, got us well and truly lost. The routes to the South in the thirties were nothing like they are now, and he had to stop rather a lot to try and find his bearings. John and Jim had the unenviable task of getting out of the car to climb up signposts and read them by torchlight. At one stage, as we slowly made our way through a small village in which there were still some late-nighters about, my father, in exasperation, called on Jim to 'get oot and ask that fella where wur gaun!' Answer was there none.

Some time around six in the morning, however, when the sun had overcome its diffidence, my father drove into the famous fun city of Blackpool, with soaking wet roads from heavy overnight rain, already steaming from the heat of the sun, and a sky as blue as we could possibly wish. The place was empty apart from the few early fitness fanatics dressed only in beach shorts. Blackpool had not yet awakened.

It was less than fortunate that my father insisted he would have the honour of driving us into the great borough of Blackpool, one of the most popular holiday resorts in Britain, attracting hundreds of thousands of visitors. Bracing climate, sandy beaches, promenades, swimming baths, cinemas, theatres, aquarium, famous illuminations, and a 520-foot tower modelled on the Eiffel Tower in Paris. My father's problem was to find someone who could put us on the road to St. Anne's. He didn't have all that much choice in view of the fact that there were very few people up and about.

My father chose a road-sweeper, busy squeegeeing water down

a drain. Father wound down his window and, in the elegant way he had when trying to catch people's attention, shouted: 'Heh, can ye tell us . . . ?' But for some reason the road-sweeper was not prepared to be detracted from the importance of Public Cleansing and ignored him. He tried again. 'Aaaaaaaaaaaaaaaaaaaay,' and waved his hand. This time the road-cleansing gentleman turned and my father repeated his request. 'Could ye pit us oan the road tae St. Anne's?'

The cleansing executive waved us away and shook his head. My father appealed to him yet again. 'St. Anne's,' he shouted. 'Ur ye deef or somethin'? Whit road dae we take fur St. Anne's?' The road-sweeper, now irritated, waved a hand and pointed at his ears and mouth while making rather strange sounds. For a moment, we all thought that perhaps my father's Scottish accent was too broad for the English, then we suddenly realised what the problem was. The road sweeper *was* 'deef'.

'B'Jeez,' said my exasperated father. 'We get this faur, an' of a' the folk tae pick we huv tae ask a dummy!' That would almost certainly be regarded as politically incorrect these days, but it was the way my father spoke.

It took us some time and innumerable enquiries—mainly by John and Jim since my father was taking no further chances—to find St. Anne's and the hotel. An emotional reunion took place between my mother and her sister Minnie and brother-in-law Charlie. What startled me was the similarity of the two women, although Minnie seemed thin and fragile compared to my Mum, so looked just that bit smaller. With their busy-bee movements and the same 'ear-phone' hairstyle, the two women could have been taken for twins.

After a thumping English breakfast the real adventure began. The promise of the early morning was fulfilled, and the day was a scorcher. We came back into Blackpool and literally 'did the town'. We gazed at everything—the Tower, the trams gliding along the Golden Mile, the beach, and, best of all for me, the bathing pool where, for the first time, I was able to discard my inflatable rubber ring and swim unaided.

There was no way I could have known that in a few short years I would be doing something very similar, but it wouldn't be in the Blackpool bathing pool. But that is another story.

Late in the afternoon we returned to the boarding house in St. Anne's for a slap-up tea, after which I was led to a large bed in an enormous room where I fell into an exhausted sleep. It was a shock, however, being wakened up only a couple of hours later and bundled into the car with the family, as we set off on the road back to Scotland. I had assumed that we would be spending a few days at least, but typically, it proved to be a short, speedy, brisk visit and back home. The adventure had lasted just over twenty-four hours. Perhaps it was just as well—my mother would have wanted to buy the boarding-house and 'do a wee bit letting'!

On another occasion the whole family drove to Invergordon and back one Sunday to view a grocer's shop which mother had seen advertised. Even I couldn't help being caught up in her enthusiasm. During the drive I had a vision of having a bicycle with a basket in front for delivering groceries around this small burgh of less than two thousand people. It was a gold mine, we were told, especially when the fleet was in. Unfortunately the owners omitted to explain that it had ceased to be a Naval base and there was no longer a fleet to be relied upon for their custom. On the other hand, my mother argued, we could find a house which would be close enough for some of us to commute to the shops while she ran some sort of B&B establishment or, as she kept describing, 'do a wee bit letting.'

It was madness!

On one of our Sunday drives we actually viewed a newly built bungalow in Largs near the Barrfields Pavilion. The villa, so called, had perhaps three tiny bedrooms, plus a lounge, kitchen and one bathroom. My crazy family went to the trouble of getting hold of the salesman and declaring their interest in buying this doll's house. It was perfect, they whispered to each other. 'We can all live in the attic,' my mother said. 'That way we can let out the bedrooms, and I'll do the cooking.' With a good deal more luck than judgement, they were restrained from signing the missive since they couldn't put down a deposit. And having slept on it, they finally realised that their lives would be more than cramped. In any case (very much a secondary consideration), they didn't have enough money for a bank loan, or a mortgage.

But my mother wouldn't give up. They discovered that a splendid family house called 'Silverwells' was for sale in Prestwick. The owner was a charming, well-to-do elderly gentleman who showed us round the whole property which boasted some twelve rooms, garages and outhouses. It was all very impressive. We gathered in the drawing-room to discuss the matter. The family put on grave, sedate, sober faces, trying to look intelligent and businesslike, hoping that they would be seen as reasonable, sensible, business people who knew what they were doing. The owner stood with his back to a huge fire as he watched the Fulton family in serious discussion. He, poor man, must have thought that there was a decision and offer in the offing. And 'off' it proved to be. My father approached the owner. 'Wid ye—ay—wid ye take a hundred pounds?'

There was a long pause. Long enough to suggest to the family that the owner was either intently considering the offer my father had just made, or perhaps had just had a heart attack. But the owner of the 'Silverwells' pile was not considering anything, other than getting these clowns out of his house.

'I think not,' he said. 'Let me show you the door again.'

Homeward bound, a rather depressed tribe returned to Riddrie, with the final vote being that at least it had been worth a try! The mission may have been a waste of time, but I had fallen in love with 'Silverwells' and its name. I dreamt about it, and made up my mind that when I grew up I would buy a big family house like 'Silverwells' and give it the same name.

18

LAST DAYS OF PEACE

NOT SURPRISINGLY 1938 was a nervous year. Two crazy men by the names of Adolf Hitler and Benito Mussolini were running amok, and it wasn't all that clear what they might get up to. But some things, good things, it seemed, were going on regardless. Walt Disney's first feature-length cartoon film, *Snow White and the Seven Dwarfs*, arrived in the cinemas and was rapturously received. My fourteenth birthday was on 15th April. The previous year I had almost decided to go into long trousers, and couldn't find the courage. But this year, long breeks it was.

I was given into the hands of a tailor in Todd, Cunninghame and Petrie, a large wholesale warehouse opposite the Trongate. My father being in the trade meant that the suit would be at wholesale prices. It was a made-to-measure outfit in petrol-green with single-breasted jacket, straight trousers and . . . plus fours! Added to that was a pair of light grey flannels which meant I had three outfits that I sported one at a time when I was attending the magnificent Empire Exhibition.

Here was magic, if you like. Here was fantasy. The memory of Blackpool dimmed to black and white by comparison. The Exhibition was opened on May 3rd 1938 by King George VI and his lovely Queen. The pipes skirled, the flags flapped, and it seemed as if half the population of Scotland had come to watch the ceremony. With a season ticket laboriously paid for by instalments at school, I usually attended the Exhibition three or four times a week; never for a moment tiring of the sheer glamour of it all. It was beautifully laid out with Bellahouston Park looking as it had never looked before or since. The great exhibition halls, the landscaped grounds, the funfair, the restaurant in the style of a ship, all provided a day of magic and wonder. I wouldn't be surprised to discover that Walt Disney may have had his brainchild as a result of a secret visit to Bellahouston. I wondered why the city fathers hadn't retained it as a permanent feature in the city, but, behind the glamour and excitement of the time, there was still fear and despondency. Britain was tooling up for a massive armaments programme.

However, the fear and despondency were lifted on Neville Chamberlain's return from Munich waving his little bit of paper and declaring the quote of the year—'Peace in our time.' Suddenly the fear and anxiety were easing and our spirits soared. Hopes and young dreams were restored to the agenda and we could look to the future.

Mr. Chamberlain may have thought he had dealt with Adolf Hitler, but he had not managed to reassure my mother. It would have been helpful if he could have called on her personally at No. 5 Almond Street, but perhaps he had another engagement.

My mother consulted her husband. 'Daddy, tell me honestly what you think. Is there going to be another war?'

My father was contemptuous.

'Of course no'. B'Jeez, hoo mony times huv Ah tae tell ye? *There's gonnae be nae war!*'

She held this slight miscalculation over his head for the rest of their lives. Ever afterward the slightest disagreement between them would end with my mother marching back to her kitchen calling contemptuously: *'And you said there wasn't going to be a war!'*

My father swore that in future his answer to any question

whatsoever would be 'Ah don't know.' He couldn't help feeling guilty; his wife was convinced it was *he* who had invaded Poland and started the whole thing without telling her. Jim and John were rather more pessimistic, as were most people, about what they saw as the inevitable. Jim actually went as far as to suggest that 'the kid' (that was me) 'might get the worst of it.' I wasn't quite sure what he meant, but I didn't much like the sound of it.

19

THOS & ROBT

MY TIES WITH WHITEHILL SECONDARY were severed on 29th May 1939 and I set about applying for a job. Letters of application had a sort of formal style. I wrote to Thos F. Murray & Co. of 134 St. Vincent Street, Glasgow, a coal merchant who, I suspect, had never seen a lump of coal in his life. My letter went as follows:

'Dear sir, I write in response to your advertisement in the *Evening Citizen* of yesterday's date advertising a vacancy in your company, and wish to formally apply for the position. I am fifteen years old, tall, of good appearance and excellent education, and would relish the prospect of making a career in coal! I am free for interview at any time if . . .' etc.

I was granted an interview by Mr. Thos Murray himself, which wasn't surprising since there was only room for two people anyway. All the offices in the building were tiny. One was presumably for reception and the other was the private office of Thos F. Murray, who appeared to be managing-director-cum-owner of the tiny business.

Thos (which I actually thought must be his Christian name) addressed me by my Sunday name of Robert. He, on the other hand, as I was to learn later, never used anything other than his formal appellation. He even signed his name thus, with a very broad fountain pen that made it more like a painting than a signature. I often wondered if his friends referred to him as Thos. . . . Thomas or Tom I could understand, but *Thos*? I wondered if he was going to call me by some abbreviated name. I had been called Robert, Robin, Bert, Bob, Bobby, or Heh you, sur! which was the way my father addressed me.

But I wondered if Thos was so keen on abbreviations it might occur to him to call me Robt! Or what if he happened to be calling a friend called Godwin on the telephone?

That could cause a problem!

Ring! Ring!

'Hello, Thos F. Murray. Can I help you?'

'Yes. Is Thos there?'

'Speaking. Who's that?'

'God speaking!'

I got on very well with Thos, although he seemed to think that I was not sufficiently soberly dressed for so great a corporate giant. He suggested my two-tone rather sporty tan and fawn shoes were inappropriate for a business gentleman. Black shoes would be much superior, especially with a dark suit. And to complete the ensemble, a white shirt and dark tie. And possibly, he thought, narrowing his eyes to visualise the effect—*a bowler!*

We settled for fifteen shillings a week, half day on Saturdays, start on Monday. I agreed but promised myself I would not, under any circumstances, wear a bowler hat! I would have looked a right idiot and the tennis crowd would never have let me live it down. Before I went into the office to start my first day I took the time to buy myself a rather snazzy navy-blue soft hat.

Meantime, there were constant reminders of the approach of war, one of which was the thoughtful placing of an air-raid siren on top of a police box just below our office window. The unexpected banshee howl when the ARP drill was practised must have caused many a cardiac arrest, and all concentration had to be suspended until it was over.

When the news of the declaration of war came at 11 a.m. on 3rd September, there was 'a profound silence, but also a sense of relief and grim satisfaction. The shilly-shallying is over. The die is cast.'

That was true. Everybody had been trying to put it out of their minds for months and pretend that life was normal. Even so, the feeling was that things were never ever going to be the same again.

The blackout was the most startling change in our lifestyle, frightening and exciting at the same time. And it had its advantages, too. In the dark hours the girls preferred to walk home in groups—especially with groups of boys. 'Snogging' areas hitherto unsuitable because of unacceptably high levels of illumination suddenly became available. The back seat of a bus was nearly as good, and a lot cheaper than the pictures.

We still spent most of our leisure time in the tennis clubhouse or the Elite Café right next door. For want of the French language, we couldn't help calling it the Eelight, and we as much as made it our own. It boasted a fair-sized function room at the back with tables around the dancing area, and a little dais where a small ship's piano with a hinged keyboard lived. There was even room on the dais for a small band, but we weren't all that interested. We preferred the 1939 hi-fi system which was in constant use playing the big hits of the day, such as 'In the Mood' with Joe Loss, with whom I was to work many years later. Other big favourites were 'The Woodchoppers' Ball', 'Begin the Beguine', and with constant practice the dancing became more flamboyant and stylish by the day.

The fact that we had come to know that the Italian family who owned the Elite were to be interned, prepared us for even greater changes. We were very sad, for these people had been our friends, and one of their sons, Tony, had been in my class at Whitehill. He was quite a character, and popular with it.

In due course a Scottish family took over the Café, and we were served and looked after by a large, buxom girl who sometimes found us just a little overbearing.

There was an attractive girl who occasionally came in with her friends. One night I asked her to dance, and in the process understood what 'libido' and 'testosterone' meant for the first time.

We danced very well together and we danced very close. There wasn't room for a cigarette paper between us. We were gliding and swaying around the room, oblivious to everything else, executing steps that Fred Astaire and Ginger Rogers hadn't even thought of, and breathing heavily into the bargain, although, to be honest, the heavy breathing had nothing to do with the dancing.

To a mass of wide eyes, nudges and raised eyebrows from the tennis club tables, we left together, and I walked her home. She lived in the scheme beyond Riddrie, and it was a fair hike.

It was also a perishing cold night. She snuggled close to keep warm as we walked the length of Smithycroft Road and up the Cumby Road. I would have no need of a hot water bottle that night, I thought.

But it was less than romantic leaning up against a railing, and to make matters worse we were right out in the open where anyone who had a mind to could see what the butler saw for free. Desirous of a little more privacy, and seeking to improve our chances of surviving hypothermia, we sought out a quiet 'close-mooth' and started the countdown.

Fumble, fumble, pant, pant!

But it was hopeless. Claw-like fingers, hands and faces completely numb and now trying to cope with a force ten gale blowing in from the back of the close. I couldn't even keep my lips from quivering long enough to kiss her goodnight. I was also beginning to worry about her face which had become an interesting aquamarine colour. Also, I had never seen frozen lipstick before.

The game was definitely a bogey. We gave up and separated

with cheery rather muffled promises that we would one day take up where we left off.

I ran as fast as I could in the hope that the strenuous exercise would help to thaw out my bloodstream. But the damage had been done. Five days later I was flat on my back with pneumonia.

When my mother telephoned Thos to tell him I was quite ill, he was all heart. 'Tell him not to worry about *anything*, Mrs. Fulton, except getting well,' he ordered. 'His job will be here for him as soon as he's fit again!'

Obviously he had not thought quickly enough. He had missed an excellent opportunity to cut 'his staff' by a third and so save fifteen shillings a week. He would have been right to do so—there wasn't work for three people. Thos F. Murray wasn't going anywhere, and neither was I. It wasn't a job, it was a pastime, a game. And I was quite happy to leave the team.

But luck was with me. Serendipity was alive and well.

Before I was out of my sick-bed—I was in it for six weeks—I had the offer of a better, much more interesting job.

Brother John had become a member of the Clyde River Patrol. It was the kind of seafaring he particularly enjoyed since he would never need to get off the jetty. Plus the fact that he only worked nights, which John seemed to prefer to daylight.

One of his fellow officers (Mr. W. P. C. B. Scott), was a director of a ship delivery contractors'. He was the second-in-command and was desperate for a customs clerk. John 'suggested' he knew just the boy to fill the vacancy! (They both knew what they were talking about.) So when my health had fully recovered, I became the customs clerk for Henry Abrams Ltd., 163 Hope Street, Glasgow, just round the corner from Thos.

Not only that, but let's face it, the offices were *much* bigger!

I loved the new job. It was a difficult and complex task, and took a bit of learning, but it all fell into place soon enough. I had a huge desk and masses of customs forms to play with as I calculated and paid out the duty on behalf of importers from all over the world, mainly for cork from Portugal, and then arranged for delivery by road to its destination. I will always remember arriving at a rather cold office in the winter mornings. The stenographer was a young male, the first and last I had ever encountered. It was also his job to get the coal fire going, and I still think of it as strange to see a homely fireplace and brightly burning fire in a commercial office.

There was a supplementary bonus attached to the salary now and again. A roster was arranged for the office staff (the typist, book-keeper, me, the customs clerk, and the office boy) to take turns at 'fire-watching', for which we received the magnificent sum of five shillings for the night, and a later start next morning. I enjoyed it immensely. I enlisted my pals to share the watch. We both received five bob, and put on another twenty phoning up all the girls we knew.

One outstanding memory I have is of two of the officials with whom I had to deal in Customs House. One was Miss Flynn. She had jet black hair pulled straight back from a florid face totally devoid of make-up, and little pince-nez which sat half-way down her nose, which was in itself an outstanding feature. In those days (and perhaps even today for all I know), the inspectors stood or sat on high stools behind rows of Dickensian sloping desks with brass rails on top to hold papers and files, with a long counter at right angles running the full length of the great hall.

Miss Flynn was desk-to-desk with a large Germanic-looking gentleman with blond short-back-and-sides hair and a heavy, round, sneering, pasty face. His name was Murtagh, although the customs clerks called him 'Murder'!

There was a joke among the customs clerks that suggested these two misfits were having an *affaire*; that after a long day of scream-ing and sneering at us, they would dress in expensive, outrageous clothes, and go off to secret, sexy parties. We could picture Flynn unpinning her bun from the back of her head, allowing her long black tresses to flow free, and indulging in a frenzy of sensualism. But we decided it wasn't likely.

In any case, we had no wish to get on the wrong side of these two. We already walked a tightrope every time we lodged a customs document.

Descriptions and the often complex mathematics had to be perfect, or we would be in big trouble.

I used to smile on the occasions when they had reason to address each other; she simpering all over her red face, he very courteously correct. Although I always thought there was a rather sinister, meaningful glint in his eye.

'Miss Flynn,' he would call. 'I'm sorry to impose on you, but I wonder if I might . . . borrow a paperclip!'

She panted for a moment, her red face becoming redder, as she sat on her high stool at the sloping desk. Then she would show us her bright clean dentures as she smiled at 'Murder'. Like a gorgon taking its prey.

'Always a pleasure Mister Murtagh. There you are. Oh, by the way, while you're there, could I have a fill of your red ink? I seem to have gone dry.'

On the contrary, she was always perspiring.

However, it was with one of these two that I had to lodge the documents. These included bills of lading, invoices, certificates of origin, the correct customs document showing the description of the goods which had to comply strictly with the tariff tables, the conversion of foreign currencies to sterling, kilos to hundredweights and so on, plus the calculation of the correct duty at the correct rate.

Sadly, it was too early to have the luxury of a calculator. Also, it was not given to ordinary mortals like me, to be able to divine when a ship carrying cargo for which we were responsible was going to dock. Notice was sometimes alarmingly short, and sometimes annoyingly unexpected. Speed was of the essence. Big money was involved, especially mine if I made any errors. The cargo had to be unloaded and set down on the quay from where it would be cleared by customs and sent on its way to its destination by road.

It could be costly to have a cargo lying for any time on the dockside.

There was always a panic when a cargo came in, as we breathlessly calculated the sums; a nightmare of anxiety until the forms were in the hands of customs for checking. It was the nail-biting wait before our jotters were marked, usually next day, that got to us. If the calculation of duty was incorrect it was assumed to be deliberate, and a fine would be imposed, which made it difficult to go back to the office and ask for a raise. It was always a great relief when we found that all was well and we could relax, sleep soundly, and dream dreams of Miss Flynn and Murder locked together in the dark customs office underneath their desks, exchanging paperclips and red ink.

20

THE ELITE CORPS

IN THE MEANTIME, the war drums were beating ever louder, and the young braves of the Elite Café were becoming more and more aggressive, screaming their defiance and their frustration at not being able to get into their Spitfires and engage the enemy that very day. They were up-beat, confident, eager for the adventure. The thought of possible death never even entered their young heads. And it is one of my saddest recollections that so many failed to survive.

My own initial wartime memory came when one of the prettiest girls there, in her tight little curls and pretty frock, and fired perhaps by the machismo displayed by the young braves, turned her glowing eyes on to me and asked excitedly: 'What about you, Rikki? Are you going to be a fighter pilot, too?'

Now, I had been expecting this, but I hadn't been able to think of a way out of it. However, I felt I had to say something. I couldn't very well tell her *I didn't want to go!* or that I hadn't made up my mind yet. It sounded so weak. And I didn't want to disappoint her, not when I was looking into enchanting violet eyes like that. There was no doubt—the eyes had it. Suddenly I heard somebody say: 'The Air Force? Naaaaaaaaaa! I'll tell you what's the best uniform. The Navy! They're much more glamorous than the Air Force.'

'You surely wouldn't want to wear those funny hats and awful bell-bottom trousers?' said Violet Eyes. His mouth took on a crooked smile.

'Nah, nah,' he said. 'I'm not talking about lower deck stuff, the AB's and so forth. I'm talking about the officers with their navy-blue suits, gold buttons, gold stripes. And the cap with that badge. That's a real uniform.'

I saw her look up at him with those glistening violet eyes, and I thought to myself, what's wrong with me? Here are all these guys shouting the odds about what service they want to join, and how they can't wait to get into the war!

The atmosphere in the Elite was heady with the smoke from all the Spitfires our boys were busy flying, as they shouted: 'I'll get you, ya bastard. I'll get you. AH-AH-AH-AH-AH-AH! We'll show you, you bastards.'

'The boys seem to be excited,' said Violet Eyes.

I didn't know what to say. If I had thought in any constructive way about what would happen, I might have come to some sensible decision, but all I could think of was that I *didn't want to go!* I had absolutely no desire to leave my home and my family and go around shooting people to whom I hadn't even been introduced.

I could hear the guy say: 'Well, of course, I am a bit excited, I suppose.' (*He was lying!*) 'But, well, you see it's all to do with the sea.' My ears stood up.

'What has it to do with the sea?' asked Violet Eyes.

'Well,' the guy said. 'To start with, my work is in the shipping business. Right? So, I suppose it's not unnatural to want to maintain my connection with the sea.' Violet Eyes was impressed. So was I! I had never heard so much twaddle in my life.

But there was more.

'You see,' the guy said. 'There's another much more important consideration about deciding which of the services you would prefer. For example, I believe that you have a better chance if you're on the water. I mean, if you're a fighter pilot in the Air Force and your plane's shot down, or you're a soldier in the front line, there's a much greater risk than there is at sea. Because if your ship gets sunk and you can swim, you have a much better chance of survival.'

I was very taken with the guy who had been talking. There was a lot of good sense in what he'd been saying. And he was *right*! Knowing that the time would come when every able-bodied man of eighteen and over would eventually receive an invitation to join the party, there was only one way to join the preferred service— and that was to volunteer. That was what the guy had been saying. It did make sense. And no one was more surprised than I was when I realised that the guy who had been shooting off his mouth and talking all this nonsense about volunteering . . . was me!

How could someone so terrified of violence be talking about *volunteering* to go to war! I could imagine being dragged, scream-ing, into some barracks or other in the South of England, but *volunteer*? I had never been in a fight in my life.

As it happened, I wasn't dead right or dead wrong about being at sea, but the problem I now faced was that I would have to practise what I had been preaching. Whatever the qualities of that particular sermon, it was to prove prophetic!

21

OFF TO THE GANGES

MY OWN WAR EFFORT, such as it was, began in 1941 at the tender age of seventeen years and three months, the youngest acceptable age at which I could volunteer. Having shot my mouth off about the Navy, it seemed I had no option but to go through with it.

The first step was to pay a visit to the Admiralty board in Edinburgh. I was volunteering to join the Navy under a scheme called the 'Y' Scheme. I have never been sure about what the 'Y' stood for, but I assumed then that it stood for Youth. This was a scheme under which young applicants with reasonable educational standards might be accepted for training as officer material, and would be required to offer documentation as proof. I wasn't all that sure that my educational standards would be sufficient to qualify. I was asked a number of questions, including the inevitable 'Why do you want to join the Navy?'

In any case the board of three (I presumed they were retired officers of some rank) seemed to be less interested in the importance of my educational 'gifts', than they were in my father's status in the community! So instead of offering the simple straightforward answer—that he was a shopkeeper—I painted him more as a tycoon, the managing director of a multiple retail shopping combine. If I had been truthful, I would have had to say that my mother was really the Boss Lady. But that hurdle was cleared and they were satisfied. The answer I received was a 'yes' vote from the Board, who invited me to join the happy throng at *HMS Ganges* at Harwich and wished me good luck, at the same time arranging the all-important medical.

I left on the given date with various documents and instructions as to where I should report, and headed for what seemed to be a huge warehouse in Dalmarnock Road that had been taken over for the purpose of medical examinations. It was divided into what looked like a series of tents with odd chairs and, of course, the traditional bucket. What followed was not what could be truly called a medical examination. Everything seemed to be dependent on the contents of the bladder. Clearly, it was the most important part of the examination and yet it was the one thing impossible to cope with at will. A young man of about my own age, who had just completed a term in Glasgow University, and sported a territorial uniform, joined me in seeking some food. Those of us who had failed to provide the necessary evidence were advised to take a lunch break and drink as much fluid as possible. After all these years, I can still hear the wailing plea from a frantic young man who had lunched as directed and taken more fluid than was necessary. His cry was not so much from the heart; more a cry from the bladder. 'Hey, nurse, gonnae get us another bucket!'

I waited with grateful patience for my eighteenth birthday. (I was in no hurry.) I had anticipated that I would hear from the Admiralty when I reached the age when I legally became an adult and could be taken from my family. For the short time I had left, I continued my civilian life with a number of 'engagements', such as being whisked off in a darkened bus in the black of night to play the piano for Scottish troops in some hidden valley. Or performing with a chum called Gordon on two pianos in the large hall of St. Enoch's Hogganfield church. Gordon played using a similar technique to my own, and another pal came with us who owned a drum set—although it didn't follow that he had any talent for playing it.

We were promised ten shillings for the night and thought that a fair fee for our work. Having positioned ourselves back-to-back, we worked our way through waltzes, tangos, eightsome reels, foxtrots and The Dashing White Sergeant, all of which we played in strict tempo—the same strict tempo for every dance!

Panting and perspiring couples, having won a gold for the fastest circuit of the hall, came to us on their knees. '*Slower*,' they gasped. 'For God's sake, can't you play a bit slower?' At which a breathtaking drop in tempo brought others to us with achingly protracted steps to plead with equal desperation. '*Faster! Please! Could you play a little bit faster?*' But then, you can't please everybody!

*   *   *

As far as the family was concerned, the war brought a flurry of defensive activity. Mother and Maisie took over the running of the two main shops while Father took over the tea dispenser at a servicemen's canteen at Millerston. John and a family friend who was in engineering set up one of the many back street munitions factories and were thus satisfactorily ensconced in reserved occupations.

In spite of John's efforts, the same did not work out quite so well for Jim who, it had been hoped, would be safe as a motor mechanic with SMT. He was called up for service in the RAF and spent practically all of his time in the seaport of Takoradi in Ghana, north-west Africa. On the other hand I wasn't going to have to go so far away. At least, not *quite* so far.

The few months left seemed to pass very quickly. Just before my eighteenth birthday I received an invitation to join the jolly band at *HMS Ganges* near Harwich, on 26th March 1942.

I certainly did not exactly cover myself with glory in the area of tact on the way down on the train. Seated in the same compartment was a 'fellow seafarer', and I assumed, incorrectly as it transpired, that he would be delighted and deeply interested to learn that I would soon be in the same uniform as he, although only for a limited period of time as I had volunteered under the 'Y' Scheme, and was therefore a CW (Commission Warrant) candidate and, all going well, would be commissioned after completing the officers' training course. He was singularly discouraging.

'Aye, just read yer comic, son,' he said.

22

TABBED

HMS GANGES was an enormous establishment. There was a huge tarmacadam parade ground that could have accommodated several thousand cars. It looked and felt like a modern airport that had been abandoned. In the middle stood a fully rigged mast about three miles high. Or so it seemed. Before a sailor could be considered fully trained, he had to climb up and over this monstrosity and return to earth before passing out as a fully trained Ordinary Seaman, and 'pass out' many of them did at the very thought of it. I couldn't count the number of sailors who complained of vertigo. But that would come much later.

Meantime, recruits in their first two weeks were admitted to the *Ganges* annexe, a large and comfortable dormitory where we would live for two weeks during which time we would be kitted-up. Initial programmes and a startling number of lectures from petty officers, chief petty officers and officers took place.

Letters and parcels arrived much earlier than we expected—unlikely friendships seemed to have sprouted with girls at home who had not previously been considered as being of interest, but who had written and/or sent tuck parcels and sweets. But from then on the bulk of my mail came regularly from Maisie and my mother whose religious beliefs appeared at the end of each letter in the form of a much repeated homily: 'God as your guide no ill can come.' Whether my mother was the author or had heard it from some other source I had no idea. I had my own ideas about her trust in the Almighty, and there came a time when I found evidence to suggest that it wasn't as simple as that.

I collected the rough-cloth bell-bottom trousers, the 'scone' cap with a ribbon carrying the name of the ship tied round the cap in what was called a tiddly bow. Tunic, collar, the black silk which went round the neck and under the collar. White shirt edged with striped tapes, socks, boots, raincoat, lanyard, knife, hammock, mattress, sheets and blanket. Suddenly I was Ordinary Seaman Fulton JX350609, wondering what I had got myself into. And there was the strangely poignant ritual of preparing our now redundant civvies in our little cases for sending home to our parents. I could imagine how they felt. Two sons removed from their home with no indication of how long it would be before we would meet again. During the two weeks in the annexe we had to suffer interminable visits from the 'old hands' in the main establishment. Caps with tiddly bows perched impossibly on the back of their heads, wide U-fronted tunics revealing gleaming white shirts, and, (the true sign of a hardened veteran) a carefully pressed collar which had been dark navy-blue but was now a washed out light blue. They gazed at the rookies with a supercilious grin through the smoke of duty-free self-rolled fags which hung nonchalantly from their mouths. 'How long ye been in?' They were so laid back they might well have fallen over.

'Er—ten days,' somebody said. The veterans gazed at us pity-ingly and offered a supercilious grin. 'Only ten days?' said one. 'Jeez-oh!' 'How long have you been in?' we asked them. There was a long dramatic pause, while their war-weary eyes raked each of us in turn clearly wondering if we were ready for the shock. '*Five weeks!*' We rookies gawped at one another. Five weeks! I thought they were going to say 'Five *years!*'

Our next hurdle was fearful. This was the dreaded typhoid-paratyphoid A and B vaccine, or TAB for short, that all ratings were required to accept with a double injection—an initial 25% of the vaccine, followed by a 75% dose. The queues were never-ending and God help you if you got in the wrong queue. Many fainted, and one received the 75% dose first rather than the 25%, by mistake—an error which, sadly, cost the young man his life. Others suffered from the reaction and needed treatment for the treatment. One was the mate that I had met at the time of our medical at home in Bridgeton. I went to see him in the sickbay and he was in a pathetic state. I could hardly believe it was the same man. With his face and body covered with sores, he was not a happy sailor.

The rest of us could only cross our legs and fingers, suffer the discomfort, and hope the pain would soon be over. The TAB, which would be registered in the rating's pay-book, produced a condition that wasn't very different from a bad dose of 'flu. Each jab stiffened the arm (mostly the right arm), which became so painful and stiff it was almost impossible to use. All of this was borne with great fortitude and pride, and worn like a battle honour.

The ability to swim was another important item that had to be checked out and that, too, would be recorded in our pay-books. Most had learned to swim years before, and many of us had learned life-saving, but those who had never learned would have to be taught. It could save their lives. For anyone spending time at sea the ability to swim was paramount, as I was to find out.

One of the highlights of our initiation period in the annexe was the weekly talent contest. I entered simply for something better to do with the time, and played what I carefully described as 'my own arrangement' of *The Warsaw Concerto*. I was also designated accompanist for the many entrants who thought they could sing, being the only one in the hall who could play the piano—if only in the key of C! It was fortunate for them that I knew most of the songs with which they wanted to regale their audience. For those I had never heard of, it was a case of 'I'll give you a note and you take it from there. I'll catch you up.' followed by an arpeggio in 'C', whatever their voice range.

I won the contest and received the handsome First Prize of a ten-packet of Craven A and a 'Thank You' for accompanying the other contestants. I won it in the second week as well. I even paid a visit to the annexe after I had been relocated to the main establishment, and won that one, too. I began to think I must be the only pianist in the entire Navy. I wondered if I could keep going like this and get my cigarettes for nothing.

*   *   *

Having reached our digs in the main part of the establishment, we would now live in the dormitories on either side of the 'covered-ways' for the rest of our training. They were like giant one-room bungalows, or large hospital wards, built to accommodate a great many beds. Within the main part of *Ganges* could be found the galleys, offices, gymnasia, hospital, rifle ranges, and, to my delight, a concert hall wherein was a splendid grand piano. I immediately applied for, and received, a chit (anything made of paper was a 'chit'), that entitled me, after a short audition, to play it.

The main establishment was truly a large, complete, and self-constituted city. After we had served all of two weeks in the annexe, we considered ourselves hardened, world-weary seafarers, especially when we were now resident in the main establishment, and reacted in exactly the same way as the 'old hands' who had bored us to death when *we* were in the annexe.

For the next three months we were drilled and drilled again, and taught everything there was to know about seamanship. It was back to school time. We were becoming giddy with what we had to crush into our already overheated brains, but the subjects were very interesting. Your average sailor truly needed to know about rigging, wire rope, cordage, bends and hitches, splicing, blocks and tackles, anchors, cables, ships, boats, flags and pennants, the compass, and a hundred thousand other things beside.

When at sea two of the most important skills would be Morse code and semaphore, and I was already ahead because of my time in the Boys' Brigade years before. It had paid off, and it was to prove enormously beneficial in the very near future.

Among the many new skills to be learned was the unexpected one of domestic science. It had never occurred to me that I might one day have to do my own laundry ('dhobeying' as I learned to call it), or mend a tear or darn a sock. Coincidentally, I later learned the phrase I was to use often in the years to come—'make and mend'.

At any rate, it was abundantly clear that, henceforth, I was to be totally responsible for my own life and survival—and, in due course—many others'. All in all, the strange new life I was now living proved to be much better than I had expected. But then, I hadn't expected all that much. My natural desire was to be at home with my friends and family, trying to recapture the way of life that most people had been used to, even if it hadn't been all that good. Naturally there was a feeling of impermanence about our strange new lives—with the knowledge that we would eventually be shuttled from place to place, or ship to ship. But most of us knew that, somehow, we would settle in and get used to it, even if there was a long stretch ahead.

23

PETTY OFFICER

TO RECEIVE AN INVITATION to the Wrens' mess in the evening was an enormous compliment, a much sought-after accolade. They tended to seek the company of public school and rugby types, which left most of us out.

There were two ratings in our mess, whose names I cannot remember, who fitted the category absolutely. Young, tall, fearless and sure of themselves. As a matter of fact, one of them looked like a pugilist from an earlier period, but spoke with the pronounced accent of the public school. They had long ago offered their credentials, and were regular, almost nightly, visitors to the Wrens' mess. Remembering my ability at the keyboard, they asked me to play for a birthday party, to which I readily agreed. The party went well enough, but the next day I received a letter addressed to Ordinary Seaman Rikki, apologising for not knowing my second name and inviting me to the Wrens' mess as her guest. She was a young blonde girl called Margaret who was very pleasant but left my libido undisturbed. She, however, clearly had not had the same problem—I was bombarded with invitations to the mess, and to her parents' home in Cambs for the weekend.

It was there the 'romance' ended. She and her father drove me to the station, and as I leaned out of the window I noticed that her father had considerately turned away while farewells were made.

The weekend had not been an easy one since I had little or nothing in common with Margaret and her parents, and conversation had flagged at first hurdles. It was no easier leaning out of the window of a train.

Her letter a few days later was questioning. We seemed to like each other, she thought. Enjoyed each other's company. So, was there something wrong? Had she said or done something to upset me?

I was bewildered. I scarcely knew the girl. Enjoyed the weekend and the food. End of story! Fortunately I was drafted shortly afterwards, and so was spared having to dream up some sort of explanation. I was left with an even stronger awareness of the 'live for today' philosophy during war time, and a firm belief that English females, especially those in uniform, were predatory in the extreme!

After training, and a few weeks extra when I carried the spurious title of 'Assistant Instructor', I left *Ganges* to take up residence at *HMS Pembroke*, the establishment at Chatham, there to await my very first fourteen days' leave of my, so far, short Naval career. We filled in the few days waiting time doing odd jobs, mostly sweeping up and other demeaning tasks under the rheumy eyes of one of the many retired petty officers who had been recalled at the outbreak of the war.

And this particular gentleman was petty indeed. I heard the call for those of us who were 'going ashore'. Which, in many cases, meant home leave. I already had all the documents I needed, so I asked permission to proceed, explaining that this would be my very first leave.

The PO was not remotely interested. He didn't care if I never went on leave, he said. As far as he was concerned I was in his charge for the duration. It occurred to me at that moment that, although the lower deck ratings could be very scathing about their officers, it was the non-commissioned personnel, men elevated from the ordinary ranks, who treated their men so badly. For the life of me, I could not believe that someone of higher rank would deliberately deny a poor virgin sailor his rightful leave. My sudden dislike of this very petty petty officer developed into a serious grudge against the entire breed. Later, when I was commissioned, I found myself, usually unreasonably, overruling them on every possible occasion.

At any rate, I dodged this fat old sea dog, slipped away and went on leave, leaving a note to say that 'Ordinary Seaman Fulton has taken ill with bubonic plague, and anyone who has been in contact with him should seek urgent medical advice.'

24

IN AT THE DEEP END

HMS IBIS was one of the very latest sloops in His Majesty's Navy. A sleek thing of great beauty bristling with an amazing collection of anti-aircraft ordnance, and so new there was only one photograph of her in existence (a copy of which stands on a bookcase in my study).

I joined her at Gravesend on 26th September 1942, and left her rather precipitately on 10th November the same year. My first experience at sea was not agreeable! The North Sea is not, so far as I'm concerned, the ideal introduction to a life on the ocean wave, or a holiday cruise, especially in late Autumn. 'Heave-to' had never had such significance for me, so ill did I become.

For the first few days I actually lived on the searchlight platform and was tended by the kindly Oerlikon gunner who had been at the game a good deal longer than me, and whose mate I was supposed to be. But in my case it was a daily 'heave-to!' and I was sure it was going to be so for most of the voyage. Tea and dry toast were all I could keep down. For four days I lay prostrate, sleeping under changeable, dull grey skies or watching the stars on a clear night, struggling to the 'heads' (loo), and staggering to my lookout post when on watch. Four hours on and four off they went.

Quite suddenly, I discovered I was no longer sick, and I could walk without bumping into everything and maintain my balance on the heaving deck that was my world. Not only that: wonder of wonders, I was actually *hungry*! I remember vividly what I ate that evening. It was the most succulent, cold, fresh gammon and exquisite tomatoes I had ever tasted. I even grinned at the call of 'haaaaaands ta dinner, CW candidates to lunch', and went down to the mess. The food was wonderful, it went down brilliantly and sweetened my embattled stomach. I was renewed and fit and ready for what was to come.

To my pleasant surprise I saw a kent face fleetingly. It was Bernie Cookson, a large, saturnine gentleman who had been in the mess next to me in *Ganges*. We shared a problem with the mess deck food, not the quality by any means, but the quantity, and the closing time. Perhaps it was because I had been starved for four days, but in any case my appetite was almost as great as Bernie's.

We put in at Londonderry, our port of call, and were astonished to find the entire country exquisitely illuminated. No black-out here. And no rationing either. It was a telling moment, the first time we had seen cities lit up for three years. We managed to hang on from one meal to another until supper, which was at the unearthly hour of 1800. The long wait for breakfast was more than a couple of eighteen-year-olds could bear. We begged, borrowed, stole and wangled shore-leave passes almost every night, and trawled the port for places that would help to satisfy our insatiable hunger.

There was an area dubbed 'up homers' where the good people of Londonderry played host to sailors coming in to port, and fed them on bread, butter, jam and cakes, and we managed to eat them out of house and home. We would do anything for food. We sat in Sailors' Hostels, in Irish Evangelical Halls, Seamen's Welfare, the YMCA (even the YWCA if we could have found some way to get in). We sang hymns, we listened to sermons. Anyone anywhere who would give us food. We even sat and listened with great interest while a young born-again Christian described his conversion in a broad Irish accent saying unto us: 'Friends, I wasn't always a goooood maaaaaan!' And all for a cup of tea and a Digestive biscuit!

*   *   *

We set course for the Tail of the Bank, where we joined three huge battle convoys of warships of almost every class.

Having got over my sea-sickness, and being so close to so many towns I loved, I now had to get over my homesickness. Against rules and regulations, I had managed a quick, cheeky phone call to my mother to let everybody know that I was well and heading for an unknown destination, and would be sailing soon. Whether that had given my family confidence or had made matters worse I wasn't sure. I was glad to have taken the chance. It was good to hear their voices and have a short news bulletin from Riddrie. On board, there was the usual conjecture, and bets, as to what our destination might be, but the secret orders remained secret from the lower deck.

On the early evening of November 7th all was revealed to us.

We were part of the 'greatest armada of ships and aircraft ever assembled for a single operation.' It was a three-pronged attack on the North African coast by three convoys which, because they were identical, and sailing only sixty miles apart, were assumed by the German reconnaissance to be one only. They struck at Oran to the west, Bougie to the east, and the *Ibis* was bang in the middle, aiming for the Bay of Algiers.

I was wakened by the mind-bending, ear-splitting, thunderous chaos of total war. Men running, climbing, cursing, Tannoys screaming 'Action Stations!' Spilling from my hammock and pulling on a duffel coat and oilskins, I dashed to my station, the searchlight platform where a thousand years ago I had found my sea legs—and stood by to load the strangely shaped Oerlikon

119

magazine while my good friend, the gunner who had seen me through a difficult time on my first voyage, wore the gun like a slimming machine.

We were under heavy and determined aerial attack. Such was the artillery the *Ibis* carried, she was clearly a huge, fearsome and deadly enemy. The German Luftwaffe could see from the air where the main challenge lay, and it became chillingly obvious that we were their principal target. Bombers and torpedo-carrying Heinkels were all around us, making a determined effort to eliminate this dangerous war machine, the bombers diving low creating heart-stopping plumes of water that mushroomed on either side of us as the bombs narrowly missed our deck.

The *Ibis* was now zig-zagging away from the Bay at tremendous speed as the air crackled with gunfire and the hellish sound of the German bombs on every side of us. As the battle raged a firework display of tracer shells picked off the enemy aircraft. It was as if our gunners were destroying them by torchlight as they buzzed around us like giant dragonflies, and one by one fell into the sea mortally wounded.

Darkness came. It wasn't clear which side would gain the advantage as the great purple celestial blind crept over the Mediterranean sky from east to west. From the dark side came the Heinkels who were to make the kill. Suddenly I could make out a streak of iridescent froth running across our bows. A near miss, and too close for comfort. Another streak told us a second torpedo had just missed us astern. But, as if thrown by a champion darts player, the third torpedo found the bull's-eye. We were hit right amidships, and with an almighty roar of indignation and pain, the beautiful *Ibis*, its side blown out and its engines silenced, began to list heavily to starboard.

I was blown off the searchlight platform onto the deck below where a fatally injured shipmate lay between the decks, his sea-booted legs sticking out from the hatchway. I called up to my gunner who was still strapped to the Oerlikon.

'Hey, Ginge, what d'you think happened?' He looked down at me with a strange expression. I wondered if I had done something wrong. He peeled off his duffel coat and dived over the side.

Was it something I'd said, I wondered. With my headphones gone, I had been unable to hear the command to abandon ship, but it didn't take a genius to realise that the call had been given. Men were jumping, diving and sliding off the ship as it began to lean over on its side. A sloop like the *Ibis* had about two-thirds of its superstructure forward, and the after deck was so low it was possible simply to climb over the guardrail and walk into the sea.

That was my plan, but the torpedo had done a good job below decks, and I could neither see nor breathe through the suffocating chlorine gas that had been released. I headed forward up the gently curving slope of the main deck to find the First Lieutenant and some ratings struggling to free a Carley-float which had been secured with determination and unnecessary artistic flair. It looked as if we were the only members of the crew left aboard. Eager for company in this nightmare situation, I offered to lend a hand, and kept up what was supposed to be light conversation. But they were not in conversational mood, and as the float came free at last, they threw it over the steeply rising port side, and followed it into the sea. I had the feeling that it was not to be my day for making friends and influencing people, and if I didn't get a move on, I could spend the rest of a very short life on board the sinking ship.

I climbed up over the guard-rail which was now almost above my head, hauled myself onto the ship's side and sat just above the flare for a moment wondering why we had been taught so much about seamanship, and customs, but no one had made any suggestions about how to leave a sinking ship. I was later told that many of our crew died by breaking their backs when they jumped or dived off the superstructure into the sea, forgetting that the keel was now just under the water. Others swimming close to the funnel were sucked back in and drowned. Another horrific fact was that when a ship was at 'action stations' the magazine and shell rooms were locked. That must have been enough to give anybody in there more than claustrophobia. One of my chums, a spunky wee Scot from Edinburgh, was stationed there during 'action', sending the ammunition up to the guns in mechanical hoists. When I think of my little mate it still causes nightmares.

My own way of leaving the *Ibis* was pure luck.

Already sitting on the edge of the flare, I peeled off my duffel coat and threw it back on board, cursing as I did so that I had left a nearly full pack of Three Castle cigarettes in one of the pockets. I looked down at the heaving Mediterranean for a second, then with a great shout of 'HO!' pushed myself off and slid down as in a chute. My body plunged into the now dark waters so deeply I was convinced I wasn't going to come up again.

When I did surface I could just make out a raft some distance away on which about twenty to thirty men were clinging together. It took me twenty minutes to swim over and call out grateful greetings. I was immediately pushed savagely under the water. As I surfaced, I tried again and again to get even a finger tip on the raft, but these men had only one thought in their shattered minds—personal survival. Those on top of the raft were kicking and punching men who, only a few hours ago, had been their mates, and now were their most ruthless enemies. Understandably, they were in a frenzy, terrified that their refuge would be plundered, while those who were still up to their necks in sea water fought them for a place on the raft. It was a frightening, sickening situation.

Sadly, it would be true to say that, in a situation like this, man's most ruthless enemy would seem to be himself. I was shoved under three or four times in my endeavour to stay alive before deciding that I had come to the wrong party, and I left them to their own devices.

I never saw any of them again.

As I swam farther and farther in the darkness, the loneliness began to get to me. With no sign of land, ship or friendly aircraft, I began to realise that this was no party. It was, indeed, life or death. I couldn't believe that I was swimming in a pitch-dark sea more than fifteen hundred miles from home with neither sight nor sound of another human being. I had no idea if I was swimming towards land or towards oblivion. And I simply couldn't understand what was holding me up mentally. There was no reason to hope. I had no idea where I was or where I was likely to end up. Other than the darkest of dark horizons there was nothing I could see. I tried to console myself that there would be sixteen days' 'survivors' leave'—providing I survived!

I had not made contact with any of my erstwhile mates for several hours now, when out of the blackness appeared, of all people, another Scotsman! Going in the other direction. Unable to swim he was doing his best to plowter through the sea-swell like a young dog, supported by an issue lifebelt which, after this disaster, came to be considered highly dangerous since it could just as easily hold a person upside down as right way up. The problem was that should someone be depending on his lifebelt, it might save him, providing he still had a drop of energy and mental awareness left. If in the water for a long period, a survivor may give up in the face of serious fatigue, nod off, and the lifebelt could then turn him upside down. I couldn't count the number of legs I saw as they floated in whatever direction the sea demanded.

The other problem was, lifebelt or no, the longer the swimmer was faced with creeping hypothermia, the more serious was his situation. I heard of many men who, with little or no energy left, waved their farewells to their mates and simply went under. I was already feeling the growing numbness in my feet. It had started slowly in the toes, then the feet and legs, and if it reached the stomach, it would be upside down and goodnight for ever! But it was good to make contact with another human being, especially a plucky, red-blooded Scot in the same dilemma. I had never met my plowtering friend. He had worked in a totally different station on the *Ibis*. It is impossible to get to know the names and background of over two hundred men in a ship's complement, but in this case names were unnecessary.

'Hi Jock,' I called. Even Scotsmen called each other 'Jock'.

'Hi Jock,' he answered.

'Where are you going?' I asked as if the question made sense.

'Well,' he replied. 'I thought I'd go up the road a bit and see if I can get a tram for Partick. How about you?'

'No,' I said, quoting a hoary old joke, 'it's such a lovely night, I think I'll walk.'

Sadly, I never saw him again.

I had remained reasonably sane all the time I was swimming. Suddenly I was aware of a monstrous, ghostly shape materialising just ahead of me. Out of almost tangible gloom came the high, arrogant superstructure of a very famous ship indeed.

HMS Scylla's fame was the result of its heroic escapades with the Russian convoys. Kept at bay by the threat of further air attack, she had waited until she could safely slip silently back to the area where *Ibis* had been hit, and was searching a wide area for those of us who had survived, and were still swimming around in the sea. The long exposure in the water had taken its toll. The creeping numbness that had started at my toes had now reached half-way up my body. I began to think that it was probably too late for the *Scylla*'s efforts to make any difference now. I knew that I was beginning to give in, but I tried hard to keep up some sort of courage and belief that the salvation that was heading towards me wasn't a sort of final bad dream.

I had gone under a couple of times, for I was very tired. I thought I was dreaming when I could just make out a whaler and the upright figure of the cox'ain, his eyes straining for any sign of

124

life, back-lit by the beam of the mother ship's searchlight as it swept the oily sea. The cox'ain spotted me and, at his command, the strokes of the oars became more purposeful. I had been reasonably philosophic, even optimistic until that moment. I had managed to remain calm, thinking of the sixteen days survivors' leave, but the second these wonderful messengers of mercy came within hailing distance my brain exploded in hysteria. I realised that I had been trying to fool myself into believing that I was not afraid. But, oh God was I afraid. Suddenly I was sure that, at the last minute, with salvation only feet away, my leaden body would sink and I would drown. I heard myself screaming. My voice went hoarse with the force of it. 'Over here,' I shouted. 'I'm over here. Help me. HELP!'

Then the cox'ain's voice reached me, calling on me to stay calm, that they were almost with me and everything would be alright. Now I could feel hands reaching down and dragging my sodden body over the side and into the whaler. I collapsed like a broken doll into the bottom of the boat, bewildered and unable to believe that I was actually out of the water. Minutes later we were alongside the steep cliff that was the *Scylla*'s port side, and I heard the cox'ain call up to his mates: 'We'll need help with this one. He's pretty far gone!'

But he wasn't! The whaler's crew gaped in astonishment as the survivor's crumpled body came upright and, grabbing the scrambling-net with desperate hands and fingers, shot up the *Scylla*'s side like a spider-monkey. Friendly hands reached down and hauled me up and over the *Scylla*'s guard rail and I stood blinking down at my feet on the solid deck. It was a strange and wonderful feeling.

A series of really hot showers started to bring our bodies back to life from the near hypothermic state, and began the process of cleansing the oil on skin, hair and eyes. Some had had a seriously bad time. Bernie, my old eating mate (with whom I am still in

125

constant touch), spent most of the time in sickbay, and still has nightmares after all these years. The survivors kept together in groups. We were still very shaky, and jumped at the slightest sound, especially when we heard the powerful mantra of *'Action Stations!'* Those of us who were fit enough—especially after having downed a lavish measure of black Navy rum—began to feel almost human again. We talked together a lot, wondering what had happened to So-and-so, hoping for news about a particular mate, discussing what we would do when we got back home to the wife or girlfriend for sixteen days' leave. We began to realise that we still had a life to live, and we grieved for those who hadn't—so many of our shipmates who, like my small but gutsy little mate, would have to accept the *Ibis*, now lying at the bottom of the Mediterranean, as their final resting place.

Having managed to get rid of the oil and been given fresh clothes, we learned that we had been in the water for something over five hours and that, from the ship's complement of two hundred and twelve, over a hundred men were missing. It was a luxury to wear clean, dry clothes, and there was a series of rather melodramatic accounts of how the survivors survived.

Many a colourful story was told on these occasions. So many stories, so many tales for the grandchildren. How some had prayed for forgiveness, promising to live a better life if only they were saved. How, just as he was giving up, a piece of wood from the poor old *Ibis* floated towards one man, and he took hold of it and was able to stay afloat. Another who had gone under for the third time looked up to heaven and prayed to be allowed to live; and another who was ready to give up the ghost, looked up to heaven and thought soulfully of his wife and three kids.

As dawn began to lift the sky's curtain, we were amazed to see the *Ibis* before us in the water. We could see that a number of survivors had kept a vigil for some hours sitting on the hull, and they were picked up by the *Scylla*'s whalers. They, and those of us who were already aboard the *Scylla*, watched in silence as *HMS Ibis* slowly turned over completely, presenting its keel as if in surrender. There is something unbelievably sad watching a ship go down. We stood silent and privately and very emotional, as our beautiful ship slowly and majestically took itself, and so many of our mates, to the depths of the Mediterranean Sea where we hoped they would live forever.

It was the saddest day of our lives.

It was only natural that these survivors, even though threatened with death every day, had suffered not only physically, but mentally from their ordeal. So many concerns, so many questions—not least, why had they been chosen to survive while so many men had not?

Whatever, when the final count was made, it was clear that we had lost two-thirds of our ship's company, as well as our captain. I remember, with an aching heart, the fond farewell I had secretly, and unexpectedly, witnessed between him and his wife on the deck of the *Ibis* before we left the relative safety of the Clyde.

As we made our way to Gibraltar the *Scylla* came under air attack, and every seaman who had suffered having his ship blown from under him began to doubt the truth of the theory that 'lightning never strikes twice'. In the mess deck in Gibraltar we were invited to sit and watch a film called *In Which We Serve*, Noël Coward's 'splendid flagwaver' which concerns the torpedoing and sinking of a British destroyer, after which Commander Noël tells his sodden troops:

'The *Torrin*' (for *Torrin* read *Ibis*) 'has been in one scrap after another, but even when we've had men killed, the majority survived' (sadly not true) 'and brought the old ship back. Now she lies in 1500 fathoms and with her more than half our shipmates' (sadly true). 'If they had to die, what a grand way to go!'

There was no comment from what was left of our ship's company.

We were all allowed to send telegrams to our families, but my family got to know about the sinking of the *Ibis* even more quickly. None other than the Lady Margaret from Cambs, with whom I had spent a meaningless weekend, was anxiously asking if Rikki had survived.

My mother didn't understand what this girl was talking about. She hadn't heard the news, and was far more worried now that this girl at the other end of the phone had made her enquiry. Fortunately the telegram which told them I was alive and well arrived at almost the same time, and relieved the worry that my Mum and Dad had been suffering. We were to be sent home as part of the crew of a patched-up sloop, and sent back to *Pembroke*. The sixteen days' survivors' leave helped the depression we were all still feeling, and it was great for the ego when I got home.

'Strong and silent, but with the air of a man who had done what he had to do.' People who knew me shook my hand and told me how brave I was. Closer friends wanted to be near me, aching to hear about My Experience but afraid to question me, which was very frustrating for I was dying to tell them, and the 'glamour' of knowing 'Someone Who Had Very Nearly Died In The War' brought forth a brief, incandescent revival of the never-never romance I had had with Violet Eyes, and from the safety of my home environment I actually thought for a moment—that it had all been worth it!

25

ARISE, SIR THOMAS BEECHAM

BECAUSE OF THE SLIGHT interruption in my sea training caused by the North African invasion, I had to put in a further two months at sea on the destroyer *HMS Hambledon*, and boarded her after I returned from leave. I was then summoned by the Admiralty to confront a board of a number of elderly high-ranking sea dogs whom I had to convince that I would never bring opprobrium upon His Majesty's Senior Service by eating my peas off my knife, and that my father and mother were truly married.

The officers' training centre in Hove, called *HMS King Alfred*, sounded so terribly English and upper-crust and clubby that it was startling to find that it was, or had been, an underground garage with a restaurant on top in its previous life, now refurbished for its war-time role. Even so, *HMS King Alfred* spread a longer distance than one would expect. Especially when both Brighton and Hove were closed areas—it wasn't possible to get in or out of these two places unless you were either a resident, or had documents giving you good reason to be in the area and you could present a pass.

One of the mysteries surrounding the early days at *King Alfred* was that we had to pay a visit to Gieves, the very posh tailor who must have been making a fortune as well as making made-to-measure uniforms for putative Naval officers. Everyone who dreamed of becoming a commissioned officer prayed that one day they would wear that wonderful uniform. Actually there were two. There was a 'working' uniform made in navy-blue serge, and a 'Sunday' uniform made of navy-blue doeskin.

The psychology of the training course was unbelievable—until I realised that much of what appeared to have little importance was really a part of the training. The question was: what did Gieves do with the uniforms of the poor blighters who had failed to make the grade? Answer was there none. But when we thought about it, we realised that it had all been planned; to spur, influence, motivate, encourage and inspire.

For the first two weeks we were billeted with households near the establishment while we underwent preliminary training in a convenient field. I confess I got a very real buzz from my entitlement to wear the prestigious white band on my cap, and began to frequent the large Regent Ballroom in Brighton on nights when I could get a pass, to show off the white band to a larger audience.

At one afternoon session I spotted a very disturbing young Land Army girl sitting alone at a table. I was half-way towards her when a young Naval officer, probably newly commissioned, approached and asked her to dance. I sat down hurriedly lest I be accused of mutiny or worse, and then noticed that the young officer had been politely refused. I was relieved that I hadn't had to suffer the rebuff, especially when I saw several other young members of the armed forces suffer a similar fate.

It began to look as if she was waiting for someone, but no one arrived to meet her. Perhaps she couldn't dance for some reason. Maybe she had a wooden leg. But then she wouldn't have been accepted into the Land Army with such a deformity.

I sat for what seemed hours waiting to see what would happen next. Nothing! So, throwing caution to the winds, I gathered my confidence in my hands and went over to her. 'Excuse me, but would you like to dance?'

'I'd love to,' she said. Automatically I had begun to walk away, assuming that I would be told to disappear like the others, but, having done a double-take, I realised this lady wanted to dance. And dance with me! Her name was Betty Richards and she was a cracker.

We had dinner together that night, and the *affaire* that developed from our first meeting made me wonder if I had fallen in love. But then I recalled Margaret from Cambs, and cautioned myself to remember the predatory nature of English girls in war time! Going out together was a welcome respite from the exacting work that was demanded on the training course, but to get involved with a girl, however attractive, would, and did, make it difficult to concentrate on the essentials, although I couldn't help thinking that ship-handling was pretty dull compared with Betty-handling.

Lancing College became our next stop and would be our second home. It was the most impressive, fascinating place I had ever entered. A wonderfully traditional boys' school, it had been founded in 1848 and was redolent with the atmosphere of previous generations. I think I could have stayed there for ever. Every aristocratic stone, every walkway, every classroom desk, spoke of the thousands of boys who had received their education there, and whose spirits seemed still to occupy its dormitories. I think it was six weeks we spent in these hallowed acres, and I loved every moment of it, although it was disturbing to discover that our large class was being mysteriously whittled away as a number of candidates 'dipped' and were led away quietly during the wee small hours. It seemed that every time we were wakened to the sound of 'reveille' we found yet another empty bed, its sheets neatly made up, and its one-time occupant inexplicably dismissed, leaving a sad little white ribbon that bore the name *HMS King Alfred*.

There were constant reminders, overt or implied, that those of us who did not have the 'right' background had to try all the harder. The carrot held out to us made us ever more conscious of how we conducted ourselves; careful not to eat peas with our knives, to hold the cutlery correctly, to *appear* reasonably well-bred and well-spoken—none of which was helped by the odd 'upper-class' snob who felt he had been forced to live among the rabble.

I still have a vivid picture of being on guard duty at Lancing one pitch-black night. I was aware I had company but couldn't tell if it was an officer on rounds, another cadet returning from a night out, or, heaven forbid, a German parachutist! My .303 rifle came up to the ready and I gave the command to 'Halt—friend or foe?' Then I heard this very educated, very English voice say: 'Oh, don't be an idiot. I'm on guard further up.' Then came: 'What school did you go to?' 'Barlinnie Public,' I told him. 'I'm sure you'd benefit awfully from a couple of terms, what?'

I was pretty sure I'd won the round. After all, he wouldn't have heard of Barlinnie. He wouldn't have known it was a prison. He wouldn't realise that I had pulled his leg and that he'd been insulted. Tee-hee-hee!

It turned out he was a Glaswegian!

Admittedly, some of us who had regional accents did our best to achieve some semblance of 'received pronunciation', although we preferred to describe it in the old-fashioned way, 'toffee-nosed' or 'la-di-da', and it resulted in some very strange speech from time to time. One young Aberdonian, a bank-teller by trade, had the thickest of Aberdeenshire accents, and at one point started to relate an incident in which his sister had come home one day with her hair shorn. When we asked him what he had said to her he replied: 'We-ell, Ah jist ast 'er, fit ti haill hid she din wi' herr herr.' His efforts to straighten these vowels resulted in yet another some-what classic pronouncement which told us that his sister was very lazy, and that 'she even nawmally expecktit herr mither tae pit the mawmalade on herr towst!'

Apart from studying the intricacies of navigation, rules of the road, signals, radar, ship-handling and so much other required knowledge, the two phrases that were instilled in us at every opportunity by our immediate and higher-ranking superiors were 'Quality of Leadership' and 'Power of Command.' These qualities, we were told, were absolute essentials necessary for becoming a Naval officer. As it happened, I was given a golden opportunity to show if I had both of these qualities—in a most unexpected way.

As soon as we had settled in, we were introduced to our guide, philosopher, friend and gunnery officer, a warm and understanding man whose name was Sunshine of all things. He was seeking volunteers to organise various sporting and other activities which were outwith the actual training course, but were still an important part of it. Each division had to present a concert just before they moved on to *King Alfred* proper. My hand shot up before the words 'divisional concert' had left his lips. I think Sunshine was surprised that he had managed to get someone to organise the show so quickly. I held a meeting of all those who were prepared to take part, and we went to the previous division's show to see what was expected of us. Some could sing, some could give a bit of poetry, some were interested in doing jokes, or sketches, and over the following six weeks during such time off as we had to prepare, I wrote some sketches and jokes I remembered from my Red Cross days with Leslie, and managed to put a programme together. It seemed a pity that the remainder of our class couldn't take part although they were keen to be in on it.

I had been wondering how to open the show, and suddenly somebody came up with The Great Idea. We would get everybody who had nothing to offer on his own, and have them sing 'You Are My Sunshine'. Even if it wasn't going to be operatic standard, it had to be a great idea. I could have kissed the rating who had come up with it. Our audience comprised the entire complement of the College plus the heavy brass that ran the establishment who would be sitting in the front row.

There was the usual buzz from a large audience chattering in anticipation, which covered the unexpected panic served up by Sunshine when I was backstage fiddling with a prop.

'The curtains will open, but won't close again,' he quavered. 'What are we to do, Fulton? We have to start in fifteen minutes.'

'Leave it to me, sir,' I said with a confidence I certainly didn't feel. 'I've dealt with similar and worse in many a church hall; you needn't worry.'

I darted to the auditorium and had spotlights brought to each side half-way up the hall, and pointed them directly onto the stage. We dimmed the auditorium lights and opened the curtains in darkness, then brought up the stage lighting (such as it was), and directed our two spotlights on to our choristers. They started well enough with their raucous version of 'You Are My Sunshine', when something happened that I had not even contemplated. I was still backstage when Sunshine bustled round with even worse news.

'Fulton', he cried. 'They've stopped singing! They've stopped singing the bloody song. They're out there just looking at one another. What are we going to do?'

They were suffering from stage fright! They had started with great gusto, and then, one by one, had tailed off into embarrassed silence. Without even waiting to hear the end of the distress signal, I walked out into the hall and stood in front of the entire complement of Lancing College, plus more gold braid than I would ever see again, and confronted my shaking choristers. I felt like Sir Thomas Beecham conducting the Royal Philharmonic. I waved my hands at them, and signalled that they should follow me. With their eyes glued to what I hoped was an expression of absolute confidence on my face, they began to sing, their voices rising with every note, and our extravaganza was not only saved, but went on to be a reasonable success.

What did not occur to me at the time was that I had been given a heaven-sent opportunity to display—unconsciously—the all important 'Qualities of Leadership' and 'Power of Command' right in the faces of God knows how many high-ranking officers. Out of disaster had come forth the success I was desperately hoping for, but I hadn't expected to achieve it quite that way.

I celebrated the end of the course with Betty Richards, dancing at the Regent Ballroom. After all, I thought, the die had been cast, and there were no second chances.

A pink gin was well known as the favoured refreshment of Naval officers, but I didn't care for it, and came to the decision that my tipple would be port, and I think, perhaps, I had indulged rather more than I should have, especially when I had to be able to join the muster early the following morning. I remember being told that if you drank a bucket or two of port, you would wake up in the morning with a terrible thirst, and when you drank a glass of water, you would get drunk all over again. However, I managed to stay relatively upright in order to try and cope with whatever would prove to be the last day of the mental torture.

The torture continued until the very last moment. We took up our formation, and the Commander gave the order: 'The following men will take one step forward.' Followed by: 'The following men will take one step to the rear.' This meant that our class had been split into two groups.

Now we couldn't tell which of the two groups was which. It was still impossible to tell who would pass and who would fail. I tried to work out the psychology. If I could have put a bet on it, I would have said the front group would be made up of those who had passed and the rear group dismissed.

The atmosphere was heart-stopping. It was only when I heard the command, 'Rear group, LE-EFT TURN! QUI-ICK MARCH. Left, right, left, right!' that I realised the rear group had been marched off, leaving the Captain to shake our hands and offer his congratulations. I couldn't bring myself to confess to him that I had become a Naval officer while suffering from an outsize hangover.

The agony was over and the next stop was Gieves the tailors. Being one year under the required age for Sub-Lieutenant, I was commissioned a Midshipman RNVR on 27th August 1943.

The first great thrill was having moved from the ratings part of the restaurant, which had been halved with a rope, like an aisle in a classy picture house. Once again the brilliant psychology of the training was obvious. The Midshipman's uniform is exactly the same as any higher ranking officer's apart from the symbols of rank. In place of gold rings on the sleeve a midshipman carries maroon tabs, with a gold button on the lapels.

While still under training during the day, we wore our jackets, caps, white scarfs and grey flannels. But I was dying to wear my handsome new, beautifully cut, doeskin uniform and enjoy a celebratory visit to the Regent Palace Ballroom with Betty.

I was proud as Punch, and you know what they say about pride.

As usual I had to wait for Betty, but I didn't mind, I was enjoying standing there beside the lift, knowing that anyone with half an eye would recognise one of His Majesty's Commissioned Naval Officers, and a *gentleman* to boot, by Act of Parliament! Suddenly, a large, rather pushy, heavily made-up woman tapped me on the shoulder.

'Second floor, please,' she ordered!

I was similarly deflated getting on the train home. Officers were supposed to travel First Class, and at one of the interminable stops hundreds of ratings crowded into the carriage, indifferent as to whether it was first or second class.

'Here, here,' I said to one rating in my best eighteen-year-old 'Power-of-Command' and 'Quality of Leadership' voice.

'Up yours,' he suggested.

'How dare you,' I stuttered. 'How dare you speak to an officer like that! You're supposed to salute me!'

So he did—*with two fingers!*

But it was wonderful to see my Mum and Dad when I got home. How proud they were. My Mum was not only proud, but relieved that I had got rid of 'those awful trousers'. It wasn't what you could call a long break and I did enjoy seeing my family and my chums, but I was also looking forward to getting to know everything that lay ahead. The full training had still a long way to go. In quick succession, I was shuttled off to the famous girls' school at Roedean for a torpedo/depth charge course, to Hayling Island for gunnery, then had a very happy stay in Fort William where I lived in one of the many hotels which had been taken over by the Admiralty for officer training. That part of the training was fun, learning to handle an ML (motor launch) and its crew as we cruised around Loch Linnhe.

We had to live in a chosen ML for some weeks and learn from the Skipper and his First Lieutenant. In particular, I loved being in charge on the bridge with an experienced cox'ain on the wheel reacting to every order. It was a huge plus to be training in Scotland and an extra plus to be able to play the piano.

I was quite ready to play all night if they wanted, and every time someone ordered a drink for themselves, one was placed on top of the piano for the pianist!

Generally speaking I slept incredibly well!

I was only in Fort William for a short time, when I learned that I was to be drafted to a brand new ML—*HMML 1421* to give it its proper label. It hadn't yet been commissioned, indeed it was still in the construction stage. This meant making tracks for the South again—to Gosport, Hampshire where the boat was being built. I had a skeleton crew with me and we set about the job of loading equipment, stores and ammunition. *1421* was a small, twin-engined craft with outward-turning screws which made it a joy to handle.

They were known as HDs, because their main function was to be Harbour Defence, but the usefulness of these launches in other spheres of operation promoted them much further up the pecking order. They were now fitted with the sonic egg known as Asdic, which was lowered beneath the hull and could pinpoint a submarine with ease, and they carried depth charges to give the enemy a really bad time. Not exactly fast—their top speed was only twelve knots—and hell in high seas, but great little craft nonetheless.

Our ship had room for a crew of sixteen ratings, who included a signalman, radar expert and gunners, housed for'ard, and there was a tiny little bunkhouse in which slept two very important crew members—the Petty Officer engineer and the cox'ain. Abaft of that was the officers' quarters—it seemed ridiculous to call it a wardroom, but it was comfortable with its two bunks, a table and a heads (the name given to a latrine).

My skipper was Lieutenant Mickey Hargreaves, a twenty-six-year-old Tasmanian, who was of very small build and looked like a schoolboy. His first move was to officially take command of the ship, and for us to get to know each other and discuss the rules he wanted to make. It was up to me as First Lieutenant to gather the crew and explain what these rules would be, and make sure they were carried out.

I was happy to see that there were a fair number of Scots among our crew, many of whom were fishermen and, therefore, no strangers to the sea. The PO engineer and the cox'ain were older and very experienced. It was up to the cox'ain to arrange the watches and obviously when a ship was under way there had to be an officer in charge on the bridge, so the cox'ain and his deputy had come to an arrangement. The cox'ain, in view of his rank, would quite properly take the watch with the captain when at sea, and his deputy would take the watch with the First Lieutenant. My dep. cox was a great character from 'Ainster' (or, as visitors would call it, Anstruther) in Fife called Watson. He was a seaman of great experience, not all that much older than me, and apart from my conviction that he knew exactly what he was doing at the wheel, we were both particularly happy that it would be a couple of Scots working together.

Mickey suggested I take two or three days off to make up for his late arrival, so I set off for Hove to have an evening with Betty. I would surprise her, comfort her in her loneliness and take her to our favourite spot, the Regent Palace Ballroom. I rang the bell, and eventually a rather fat women opened the door. It was her mother. She crushed me to her 'Guinness Book of Records' bosom.

'Ouw it's Ye-ew.' She smiled a huge smile. 'W'ere you been, then?'

'Oh, here and there,' I said. 'Is Betty in?'

'Now-ooo, she shouldn't be long, though. Come on in.'

We sat for an unexciting moment. She looked at me and said: 'Wye is it everybodee seems to want ma Be-tt-ee?'

Thankfully, the door opened at that point and Betty came in. She was, shall we say, underwhelmed to see me, and, unlike her mother, she was speaking English!

'I'm married,' she said. 'I hope you're not upset!'

'Not at all,' I told her. 'I'm very happy for you.' Truth to tell I was just as happy for me. 'It's just that I was in the area and thought I would say hello. After all we haven't seen each other for ages. It must be at least four or five weeks now!'

I most certainly was *not* upset. I was gasping at the speed at which they operated. Grab a man, get pregnant, get married. I can remember the talk the medical officer gave us when we first arrived at *King Alfred*. Actually it was more of a warning. If any rating had fathered a child and had not acknowledged his responsibilities, he would be dismissed summarily. The MO would have no problem with me. I was too scared. At eighteen all I was seeking was some convivial female company now and again. I suddenly recalled Margaret from Cambs and shuddered at the thought of becoming a married man, and possibly a father, at this early stage of my life.

Betty's mother intervened with a stunning philosophical observation. 'Ownly taikes a daiy to get married in war time, love,' she said.

As I had believed all along, the young English girls of the time lived on a diet of anxiety and neurosis based on the fear of a life on the shelf. Betty had wasted no time.

'You probably think I've got fatter,' she smiled.

No, I didn't think so for a minute.

'Well, I am. I'm pregnant!'

'Oh, splendid. Congratulations,' I said. 'Anyone I know?'

'You remember the young Lieutenant I refused to dance with the afternoon you and I first met?' she asked. 'We were married six weeks ago!'

A PAUSE!

I thought I had been pretty lucky having had two very narrow escapes.

26

SUB

I WAS GLAD to get back to *1421*. The work was going well, and the skipper and crew were now able to settle in our new 'house boat'. I felt very much at home there. It was a neat and comfortable craft, although we had yet to find out what it was like at sea.

Our next task was to complete the necessary trials for *1421*, and be prepared for whatever the Admiralty had in store for us. We dared not reveal any war plans, so we couldn't explain to our crew what was in store for us. All we could tell them was that we had been ordered to Ardrishaig for a refit to special secret specifications. The route took us past Arran, and I knew from my mother's letters that they were on holiday there. It was achingly frustrating not to be able to pull in to the jetty and see them to say 'Hello!' It was just as frustrating to realise I was less than fifty miles due west of my beloved Glasgow as the crow flies. I would have been quite happy to have been a crow for a few hours, but it was necessary to put that to one side for there was much to do.

On reaching Ardrishaig, we were fitted with radar. Not something with which we were greatly acquainted. Curiously, it turned out to be our 'wardroom butler' who was the radar expert.

Many of the other MLs had been fitted with what we came to call 'goal posts' over the ship's bridge. This was a brilliant device with which the MLs could transmit a radar image to the enemy which would look for all the world like a huge invading army. Which it was—but which was it? When the time came there would be dozens of our Coastal Forces MLs with their 'goalposts' at different points all along the Normandy Coast going on and off, hopefully totally confusing the Germans as to what was about to hit them and, most importantly for us, from where!

We 'worked-up' hard on our little ship, 'Action Stations', gunnery exercises with live ammunition, everything including 'attack' and 'evasion'. The convoys gathered at Plymouth, and on the 5th of June 1944, thousands of people on the Hoe watched and waved as the giant armada made its majestic exit through the Sound and headed for the Normandy coast preparing for the big push. Or as Churchill told the nation: 'The hour of our greatest effort is approaching.' The weather, however, was against us and our orders were dramatically cancelled. We were ordered to shelter in Portland until the bad weather abated. Thankfully it did the following day, which is why what was sometimes called 'the Second Front' took place on 6th June 1944 and not on the 5th as had been planned.

This was D-Day! The task of the MLs was to take up a position about two-thirds of the way across the Channel heading south and heave-to to mark the channel for our invading forces. To find a spot in a heaving sea was not the easiest thing in the world. I thought of the old joke about 'putting a cross on the side of the boat'. I had never seen so much military hardware. It seemed a thousand times greater than the North African invasion. Hundreds of ships, all shapes and sizes, tank and personnel landing craft, droves of heavy bombers and fighter escorts overhead—like something out of an El Greco painting. In the distance we could see the sky over northern France burst into a great orange sunrise, as Caen was reduced to rubble, and even from our position several miles out, we could hear the hellish, thunderous roar of battle while smoke covered the heavens.

For almost a year afterwards we plied back and forth from our base in Gosport to the Mulberry at Arromanches, that great makeshift harbour built from huge concrete structures like blind, unfinished houses, and elderly vessels that were past their sell-by date, their life's work done, brought to rest horizontally on a beach of war. Our own much-loved craft was doing the work it had been built to carry out, but it was never designed to cope with the weather we had to suffer. Often we found ourselves able to look down on a huge heaving sea twenty feet below us, and then had to look up twenty feet to see where we had just come from. Sometimes we wondered if we would ever see land again.

We came under aerial and E-Boat fire on a number of these trips, but it was obvious that the enemy was beginning to get desperate. They had started to hand out Iron Crosses to those who were prepared to die for the Fatherland in what were euphemistically called one-man submarines. This was just another way of describing a man—or even a woman—sitting atop a live torpedo and guiding it to its target. There was no cover of any kind for these poor souls and it took only a pack of five sticks of gelignite to put them out of business.

The bigger ships had a far greater problem. 'Register ships' patrolling just outside the Mulberry harbour entrance were constantly picked off by long-distance torpedoes, and we had to get under way fast to save as many survivors as possible. We had a hairy time on the MLs, and the stress caused by living and working on board these small craft was unbelievable. When we stood watch on the bridge we were standing immediately on top of the engine room and had to try and get used to the sound and the shudder of the engines. We were also in constant fear of enemy sea or air attack. We were, after all, in only a small wooden craft.

Heavy seas had a devastating effect on us. It was almost impossible to eat or make the beloved cocoa, drenched as we were by the sea from all sides. We were at sea most nights, usually leaving around midnight, and the awkward problem was the weather forecast. We were never sure what we would have to face. More often than not, the forecast had been given out much earlier in the day. Consequently we had to get under way without knowing what the weather situation was now. I remember escorting a very slow-moving tanker en route to the Mulberry in mountainous seas, and the skipper and I were on the bridge together. It was difficult even to keep up its painfully slow speed of some three or four knots. Mickey asked me what sort of speed we were making. I had a look over the side and was forced to admit that the opposing tide was certainly winning—we were going astern! Our signal to base that we were making no headway was met with the order to 'heave-to or return to base'. That, of course, meant that we could either drop anchor and stay heaving in the churning sea, or go home. I chose the latter. It didn't seem possible that friend or foe would be out and about on a night like this. So we turned the boat round and went 'home'.

What I recall vividly was the camaraderie at the base. There was always a joke to be told, a bit of gossip, a sad story about a chum. We made a point of never talking openly about the dangers of the job, but it was difficult to shake off the constant nagging in our hearts. As we pulled away from our berth I always had the feeling that we might not be coming back. It was the nightmare of the invasion all over again. Later, in hospital, I was told that the effect on crews of coastal craft was almost exactly the same as on the air crews of fighter aircraft, with one important exception: we were allowed no rest-periods after long hours of duty. Consequently, a number of special hospitals, about which very little was ever heard, were full of Naval personnel physically—and more seriously, mentally—shattered. My skipper, Lieutenant Mickey Hargreaves, was the first to go. His collapse took place while we were still anchored in the bosom of the Mulberry. Shaking and disorientated, he was relieved of duty on the orders of a Commander MO. I took command and brought 1421 back to its base in Gosport, where Mickey left the ship, and was taken into hospital. We were taken over by a Lieutenant who hadn't been further than the Isle of Wight, and questioned everything we were used to doing.

After a fairly long time shuttling between Southampton Water and the Mulberry it became like driving a car up Sauchiehall Street. I knew every buoy like I knew the streets in Riddrie and charts were not required. But our new skipper had to be consulted about everything. Even the food we were eating had to be approved.

As soon as I reached my nineteenth birthday I was automatically promoted to Sub-Lieutenant.

I got along very well with all my crew. They were a great bunch and I was very fond of them. Together, we had all had a fairly rough time over the last couple of years and, if anything, it brought us even closer. Although one of them always got the better of me. His name was Cameron.

All ships were kept in pristine condition when not at sea and 1421 was no exception. The crew would be obliged to use the time to get down to cleaning, painting and tidying, and I would arrive to check how the work was going. Every day I checked, I knew I was going to have to cope with Cameron.

There he would be, carefully polishing the two or three inches of practically nothing. The two or three inches of brass plate on the bridge, he had decided, was the most important item on the boat. He never moved from his chosen area which he made shine like the sun. As a matter of fact, I was convinced he would eventually polish a hole in the brass. That would be his day's work, and he would happily follow the crew to their rest period, having done precisely nothing. He had a slight stammer, or it was something he had developed as a cover, and when I accused him of evading his work, he would say to me: 'Yes, sir, a-a-a-and how are *you* this morning?' I was always frustrated. 'I'm very bloody well, thank you,' I shouted, and left him to his little bit of brass.

On one occasion when we were at sea and I was taking over the watch, I found him sound asleep in a corner of the bridge, which was a very serious offence in war time. He could even have been shot for falling asleep on duty. 'Cameron!' I shouted. 'What do you think you're doing? Do you realise . . . ?' But he was quick. 'Oh, g-g-g-g-ood evening, sir. I-I-I-I di-di-didn't see you there. I was too busy keeping watch. I-i-i-isn't it a wonderful night, sir?'

Wonderful? *We couldn't see a perishing thing in this light!* I never ever got the better of that man even in the blackest of nights. But every time I gave him a dressing-down, I couldn't help laughing at the sheer cheek.

The one sadness in our crew came from a tiny little fellow called Heap, whom I called 'Big Heap'. One day Big Heap came to me with a letter he had received from his father. It had been carefully worded, and Heap asked me to read it and see what I thought the letter was truly saying. It wasn't difficult to read between the lines, and I told him that it looked serious to me. Against all sorts of difficulties involving Petty Officers (my vendetta was working at full throttle), I demanded immediate arrangements to get him home on fourteen days' compassionate leave. It was to be a sad journey home for him, but, at least, he had been able to see his mother before she died, and see her put to rest. He returned to *1421* feeling better than I could have hoped. He was coping wonderfully well, and I have to confess, I felt really good about what I had been able to do.

My turn came only a few months later. It would not have been prudent to voice my worries to any of the crew or our new skipper, but I had begun to suffer from blackouts and confusion, often returning to consciousness to find I was on watch on the bridge, not having the least recollection of where we had been or where we were making for. If it hadn't been for Watson, I might well have put us in danger. By this time we were under way on the Seine which was full of mines that hadn't been primed and were, therefore, no threat. It was obvious that the Germans were in a hurry to get out.

We arrived at what was left of Le Havre harbour, some of which was still burning, with all jetties and wharfs completely destroyed. The Americans, however, had arrived fully prepared and started to manoeuvre great steel jetties into position, which were a threat in themselves. Peter Scott, the famous artist and ornithologist, was already comfortably tied up alongside one of them, along with many of the Coastal Force crowd who were seeking a place to berth.

On our arrival we found ourselves almost completely locked in, and as our look-out watched, one of the huge steel jetties was moving slowly towards us. It was alright for the ship we were tied up to—the *Grey Goose* (if I've remembered the name correctly)—it was a much larger, steel vessel. Our hull was entirely wood. My crewman on look-out yelled for me. We freed all our ropes and got the engines going fast as we watched this giant steel structure heading straight for us. An American sailor standing on it with his arms folded, casually remarked: 'Ah thenk it's gonna come a be-at close!' A bit close! This was where the *1421*'s brilliant outward-turning propellers came into play. As the jetty continued to approach, we went straight ahead at full speed, almost touching the *Grey Goose*, and following a perfect turn to port, we were out of danger. I would have given Watson a medal if I had had one to give him.

Le Havre was to be the base of the Commander Minesweeping North France, to whom we were attached. After carrying out a difficult ship-handling manoeuvre like that, I felt I must have been dreaming about the blackouts. I was just tired, that was all.

I got on well with the Commander. He was a jovial man and a delight to work with. For whatever reason, he decided he would come aboard *1421* if and when there was a problem. The first ship to suffer a long-range torpedo was a minesweeper, and from then on the Commander called for *1421*, even in the worst weather. He came up with the greatest accolade I had ever received. 'Don't worry,' he called to a stricken vessel. 'The Sub could get alongside without cracking an egg.'

I would have been happier about the commendation had I not rammed his ship and put a fair-sized hole in his port bow. We were coming back from outlook duty and would normally have come alongside to report, but I must have blacked out and was scudding along much too fast. I 'came to' with *1421*'s nose firmly embedded on the port side of his ship.

I thought perhaps I should mention it.

When the bump came, he possibly thought he and his ship were being attacked. And, of course, he was in a way. He had been called and had a look over the side. When he saw who it was he called down: 'Sub, if you want to come aboard, you're very welcome, but do try to do it in the usual manner.'

My second kill was when I managed to sink an American MTL, a small craft such as might be found in Loch Lomond or Hoggan-field Loch. I was glad to be able to report that the Americans driving this little boat came to no harm. Naturally we offered them assistance—we offered them a couple of towels and courteously pointed the way to the shore.

Admittedly, Watson had kept telling me that they were heading straight for us, and I had refused to budge. 'Hold your course,' I insisted. It had nothing to do with my personal problems, but was a consequence of the fact that, even at sea, Americans drove on the wrong side of the road.

The Admiralty might well have wondered whose side I was on.

*   *   *

North Africa apart, I had never been in a foreign country (unless you count Paisley), so I thought it might cheer me up a bit if I took the opportunity to go ashore and see what a French town was like. Just as I was about to leave the boat, I noticed a long line of British and American sailors queuing up on the bank in front of what looked like a tiny garden shed. I decided I would walk further into the town. I tried hard to push my way through the queue of sailors when a huge coloured American seaman put his hand out to stop me and said, 'Hold on, Bud, you'll have to wait your turn. O.K.?'

'What are they waiting for?' I asked. 'Is it a fortune-teller?' He looked at me as if he thought I was joking. 'Yeah,' he said. 'That's what it is. A fortune teller!'

The large American sailor allowed me to go through the queue and I continued my walk towards the town. As I left the waiting queue, I saw a number of people running in various directions screaming 'Allemand! Allemand!' I had no idea what was happening until I realised that it was because of the way I wore my uniform. My cap like Rommel's, my long overcoat and boots.

The poor people of Le Havre must have thought I was a German who had been left behind. Just as they were getting over it, too!

The French shops were doing a roaring trade now that the Americans had arrived on the scene. I bought a couple of things for my mother, using pointing language, and then I wondered what it would be like to speak to someone in her own language. 'Quelle heure est-il, s'il vous plait?' I said. She told me what the time was. And that was the problem. I only knew that one French phrase. I had no idea what she had said.

And I still don't know what the time was, or what all the sailors were queuing for.

27

R&R

WE PUT IN at Shoreham-by-Sea, so close to the unforgettable Lancing College. I left *1421* with such deep regret, and there was rather an emotional parting from my crew. We had been through much together. My deputy cox'ain, Watson, was the first to take my hand, and, of all people, Cameron was the second. I was despatched to the Medical Officer at Hastings. He gave me a complete and thorough examination. Then he said: 'Hold out your arms.' I presented two quivering limbs with ten jerking fingers.

'Hmmm,' he murmured. 'I think maybe you've had enough.'

I must say I was inclined to agree with him.

His decision was that I would be required to attend a psychiatric hospital in the West Country. In the meantime I would be sent home on leave, until I received instructions.

My mother, although she was delighted to see me, was worried about the gaunt, depressed young man who had appeared unexpectedly at the door. She smothered me with questions. How was I? How long was I home for? When had I to go back?

I explained that I had to go to hospital. She was very concerned and wanted to know what was wrong with me. I was very depressed and didn't want to talk about it. But she persisted, and I came out with:

'They've decided to throw me in the loony bin.'

Not surprisingly my mother burst into tears, and I realised at once how badly I had upset her. I needn't have said it so brutally. I should have assured her that everything would be all right. I would only be away for a few weeks.

I left for Wraxhall Court Hospital, an RN establishment for the care and restoration of anxious and bewildered Naval officers. It stood in delightful countryside just outside Bristol. I arrived there sullen and silent, having no wish to see, hear or speak to anyone. I had been unable to sleep properly for weeks. I was given a heavy sleeping pill which seemed to keep me awake rather than put me to sleep. The following day I was interviewed by the chief MO who asked all sorts of questions.

What I desperately wanted was sleep. Blessed sleep.

I was still taciturn, rude and unapproachable, but on the second night a medical orderly arrived with a draught of brownish liquid which tasted disgusting. I learned later that I had been given paraldehyde. Within seconds I was staggering round the ward, shaking hands with the other patients, asking their names and introducing myself. Babbling cheerfully and telling them that it was delightful to meet so many nice people. I was sound asleep before I got half-way and had to be carried to my bed.

The weather at this time was almost spring-like and fresh, and I went out walking with another Sub who cried a lot. Sometimes we chatted about our families, our homes, and our work. At other times we would have a cry together. We even had a sort of competition to see who could cry the most. Mostly we went down to a typical English pub which was close by, and enjoyed a 'point o' zoider' and cheese and watercress sandwiches. Afterwards we used to wander along by the fields, and pause for a moment to have a 'Moo' with the West Country cows. They were friendly and polite and always mooed back.

It is just possible that one day someone saw and heard us, or one of the cows may have reported us.

Whatever the reason, the medics decided it was time 'these two idiots' were sent home. We were both invalided out of the Service just as the European war was coming to its finale, and we weren't sure if we were being released because of the approach of the war's end, or if it was because of the cows. Anyway we were not going to argue. We packed, and headed for home.

I didn't think to ask if the cows were going home as well!

Dressed up in my finery for *The Rikki Fulton Hour* on STV in 1965

Above: Tree climbing with
my big brother Jim

Above: In a huff after they refused
to take my picture at Dryburgh Abbey

Below: Jim with Togo

Below: John and Margaret,
my father and mother

In the Navy in 1942, at the tender age of eighteen

Left: On *HMML 1421*, with me in front of fellow officers from Coastal Forces

Below: HMS *Ibis*, sunk by a German torpedo in 1942

Above: As Weelum Sprunt in *Bunty Pulls the Strings* at Dundee Rep in 1948, with an anxious looking Graham Squire. My first professional engagement

Left: With Edith Macarthur in a scene from the Ardrossan and Saltcoats Players' production of *Gaslight*

Master of Ceremonies at the Royal Albert Hall, London, in 1955 at the
BBC Light Programme Festival of Dance Music with the legendary BBC Showband

Left: With Jack Milroy, Margo Henderson and Fay Lenore in Edinburgh's *Five Past Eight*

Below: 'Sure Josie, sure Josie, sure, sure, sure!' With my old china Jack Milroy, filming our TV series in 1963

Above: Celebrating record ticket sales for *Robinson Crusoe* in 1974
with Larry Marshall, Una McLean and Walter Carr

Opposite: My first ever 'Dame' picture—a promotional photo from 1955

Above: A long drop off a short pier. Filming STV's *A Grand Tour* at Crail Harbour

Below: Kate and I on tour with *A Wee Touch of Class* in 1986

The Rev. I. M. Jolly gets into the Christmas spirit with Cathy MacDonald in 1991

Above left: In *Scotch & Wry*, with Claire Neilson

Above right: Drunk again, in *Scotch & Wry* with Gregor Fisher

Left: Supercop gets carried away at Erskine Hospital

Above left: As McPhail in
Para Handy, 1993

Above right: As Bonnie Prince
Charlie in *Scotch & Wry*,
December 1988

Right: Having a laugh with
Jack Milroy

Above: Accepting the BAFTA award for Lifetime Achievement from Princess Anne in 1993

Right: Saying my thank-you's—in my own particular way

Opposite above: A night out with Jackie Stewart, Moira Anderson, Jimmy Tarbuck and Sean Connery at a Variety Club dinner for Jimmy Tarbuck in Glasgow

Opposite below: Meeting Princess Diana at a Royal Command Performance at the King's Theatre in Glasgow

At home with Kate and Jake

28

CIVVY STREET

PORTERS WERE STILL TO BE FOUND in railway stations in the forties, and, as in so many areas, the women had taken over from their men. As I clambered out of the carriage at Central Station, I was confronted by an enormous female in the drab home-made uniform and peaked cap of the station porter. She waddled helpfully towards me. 'Cairry yer bags, son?' she enquired. To be honest, I was amazed she could get her bulk out of bed in the morning, far less 'cairry' the extra weight of a suitcase, but I was so overcome with the sheer pleasure of being home in Glasgow for good and being in the company of a fellow Keelie. I would have hugged her if I had thought I could get my arms round her.

The return to civilian life in Riddrie created a mixture of emotions, and I was conscious of the fact that it would take some time to come to terms with the nightmares and spectres that still bugged me, but I have long since been able to blanket these with more acceptable thoughts and interests.

The major problem that first arose was that each time a Corporation bus hauled itself up the hill of Cumbernauld Road on the other side of the bowling green, it sounded to my ears for all the world like one of the Germans' secret weapons—the V2 monstrosities—and I had the devil of a job getting out of the habit of diving behind hedges—or under the table when I was at home.

I began to consider what I was going to do with my life. Although grateful for having had the job to come back to, I wasn't sure if I could see any great future with Henry Abrams Ltd., much as I had loved the work and the people. I remembered that art had been one of my best subjects and, along with Joyce Moffett's teaching of English, it had carried me through many an examination at Whitehill. My thoughts were definitely turning to the teaching of art.

I sought and obtained an interview with the charismatic head of Whitehill Secondary, Robert Weir. He greeted me warmly—even more so when I told him what I had in mind.

'Wonderful idea,' he boomed. 'Let's have a look at the old report card. Oh, no,' he said, studying the card. 'Not *art*, Robert. Not *art*! *English*, my boy. Look at the marks—very high. No, you shall be an English teacher. Now what we have to do is arrange a cramming course for your university prelims, and then we must see about . . . mumble, mumble, rhubarb, rhubarb . . .'

I thanked him very much and said I would think about it, for I *was* grateful—I did think about it and decided it would be easier to stay where I was for the moment. After a couple of weeks' rest I enrolled at the Commercial College in Pitt Street, taking English, Commercial English and Book-keeping in an effort to improve such prospects as I might have.

I was really happy to be back in civvy street, and at my old desk with Henry Abrams Ltd., on the sixth floor at 163 Hope Street. The Managing Director, Mr. Abrams himself, was a delightful, gentle man. The fact that his own son, Harry, and I had worked in the office together, and had both decided to offer our services to the Royal Navy, created an even better relationship.

I liked Mr. Abrams and admired him enormously. He always gave me my Sunday name, 'Robert', and also gave me the keys to the safe. That was a tremendous compliment and indicated great trust. For book-keeping purposes he would give me an IOU and

I would give out the cash he asked for. The amount was never very great, but, clearly, it was more than enough for 'a good lunch' in those days. I can still hear him enter the office having had a *very* good lunch! 'Come in, Robert,' he would say. And I would follow him to his private office. There was, of course, a stenographer, but there were times when he wanted to send what he called a private letter. I would then write down what he wanted to say in long hand and type it out on the company's letterhead. The problem was that the letter he had dictated to some client who had aroused his wrath was usually outrageous and insulting, even libellous, but brilliantly composed.

'Get that off right away, Robert,' he would say, and promptly leave to board his taxi to the station and thence to his home in Kilmacolm. The following morning would find him chirpy, but with a slightly worried frown on his brow.

'Come in, Robert,' he would call as he headed for his office. 'That letter I gave you yesterday—em—I've been thinking about it. Did you—em—manage to catch the post last night?'

'I'm terribly sorry, sir,' I would have to say, 'but something came up and I didn't manage to catch the post.'

'Oh, thank G—! I tell you what, let me have it, would you? There are one or two things I want to add. Thank you, Robert. Ask Miss Sutherland to come in.'

And the previous night's letter would be filed in the fire.

My salary from Abrams' was £3 a week, slightly lower than my Navy pay, but I was surprised and not ungrateful to receive a monthly disability pension of fifteen shillings from HM Government, which says much about the value of money in the forties. Still, it was a valuable contribution to my finances such as they were. All during my war service I had arranged for an allowance to be sent to my mother. In many cases it would have been for the benefit of a member of the family, but my mother faithfully lodged it in the bank every month, and I came home to a bank account—

which I had never had before. And, what was more, it had money in it!

The fifteen bob, however, was not without strings. Every so often I was bidden to appear before a group of three doctors in utility suits seated at what looked to me like a painter and decorator's pasting table, whose job it was to assess the progress or otherwise of my disability. Since I was unaware of it, I couldn't help them all that much, but it passed a morning or afternoon. 'And how are you today, Mr. Fulton?' they always asked me, and always received the same honest answer that I felt absolutely first class. On one of the assessment sessions they changed the question. 'And what do you feel like now?' they asked. It took me all my time to avoid the mistake of replying that I would be happy to join them in a gin and tonic.

There seemed to be an abundance of parties going on throughout the city. Probably because the war was as good as over and people were getting back to normal. I thought it was time I built up my long-neglected wardrobe. Having refused the 'demob suit' thank you very much, I was given a generous amount of clothing coupons in lieu. Carswell's of Renfield Street received the benefit of my patronage, and I lashed out on three natty suits at four pounds ten shillings a time. In this sartorial elegance, I could be found at many of the seemingly non-stop parties at the Stewarts' elegant home in Dennistoun wherein lived two very beautiful girls and two very understanding parents.

29

MYSTERIOUS RENDEZVOUS

I MET A WREN under a table at a party in Bishopbriggs. I'm not terribly sure *why* we were under the table, but we introduced ourselves and chatted and we were sufficiently interested to make plans to meet again. Her name was Katherine.

She was small, attractive, dressed with style and affected a slight drawl.

We decided to take in a film in the centre of town and I would call for her at a time that was suitable. She said she had something to do in town first, so it would be easier if we met at the picture house. Not necessarily under a table.

I had no problem with that, but I did have a problem with our return. We had enjoyed the film, and I called a taxi to take us home. I had no idea where she lived, but clearly it was a route she knew well. It took us from the centre of town along George Street, crossing the High Street to Duke Street and we had to say 'goodnight' at the corner of Westercraigs.

No problems there either. Except that any time we had a date, the same routine took place. She would insist on my meeting her at whatever picture house or dance hall we were headed for, and being taken home by bus, tram or cab to the corner of Westercraigs. I even began to wonder if there was, perhaps, some religious reason and she dared not be seen with me. Or if she lived in one of those beautiful big houses where she and her family were trying to hide the fact that there was a poor deranged member of the family locked up in the attic that they dare not let anyone see or hear.

The mystery was eventually solved when I insisted that I would at least see her to her door. We walked up a path and, as I pecked her 'goodnight', the door opened and an elderly man appeared with a walking-stick in his hand and berated us for using his front door for our 'filthy carryings-on', and threatened to call the police.

I apologised and explained that we had been visiting friends and had obviously come to the wrong house.

It was so ridiculously simple. Actually what she didn't want me to know was that she lived up a close further up Duke Street!

During the short period we had known each other Katherine had made it clear that she was the one and only Arbiter of Elegance. She pronounced on social etiquette and *haute couture* with equal assuredness. Her own dress sense, she informed me, was impeccable. She spoke of breeding, refinement and good taste like the daughter of some exiled Royal forced to live temporarily in reduced circumstances.

She remarked on the texture of my four-pound-ten suits and criticised my choice of ties. Although I wasn't aware of it, she had decided that I self-consciously held my hands in a particular way in order to disguise their size. The fact that large hands were a blessing for a pianist was summarily dismissed.

But none of that mattered to me. We were only going out dancing, or to a party or the pictures, after all. I hadn't asked her to marry me or meet the family. I had had experience prior, thank you! I was on my guard at all times.

Katherine healed very quickly.

She had the outlook of one who convinces themselves that they, and only they, are in a position to appraise and offer their opinion as being the Epitome of Good Taste. And there are a lot of them about!

It sapped the confidence to a certain extent, but there were moments when her obsession with refinement and the refined left her vulnerable to injury.

Such a situation was when she received an invitation from a girl friend in the Wrens to what sounded like the The Society Event of the Year. It was to take place in the grounds of the family country seat in Middlesex. I was disappointed that it hadn't been Westminster Cathedral. Katherine informed me that the bride was very cultured and came of excellent stock. What would you expect, being the daughter of a *three car family*?

Since her invitation allowed for a partner, I was called upon to accompany her.

This worked out splendidly for me. Only a few months previously, I had travelled to Nottingham at the behest of my old 'eating-buddy' from the *Ibis*, Bernie Cookson. He had decided to tie the knot with a truly beautiful girl and asked me to be his Best Man, and I had obliged. Katherine's Middlesex wedding gave me an opportunity to take up Bernie's invitation to visit, so I was able to spend a few days with them before meeting up with Katherine in London.

We set off for the Middlesex Wedding of the Year in good time, but our sketchy knowledge of London and its environs caused a great many delays while we asked directions, occasionally boarding the wrong train and having to backtrack and start again.

Eventually we found the delightful and impressive church, but were denied the pleasure of seeing the inside of it and attending the service—since everyone had long since left the church to head for the family home. Photographs of the happy couple and their families at the church had only just been completed, and Katherine was able to say hello to her friend. We were introduced to her friend's new husband and their families, and after a few pleasantries singularly lacking in warmth, we were left to find some way to get to the family country seat.

This turned out to be a red brick and pebble-dash semi-detached council house of some five apartments circa 1930. It had a small garden to the front, and a relatively larger one—which Katherine had euphemistically described as 'the grounds'—to the rear.

Katherine put on a brave smile to hide her obvious disappointment and pretended that all was well. Until she spotted the open wooden garage at the side! Here were housed the carriages that had justified the description of her Wren friend as coming from a three car family.

A small Ford, vintage 1937, sat disconsolately alongside an ancient Wolseley that leaned against the wooden side of the garage, fretting about the lack of its nearside front wheel. But, out in front, and obviously the only vehicle that was roadworthy, stood a motorbike and sidecar.

So far, the only thing that was going right for Katherine was the weather. It was a fine, late summer day, and the home-made wedding cake was pierced with a bread knife in 'the grounds' at the back of the house while we drank the health of the bride and groom with an impudent little South African sherry. There followed a slight delay as the bride's mother, sister and sundry other female relatives (the bride included) prepared the wedding feast, during which further quantities of the sherry were consumed while photographs (none of them professional) were taken.

The room to which we were eventually called had been totally cleared of its rightful furniture and filled with wooden forms and a series of wooden trestle tables covered with large paper table covers.

We gained access to this banqueting hall via a door from the inside of the house and the 'French windows' from the garden. When everyone had taken their places, all but a very few of the seventy-odd guests found themselves imprisoned—in order to reach the loo, as many had to do urgently because of the large quantities of beer that had been consumed, it was necessary to climb over the tables to the friendly cries of: ' 'Ere you go, Arfer. Pissed again.' And: 'Too late, Fanny, there's firty fahsand in there already. Use the bleedin' garden. Nobody's lookin'.'

The little pout on Katherine's face had become tighter by the second.

The food was home-cooked. Good thick soup made the day before and followed by steak-and-kidney pie with peas and cabbage. Giant mixing bowls of trifle washed down with yet more bottled beer (brought in by the guests themselves) for those who wanted it, and most certainly did.

It was a feast indeed by any standards, as good if not better than many a caterer could have provided, and worth a king's ransom in meat coupons. In fact the meal turned what had looked like a major disaster into a happy, down-to-earth occasion, and I began to enjoy it thoroughly. Katherine, however, was indignant that she had been so completely deceived.

When everyone had eaten their fill and congratulated the cooks and helpers, a number of large catering tea urns, obviously begged and borrowed and full of the hot brew, were placed at intervals round the tables. There were a number of speeches, many un-invited, followed by a rather vulgar song from the bride's father.

But the *pièce de résistance*, the climax of this entire extraordinary day, was yet to come.

At that romantic moment in what could only be described as a more normal wedding, the bride and her groom would start off the evening's enjoyment, by dancing round the floor to warm and affectionate applause, to be joined then by their guests. In this case, the groom groped under the table to produce an accordion, while his bride, having unobtrusively changed her shoes, hauled herself on to the now bare trestle tables and, still in her flowing white gown, treated the assembled company to a vigorous tap dance accompanied by her husband.

161

It was at this point that Katherine began to feel faint. Dazed and shaken, we made our apologies and left to try and find our way back to civilisation.

30

THE CATALYST

STILL HANKERING after some half-remembered dream, I went to one of the gang's parties and met a girl called Jean Wilkie who lived just round the corner in Eastercraigs. I automatically called her 'Wee' Jeannie Wilkie because she was, indeed, small like my mother. (Are *all* men attracted to girls who remind them of their mothers?—character, appearance and urges 'to do a wee bit letting' etc. apart.)

Anyway, Wee Jeannie Wilkie was very attractive, cultured and had a great love of music. It was, of course, only her mind that interested me.

And I'm lying.

She invited me to join some other friends at her home one evening, among them a man whom I enjoyed meeting very much. He was a journalist and introduced himself as Harry McNab with precise articulation—'M, small c, N-A-B'. As we talked it became apparent that this was a man whose mental Thesaurus was formidable, but it was fun to listen to him.

It was a great evening. I enjoyed it tremendously. We chatted about things I had never chatted about with anyone before, like music, poetry and theatre. I confess they lost me when it came to poetry. A few limericks and one or two of Burns' poems and I was out. But I made up for it with the other two.

It was Harry McNab who looked over at me as I sat relaxed in an armchair and said: 'I feel sure those hands, so artistically draped over the arms of the chair, could produce something quite remarkable for us.'

He had obviously been aware of my urge to play the wonderful grand piano that adorned the Wilkies' sitting room.

I needed no second invitation. Grand pianos to me were like honey-pots to a bear and I would have happily played all night.

There were even better evenings, too, when Jean and I were on our own. She was very sympathetic, and the very first person I knew who could even begin to understand my deep, deep longing to become an actor. Katherine most definitely did not approve. Perhaps she should get out from under the table a bit more, I thought.

*   *   *

On May 7th I went down to Katherine's house to see her but she was away somewhere, and I began to feel lonely. I was also conscious of a strange quiet that had come over the city. Perhaps everybody was celebrating at the town centre. So I started to walk up Cumbernauld Road towards Eastercraigs in the hope that I might find Wee Jeannie Wilkie at home. As I passed one of the closes a woman stuck her head out of her window and called down to me:

'That's it, son. The war's finished. It's all over. It's all over now.'
I nodded at her and gave her a rather unconvincing wave, but I was too depressed to give a cheer.

It seemed the wrong time to be alone. Perhaps if I had managed to make contact with Katherine or Wee Jeannie it might have been more like the celebration it should have been. It would, I knew, take a long time to come to terms with the war's end after six long years. But, at least, there was a move in a very positive direction.

Wee Jeannie Wilkie was the lovely lady who set me off on the only life in which I had any true interest. There was a time, years later, when people used to write to me asking how and where to begin in showbusiness. My advice was always to seek entry to drama college. They would assess and advise. Many years later when my own career was established, I felt very sorry for those people who longed to get a foothold in the theatre because they loved it, but, sadly, found that love unrequited.

It used to be that young people who sought a career in the theatre would be taken on by repertory companies whether they had talent or not, but they would have to pay something in the region of twenty to thirty pounds just to be allowed to do menial, and sometimes unnecessary, tasks in the hope that a walk-on part might be on offer. I can remember watching a young girl scrubbing the paint off a useless piece of canvas which would almost immediately go into the bin.

Thank heaven for the drama and training schools.

In my own case it was Wee Jeannie Wilkie who solved the problem by pointing me in a different direction entirely. She suggested that the solution to my problem was the amateur movement, and gave me the name and address of the secretary of the Pantheon Club, which was at that time—and probably still is—one of the busiest and most successful of the amateur clubs.

The amateur movement in Glasgow was very strong at this time, no doubt because of people's need to provide much of their own entertainment during the war years.

There was an annual One Act Festival which ran for two weeks of packed houses in the splendid old Lyric Theatre. Standing opposite the Empire Theatre in Sauchiehall Street, it was built in 1879-80 and originally called the Royalty Theatre. It was a splendid place. A 2000-seater, it had been sold to Howard & Wyndham, who sold it to the YMCA and renamed it The Lyric.

Entries for the One Act Festival came from hundreds of clubs all over Scotland, and audiences were treated to a high standard of acting in three one-act plays each evening, ending with an adjudication of each entry by a recognised actor or director.

In 1960 the Lyric was sold to developers, and it was demolished in 1962 to be replaced by sundry uninteresting shops. It was very sad. It was a perfect theatre which the amateur clubs could have made their own.

Across the road Moss's Empire was in trouble. The management had decided that variety theatres were no longer in vogue. They tried rather salacious plays to attract the public, without much success. As some wag put it: 'They're going to close this one, and if it's a success, they're going to close the lot.'

The Empire began its life as the Gaiety theatre. It opened in 1874, and was rebuilt as the Empire Palace which opened in 1897. It seated 2158 patrons, and gave the Glasgow folk years of such pleasure. The last show before demolition was 31st March 1963. It closed with a performance by an amazing number of stars and well-known names, who gave the Empire a wonderful send-off. Jack Milroy (who else) and I appeared as 'Francie and Josie' in that wonderful music hall for the first and last time. Neither Jack nor I ever performed at the Glasgow Empire except on that one very important occasion. After that day Jack and I always used to say: 'Well, that's the first time we've brought the house down.'

Andy Stewart had tremendous success there, but some of the English performers would be quaking in their shoes before they had reached the border.

Des O'Connor admitted that he had fainted on stage and had to be carried off without finishing his act. And that was before any of the Upper Circle had even raised their voices.

Dead silence from the Empire audience was death indeed.

The late Roy Castle went through something of the same, but it didn't seem to bother him so much. That was because his was a very busy, and rather lengthy, act. He was a wonderful performer and much liked. I only had the privilege of working with him once and that was in an STV Hogmanay programme in 1966. Roy was a multi, multi talented performer. He sang, he danced, he played the trumpet, he was a fine comedian. But his act was just a tad long for the Upper Circle. I'm sure he was too busy performing to even hear the message that had come from the Upper Circle, which was:

'Is there no end tae this man's f*****' versatility?'

Mike and Bernie Winters were almost in the same boat.

Bernie, like Des, was terrified and had no idea what to expect. Mike's job was to wander on stage, pipe in mouth, and appear nonchalant, easy-going and cool, and do a warm-up in preparation for Bernie's appearance. However, the Upper Circle were not as warm as expected, and the cue for his entrance nearly cost him a cleaning bill for his trousers.

Bernie had barely opened his mouth for the inane giggle that was his stock-in-trade when he heard one of the Upper Circle give them their critique before they had even started.

From the Upper Circle came: 'Jesus Christ there's two o' them!'

The Alhambra theatre in Wellington Street, a 2750-seater, opened in 1910. This, the home of the famous *Five Past Eight* shows, was in my opinion perhaps the best theatre in Europe. After the death of Stewart Cruikshank, Peter Donald took the reins and within a short time Howard & Wyndham had rid themselves of most, or all, of their theatrical properties. H&W offered the Alhambra to the Glasgow Corporation along with the King's Theatre in Bath Street. The King's was sold to the Glasgow Corporation in 1966, but the Alhambra, offered in 1969, was refused because of the outlay required for purchase, plus the cost of the upkeep of two theatres. Peter Donald's threat of demolition was carried out in 1971.

At least we have two wonderful theatres left in Glasgow.

31

BEYOND THE CURTAIN

MY LETTER to the Pantheon Club secretary was greeted with enormous enthusiasm, perhaps understandably in view of the dearth of men in their early twenties. I found myself in the company of people like Alan Mackill, a great character with just a touch of eccentricity, Willie Joss whose 'Tammy Troot' was such a favourite in the BBC's *Children's Hour* and Molly Weir who, along with several others, shared my desire to make a career in acting.

In November the committee were casting their next production. It was a play called *Stage Door* by Edna Ferber and George S. Kaufman. It had a huge cast of thirty-two characters, and I didn't mind at all that the part in which I was cast was small. After all I had only just started, and I was just very happy to get my feet on a real, honest-to-goodness stage. I used to stand in the wings watching all the way through every performance, fascinated by the skills of some of Glasgow's best known amateurs.

Rehearsals for productions such as *Stage Door* went on for months, beginning with perhaps one night per week and increasing to two and three nights, and as the opening night approached it became a full-time effort. The final rehearsals took place on a Sunday, which was my favourite time of all. The cast gathered in a hall near Charing Cross and prepared to rehearse through the afternoon and evening. There was always a break to enjoy the flasks of tea and sandwiches we had brought (I had a penchant for cold Ovaltine), and to chat about other things. These breaks were a platform for great philosophical debates on theatre and the arts (amateurs were well known for enjoying talking through their hats), the enjoyment or otherwise of some production or other, and sometimes heavy criticism, deserved or not, of a performance by a rival club.

There was a neat story about a group of amateurs who had recently mounted a production of Shakespeare's *Richard III*, and later had gone to see a touring version of the same play starring the Master (Sir Laurence/Lord Olivier) himself.

When asked if they had enjoyed the performance, a young amateur leading light, having got over his amazement, replied half laughing through his surprise, that 'it was actually quite good really. *Laurence Olivier played my part!'*

Sometimes at the Sunday rehearsal breaks, I took to the unlikely pastime of reading tea cups to give the company a rest from the script. I had never read a tea cup in my life. The only thing I remembered was that it was necessary to carefully empty what was left into the saucer, turn it upside down and turn it round three times. When she realised what was going on with the little group, wee Molly Weir came over and thrust her cup and saucer at me excitedly.

I went through the ritual and stared at the tea leaves. Molly's body language told the whole story. She had something very important on her mind.

'A Big Decision?' Right first time. 'I see a journey ahead' Yes, yes! 'It has something to do with acting?' Bull's-eye! But that wasn't difficult. If it was a big decision—about a journey—to do with acting. I figured that Molly was going for gold and about to try her luck in the profession. Just to put a touch of mystery into the game, I counselled her to go ahead and make the journey—the leaves say London! Would that be right? A barely suppressed squeal confirmed the prognosis. I warned that things might well be difficult and disappointing at first, but in due course her efforts would be crowned with success.

And lo and behold—that's exactly how it happened.

The dress rehearsal for *Stage Door* was unbelievably exciting. Not surprisingly I got to the Lyric long before I was needed, and watched the stage crew decorating the set and placing the props, most of which came from Alan Mackill's own home. I spent a good fifteen minutes just savouring the feel of my feet on the stage.

Just a little bit different from the makeshift affair in St. Andrew's East Church Hall!

Often during my career in the theatre, I have invited friends and their children to come onto the stage after a show and experience a totally different perspective. I would have the electricians put on the lights in the empty auditorium, and full lighting on the stage, now looking anything but glamorous.

I always found their reactions interesting. Few had any idea what to expect and the impact was tremendous as they stood on the hallowed boards. From wonder to awe through to disbelief, their responses brought forth comments like 'I had no idea it would be like this!' and on many occasions they would say, 'I don't know how you can stand there in front of all those people.'

But the memory of that first moment on the Lyric stage will never leave me. It was like coming home—like putting my head in the door of a house I knew I was meant to live in.

I had arrived on the other side of the curtain.

32

GOOD COMPANY

ALAN MACKILL cast me for a tiny part in the play the Pantheon Club were offering as their entry for the 1946 One Act Festival in April. I was pleased because it was my second appearance in a play, and surprised because the part was that of a seventy-five-year-old man in an old folks' home in Scandinavia. And I was only twenty-two. It seemed to suggest that there might be more to come.

The play was called *Autumn Fires*, and Alan and Willie Joss played the leading parts as two old boys who shared their lives in a double room where they constantly quarrelled with each other about the lines of demarcation which were obvious in view of the incredible untidiness on one side and obsessive neatness on the other.

(I have often wondered if Neil Simon found his inspiration for *The Odd Couple* in that elderly play!)

The plot centred round the birthday celebration of one of the old men (Willie Joss) with one or two of his ancient cronies from the home. When it was deemed to be ready for public perform-ance, we tried it out in front of an audience in a church hall well away from our base, to get a proper feel for it before presenting it in front of the Festival Adjudicator.

It seemed to be going very well until Alan had to offer cigars to their 'guests'. He offered the cigar box to the first character who stretched out his hand then looked up at Alan with a questioning look. Alan looked down and realised that he had forgotten the props. The cigar box was empty! But, with the aplomb of a real pro, he offered the empty box to the other characters one by one in what was supposed to be an English accent, followed by a very loud stage whisper out of the corner of his mouth.

'Would anyone like a cigar? *Yer not smokin'!'*

In spite of everything we went on to win the SCDA (Scottish Community Drama Association) Trophy.

It seemed to me that Alan Mackill produced for nearly every amateur club in Glasgow, and he was taking advantage of his new-found protégé. I seemed rarely without a script in my hand. I was either rehearsing, or acting in a play somewhere, practically every night. Even lunch breaks were frantic ninepenny plates of soup in Danny Brown's and off to a rehearsal in some hall or room. He even had me playing the lead in the Technical College's annual production. It is perhaps ironic that it was Strathclyde University, formed from that College, which later honoured me with a doctorate.

A bluff hearty man, Alan ran his own printing firm in Robertson Street, so had a double bite at the cherry by doing all the printing for the shows he produced. Not a great actor, although he did play the odd part now and again, often in the middle of the street. To the embarrassment of many, including myself, he would relate an incident in which he had bettered someone in an argument, and friends and strangers alike would find themselves cornered up against a building or railing as he re-enacted the scene, arms flailing, bawling and shouting aggressively while passers-by hurriedly crossed the road in case they became involved.

His pride and pleasure at my success—when I returned from London in 1955 and was starring in the big pantos in Glasgow and Edinburgh—was a joy to see. When he took ill and was forced to retire, he often wandered into the Alhambra Theatre whenever I was appearing in Glasgow. He and my father were the only two people the stage-door keeper had orders to admit at any time without question. I could never repay Alan for everything he had done to help me on my way with friendship, encouragement, advice and invaluable experience, but he was proud of the privilege.

Definitely one of the good guys.

*   *   *

Life was now becoming complicated. I was dealing with customs during the days and acting or rehearsing somewhere at night. On top of everything else, Jim was due home from Africa and John was still hatching plans to involve the three of us in his Grand Scheme for Fulton Brothers Incorporated.

It seemed as if Fate had heard us talking. I learned that an office on the floor beneath Abrams had become available for rent. I immediately made enquiries and found that it was one of a suite of three offices occupied by Mr. McGuffie's small civil engineering company. It had a telephone with its own line and a large slanted drawing board built into the front of the windows, and that was all. That evening at home I told John my news and his eyes narrowed in apprehension. Suddenly the talking and fantasising were over. I had finally called his bluff.

He came with me and was scrutinising the office in a very businesslike manner. Mr. McGuffie came in from his own office, and politely offered his hand. John took Mr. McGuffie's hand between his thumb and forefinger and waggled it back and forth several times and then massaged Mr. McGuffie's fingers, on the premise that if Mr. McGuffie was a civil engineer he must be a mason, and he was convinced that at some point he had cracked the masonic code. By this time John was examining the office with great care. Even I was almost convinced that we were already in business and had offices worldwide.

After due consideration John announced that the office would be perfect and we would be happy to rent it. At the same time he managed to give the impression that our presence would enhance the standing of all the other offices. I shook Mr. McGuffie's hand on the deal, and John waggled Mr. McGuffie's hand and massaged his fingers again. It was at this point that Mr. McGuffie announced he had a question to ask: 'What sort of business are you in?'

I looked at John, he looked at me, and we both looked at Mr. McGuffie. Then, with absolute assurance, John said: 'Manufacturers' Agents.'

I had thought that Mr. McGuffie's question was going to be 'Why are you waggling my hand and massaging my fingers?' But I was even more interested in discovering what business we were in.

I set to with the telephone book and sent out letters to companies I thought might be interested in having a Scottish agency. Now I was working for Abrams and for Fulton Brothers, and acting and rehearsing in the evenings. By this time I felt as if I had played for every amateur company in Glasgow and began to feel like an old hand at the game. I loved to stay in the town after work and go for a meal in the Paramount Café (now the Odeon) in Renfield Street, and I always went to the same table.

The first time the waitress served me I deliberately mentioned that I didn't have much time as I had to be in the theatre in plenty of time to prepare for the performance. She was very impressed. She had never served a famous actor before. And little did she know that she still had not served a famous actor, but it meant that I got my tea first.

I told her about the play I was doing and asked if she had seen it. 'No,' she said sadly. 'I don't get to the theatre much. You can't in this job.' I said it was a great pity, she would have enjoyed it, and I had been going to arrange something.

She paused for a moment considering, and I froze a little, wondering if I was going to have to pay for tickets for the theatre.

'D'you think you could give me your autograph?' she asked. I breathed a sigh of relief, smiled, and magnanimously scribbled my name on her pad, and mentally doubled her tip—just 'mentally', you understand, but from then on I got priority service.

The Park Theatre was also near at hand. It was the baby of John Stewart, a rich theatre aficionado who, without any specific artistic talent of his own, desperately wanted to be involved in theatre. He had created a little eighty-seater theatre by converting two large houses in Park Circus, and had garnered something of a cult following. I had served some of my time there and it was exciting to hear of the plans John Stewart and his partner Kenneth Ireland had made to give the Park Theatre professional status. It was the seedling of what is now the Pitlochry Festival Theatre, first established in a tent and now a beautiful, highly popular and successful venue.

The Pantheon Club was celebrating the return of a man called Eddie Fraser who had produced musical shows for them before the war. He was now back to his old job and making preparations to produce the first musical since he had been called up. It was to be *Glamorous Night*, a wonderful choice. I was a great fan of Ivor Novello and his beautiful music, and it was hinted that the leading part might come to me.

I was working in the Park Theatre in a hideous two-hander that I hated, and so did the audiences, when the Pantheon Secretary arrived with Eddie Fraser one evening and introduced me. Apparently all that was needed to seal the decision was for Eddie to meet me at the little theatre and look me over.

He was much smaller than I had imagined and had turned up in a khaki battle dress tunic which had been dyed green. He could not be described as immaculate. He had lank fair hair and a round podgy white face, and a slack mouth which contained teeth in an advanced state of decay, and of a colour I had never seen before. The result of chain-smoking, I suppose, which had also stained his fingers an unattractive mahogany.

He was colourful but in no way the tall, elegant, rather *outré*, flamboyant personality I had expected. Eddie stood there with narrowed eyes, examining every aspect of my appearance. There was no smile. If he had smiled at anyone they would have been treated to a glimpse of the unbelievable teeth.

He was seriously unimpressive, and I was seriously disappointed, but I got the part anyway.

At the same time it looked as if Fulton Brothers might have struck a drip of oil. A company called Bennie Lifts had added metal furniture to their manufacturing repertoire, presumably because there was not a great demand for lifts at that time. On the other hand, like many other factories, they may have been in the process of changing over from munitions. I wondered if this could be the same Bennie who invented and built the monorail train that became something of a landmark in Milngavie.

Whatever, my letter had been well received and Mr. Bennie sent us his catalogue which showed a range of modern round coffee tables and nests of square tables with wrought iron everywhere. John and I were not all that sure if, and to whom, we could sell such items. They didn't seem to be compatible with newspapers, cigarettes and stationery. But, we thought it might be worth a go— if the financial arrangements were acceptable. Bennie's response was very positive. It looked as if Fulton Brothers might well be on their way, even if I couldn't see the connection between the news-agent and stationery empire John had outlined years ago, and selling metal furniture.

We signalled our interest to Mr. Bennie subject to terms. His reply was enthusiastic and he promised to send catalogues, order forms and samples. He also informed us that he had asked his brother-in-law, who was an accountant in Glasgow, to call on us at our office the following week so that he could study our organisation and assure himself that we would make suitable representation for the Bennie company.

This was not going to be easy. We stood discussing the implications in our totally empty office with its solitary telephone on the mantelpiece and bare drawing table at the windows. We had to admit we didn't exactly have the look of a long-established, thriving business. We were strapped for time (and money), but we dropped everything including my work for Henry Abrams upstairs and went into action with a precision that was worthy of the military. I bought a knee-hole desk and a couple of interesting padded chairs in reasonable condition from the sale rooms, plus a new filing cabinet. John, so clever with hammer and saw and paint, brought a small table back to life, on which we placed Katherine's portable typewriter with a shorthand notebook alongside bearing unidentifiable squiggles which would hopefully confound all but a Gregg or Pitman reader. An ancient but handsome coat-stand waited in a corner with the dignity of an old retainer. Calendars, papers and files were distributed everywhere in carefully placed disarray with knick-knacks from home to give the place what we hoped would be a stuffy, businesslike atmosphere.

But the ingenious final stroke was John's.

He brought two suitcases full of a variety of stock from the Roebank Street shop, which he placed in a neat display on the drawing board at the windows.

Mr. Bennie's brother-in-law duly arrived at the arranged time. We talked about our business and the economy for a while, then John produced the star prize. 'Just a few of our lines,' he said airily, indicating the items from Roebank Street.

Mr. Bennie's brother-in-law was tremendously impressed and sent a glowing report to London, whereupon Mr. Bennie promptly despatched several metal and glass tables along with an invoice payable within thirty days!

The finale to Fulton Brothers' first venture was that we couldn't get rid of the blasted metal furniture, and had to take them home to Riddrie where people kept shifting them to different parts of the house each time they fell over them. But we were able to establish other agencies which proved much more successful since they were more in line with the trade in which our shops were already engaged.

Needless to say, the frequent absences from my desk had not gone unnoticed. I had discussed my plans with Mr. Abrams from the beginning, and was now able to say that things were beginning to move. He and I both agreed that I ought to do the same. Go downstairs and give Fulton Brothers my undivided attention.

A few months later Jim was demobbed from the RAF and, after a short break, joined me in the office, thus creating the well-known problem of top-heavy administration. Too many cowboys and not enough Indians.

Two of us at least wondered if Fulton Brothers was going to be worthwhile.

Meantime my application for an audition with the BBC at Queen Margaret Drive in Glasgow had been acknowledged much more quickly than I anticipated. Jimmy Crampsey, by then the head of Schools, took the audition himself in Studio 8 in the old drama lounge, with Archie P. Lee, a great friend of long standing, in attendance. I was rewarded ten days later with a contract for a historical piece for schools called *The Gowrie Conspiracy*. It went out live at 2 p.m. on Wednesday 15th January 1947, and I was paid the princely sum of £1.11.6 (one-and-a-half guineas, or £1.57p).

Events were now moving of their own volition. I was making no forward plans, not even thinking about the future, so exciting was the present.

Contracts for programmes came thick and fast, and I realised that having our own office would make it much easier now for me to take time off for broadcasts.

It was a bit off-putting at first when I could see the faces of producers peering through the portholes seeking new faces and voices, but I got used to it and found it amusing.

One such producer was the well known, much loved Auntie Kathleen, Kathleen Garscadden, who was seeking a replacement for that lovely man, the late Gordon Jackson, who had to withdraw from a six-week serial because of his film commitments. I was rushed into service. This was a Godsend—it meant I would be seen in the canteen for two or three days each week for six weeks, which gave other producers an opportunity to take a peek through the porthole.

I couldn't help being happy about the way things were going, but Katherine wasn't taking kindly to my constant involvement with the acting fraternity. The Pantheon and other clubs were taking up the time that should have been spent with her, she thought. I was forever rehearsing or playing somewhere in the city, or what she called 'fiddling about with Fulton Brothers!' She discovered that I was not the sort of settled, malleable character she had hoped for. Romeo and Juliet we were not.

I realised that the meeting in the Paramount Café to discuss our so-called relationship was a mistake. But an actor has to do what an actor has to do. Katherine's demand that I give everything up, 'get a decent job, get married and have kids' filled me with horror. Nothing was going to come of what was just a mild friendship. There was no future for us. The course of events in my life had been predetermined, and I had to be free.

She was in floods of tears. 'I'm distraught,' she kept saying. I had not expected her emotional outburst, and found it pretty embarrassing with other people having coffee and cheesecake, especially cheesecake which I loved. I found it incredibly difficult to deal with the situation. I didn't know what to do about the copious tears, because I bloody well wasn't going to soil the silk pocket handkerchief she had given me for Christmas. But she wouldn't stop. I was becoming quite emotional myself. Eventually I went to the loo, and in the tiled and marble confines of the gents' toilet I tried to stop my heart beating so fast. I had to be careful. I was concerned that seeing her in such a state I might buckle and surrender.

What was most important to me was that I wanted to find what was at the end of this rainbow I had discovered.

I returned to our table and sat quietly until she had calmed down, then escorted her with quiet, dignified charm to a taxi outside, gave the cabby her address and, without looking back, walked up Renfield Street into the sunset!

I couldn't help thinking how lucky Fulton Brothers were to have managed to borrow her typewriter before we broke up!

33

LIFE WITH AUNTIE

KATHLEEN GARSCADDEN was a one-off. Originally trained for opera, and working in radio since its inception, she was responsible for the kick-starts of many of us who have had the good fortune to make a name for ourselves. Moira Anderson, Gordon Jackson, Stanley Baxter to name but a few.

Her great talent was her timing of a programme. Since they were always 'live', it wasn't the easiest thing in the world, but Kathleen's answer was simplicity itself. At the end of a broadcast she would direct her rather piercing eyes at the clock and improvise if necessary—even reading the cast list twice for the required number of minutes, and 'Goodnight, children. Goodnight' would be heard precisely on the final second of the programme.

Kathleen was rather like my mother, only worse, in that she wouldn't have recognised a joke if it came up and hit her on the ear. In one of the programmes, we had been performing one of Wilma Horsburgh's quaint little poems which was about a little smut of soot from a chimney called Sammy. Kathleen brought the programme to its end with: 'So there you are, children. That was a wee smutty story for you.'

During the war years the newsreaders imprisoned in their tiny London studios had become a sort of lifeline for everyone. Alvar Liddell, Joseph McLeod, Bruce Belfrage—they had a calm, commanding confidence when reading the news which brought a sense of security to the listeners, as well as great affection and fame.

At the cessation of hostilities Joseph McLeod, presumed to be a Scot despite his exquisite speaking voice, was doing a sort of lap of honour in Scotland and Kathleen, great opportunist, asked him to speak the narration of a *Children's Hour* story called 'The Black Wherry.' It was a tale of smuggling, excisemen and spies.

Among the large cast was old Alec Mackenzie, a retired head-master who later went on to make some excellent films such as *The Maggie* in 1953 and *Greyfriars Bobby* in 1960. Alec had the Gaelic. In fact Alec had the Gaelic long before he had the English, and as he listened to Joseph McLeod's narration in a Highland accent, Alec became more and more agitated.

I thought McLeod was doing extremely well. It has been said that someone with an *Engish* accent could produce a Highland accent more easily than a Lowland Scot.

'And the following nytte,' intoned McLeod. 'The sin wass shining on the peecht and the brach-ken. . . .'

Alec, now red in the face and perspiring, was clearly worried. So I asked him if he was alright. 'No,' he said, 'I'm not aal right. It's this clown McLeod with his peecht and his brachken. We'd better warn Kath-leen.'

'Why,' I asked, puzzled. 'What's wrong with the "peat and the bracken"?'

Alec, staunch United Free Church, was seriously discomfited. 'Well,' he whispered to me, 'peecht is a Gaelic word for a woman's—well never mind. It's jist a terrible bad word.'

There are many stories which emphasise the more vulgar side of the actor's sense of humour. We were having a break during rehearsals for a documentary programme produced by Archie Lee and not only was he producing this programme, he produced one of the most disgusting, but most excruciatingly funny, recordings—a performance by the Orpheus Choir's conductor, the great Sir Hugh Roberton. Sir Hugh had been recorded many times before, but not quite like this.

It appears that a BBC team were recording a celebratory programme from St. Andrew's Halls which included some wonderful music from the orchestra and an interview with Sir Hugh. After various tests, the sound team had decided that by far the best sound quality for the interview was obtained in the gentlemen's lavatory, which was tiled from wall to wall and had a stone floor. So they duly set up their gear there.

During the break, however, some mischievous swine had lodged a microphone behind the old-fashioned cistern of one of the cubicles. Whoever set up the mike could not have played the trick with the intention of deliberately trapping Sir Hugh himself. After all he couldn't have guessed which cubicle Sir Hugh was likely to use.

But it had been brilliantly recorded. From the first sound of the approaching steps through the opening and bolting of the lavatory door, the rustle of trousers being dropped, the grunts of relief and a great rustle of toilet paper followed by a similar rustle as the trousers were hauled into place, the opening of the bolt and finally the exit of Sir Hugh to the tune of the final fade-out of the longest flush in Christendom.

The effect on the cast of Archie's documentary was devastating. The entire cast were rolling about on the floor of the drama lounge in helpless paroxysms of laughter, and it was a very long time before rehearsals could resume.

It was classic coarse humour.

There were many things that puzzled me about the BBC. For one thing it never entered my head that everything technical could be anything other than perfectly handled, or that there could be such a thing as a gaffe. But we know differently now, and they actually make very amusing programmes out of them. Perhaps it was because it was still early days yet for radio, but the fact is that once or twice a switch would be left on, or perhaps a mike had been left live and the line left open.

My own favourite memory from many years ago was of one of the janitors whose job was to clean and tidy the studios after the programme had ended, and who had obviously been inspired by the newsreaders in London who always made an announcement like: 'This is London. Here is the news, and this is Alvar Liddell reading it.'

Studio six was an effects studio. It contained a huge tank filled with water, with an oar in a rowlock. There was also a microphone hanging upside down above a circle of gravel surrounded by a circle of cement, which would produce the sound of footsteps on gravel or roadway.

One morning in early spring the engineers were startled to hear from an unknown source the sound of brushing and sweeping accompanied by a happy but discordant male voice humming, and before the engineers could locate the phantom troubadour, the humming stopped and a cocky wee Aberdonian was heard to say:

'Fit like ah'biddy. This is Aibardeen! This is studio six, an' this is Erchie Macgregor cleanin' et.'

On another occasion Archie Lee featured in a radio *faux pas* when he was faced with an emergency during his stint as producer of the early morning 'God spot'. With only a few minutes to go a telephone call informed him that the duty minister had been taken poorly and was unable to make the broadcast. Archie, in desperation, phoned Moultrie R. Kelsall, a well kent producer and experienced radio and film actor who lived only minutes away, and asked him to get to the studios urgently and read the script. As Moultrie arrived at the producer's cubicle Archie, quite unaware that his microphone was live, could be heard by his early morning listeners welcoming his colleague: 'Well, if it isn't the

Reverend Mr. Kelsall. Would you care to plank your reverend arse at the microphone, and I'll be with you directly.'

*   *   *

In 1947 I received the accolade. Eddie and Jean Fraser had invited me to the Saturday night *soirées* at their flat at Crosshill. The occasions were enjoyable enough. I have never been at a gathering of pros where they didn't delight in talking shop.

In the case of the Frasers, it seemed to me that those who were bidden to appear at Crosshill were there to worship. The Fraser 'Bible', otherwise known as 'Who's Who in the Theatre', which was brought up to date annually, was always in evidence, and regularly referred to with star names dropped like confetti at a double wedding.

'Michael Denison—delightful chap, isn't he darling? Very shy.'

'Yes, really very shy, darling. Then, of course, there's Dulcie! Well!'

'Oh, Dulcie! What! Quite a character, isn't she, darling?'

'Yes, you wouldn't believe it. Great fun.'

Mouths dutifully agape and eyes wide with childish amazement, we had to sit there drinking tea and eating home-made sponge cake. . . .

'You're such a beautiful baker, Jean.'

'Oh, thank you, Muriel. Yes, I've always had a light touch.'

. . . and listen to readings by one or the other, commenting on the histories of one or two well known names they had met.

I was hoping someone would say: 'Isn't it the same cake as we had *last* Saturday? I thought the one last week was better!'

Eddie's oft repeated homily was that 'if you want honest criticism, no matter how much it hurts, we'll give it to you straight from the shoulder', which claim turned out to be ironic some time later after one of Eddie's amateur musicals for Hamilton.

185

At first sight these Saturday nights appeared to offer artistic discussion on all aspects of the theatre. But they quickly became platforms for rather boring tittle-tattle, gossip and ill-considered criticism of fellow performers. If it wasn't Eddie's work, it couldn't be much good.

Although there were moments of blind justice.

Bessie Swan was a spinster lady who worked in the Corporation Transport Department and occasionally played small parts on radio. She was a large woman. Physically large, and large in gesture and vocal expression. If she had ever been a clippie, which I doubt, her call of 'Any more fares, please?' would have been heard by the travellers on the tram in front.

She was all of a twitter to have been invited to the Fraser *sanctum sanctorum* in Crosshill, and as is often the case, she unwittingly put her foot in it.

Not only was she determined to offer some input to the discussion, but she launched a vehement attack on a *Children's Hour* programme which had been broadcast earlier that very day.

'Well,' she complained, 'I listened to this thing. It was one of these plays set in Skye or somewhere with everybody running about speaking in terrible Highland accents. Well, the man play-ing the lead—I just couldn't believe it, darling. And as for the acting, well. . . . It was no more Highland than Toni Nicoletti in the fish-and-chip shop. I was actually sitting there mouthing the words as he said them, well you know I've got Highland blood! I simply *had* to look up *The Radio Times* to see who was making this awful mess, and bless me if it wasn't Bryden Murdoch! And he's usually so good.'

The rest of us were too tense to move, not knowing whether to stop her, burst out laughing or knit ourselves a kilt. I went to speak but Eddie silenced me with a venomous glare. He never quite regained his *savoir faire* that night. Bessie had missed the announcement at the end of the programme that had made it crystal clear that Bryden Murdoch had been indisposed, and his part had been taken by none other than *Eddie Fraser*!

Poor Bessie was never invited again.

34

GLAMOROUS NIGHT

'THE FIRST Pantheon musical since the war' was a rollicking success in many ways. *Glamorous Night*, with its heart-tugging Novello songs, the stirring regal marches invoking times and places existing only in the happiest of dreams, brought glamour and an upsurge of confidence and optimism to players and audiences alike.

From the moment we had our first rehearsal with the full orchestra I was hooked on musicals. I have never failed to feel the tingling sensation of joyous excitement that embraces you; a spiritual force that pumps the adrenalin to the beat of the opening music.

Eddie's directing of the show had been neat and meticulous, like the diminutive handwriting with which he annotated his script. And he was an authoritarian. Once he had blocked (arranged) the moves, it was necessary to get a court order to change anything, and suggestions were not encouraged. But if rehearsals were not exactly fun, the end result could not be faulted. The company and our audiences loved it, and Pantheon had no hesitation in deciding that 1948 and 1949 would continue the Novello cycle with *Careless Rapture* and *Crest of the Wave* respectively.

That first fee of one-and-a-half guineas from the BBC was not only the first professional fee I had earned, but also the start of a busy and successful time. Broadcast contracts were coming in thick and fast and I was making more money than I had in Abrams. I was involved in practically everything. *Children's Hour*, documentaries, drama, religious programmes and even a stint of reading the sports news on Saturdays. Since I knew very little about sport I managed to misread the results sometimes, or give victory to the wrong team, or refer to an Alfa Romeo without giving the correct emphasis on the 'e'.

However, it would be a long time before Fulton Brothers would show a profit. So, once again the Fultons were dependent on the two shops.

I would never have thought that events could move so fast in only a few months. An audition in January followed by a schools contract, a *Children's Hour*, Pantheon's *Glamorous Night*, plus Howard Lockhart's idea to invite me to join the McFlannel family as the young minister, a new character called David McCrepe.

That was the beginning of my long acquaintance with the clergy.

Since then I reckon I've appeared so often in a dog-collar I could reasonably expect a pension from the Church of Scotland, although it's just possible that one or two clerics might recognise themselves and vote against it.

It was a great thrill to meet the *McFlannels* cast, and I could hardly believe that I was actually going to work with them. Willie McFlannel was played by John Morton, a retired shipyard worker. I have no idea how he came to be in showbusiness. He couldn't be classed as a great actor, but there was a warm couthiness in the voice which had tremendous appeal. Sarah was played by the redoubtable Meg Buchanan, a well known and tremendously talented actress who had a long list of prestigious acting parts to her credit. Peter McFlannel, the younger of the family, was an amateur and was happy to stay that way, and Jean Stoddart who played Maisie McFlannel, was engaged in variety. On air she sounded like a young woman in her early twenties who lived in a tenement and came from a working-class background, but the lady I came to know as Maisie McFlannel was slightly older and always arrived dressed as if she was ready to attend the Holyrood Garden Party. It was funny to watch her standing at the microphone with her silver fox fur draped round her shoulder.

A group of us went to Molly Urquhart's Theatre in Rutherglen which was half amateur and half pro, to see a one-off variety show. From there I was asked if I would take the part of Weelum Sprunt in *Bunty Pulls the Strings*, for their 1947 Christmas production. This was a great favourite with amateurs and pros alike. There was a very small man who directed the play. He didn't seem to have much understanding of blocking and often there would be a long pause while he went off to see if he could disentangle his actors. His great cry was: 'This jist doesnae seem tae huv worked out the way Ah anticipatit!'

In the same eventful year I finally succeeded in making a date with an elusive young lady called Ethel Scott, whom I met when we were doing *Stage Door* for Pantheon. Ethel was the Social Convener for the SCDA. She was small and neat and very good-looking, her fine features offset by a Liberty Cut hairstyle. She was very self-assured. Not surprisingly, perhaps, as she was an assistant to Sir James French of Barr and Stroud. She was assertive and extremely efficient, especially when dealing with eager young suitors. Requests by telephone for dates were always treated kindly, and the response was invariably 'Sure!' But there were always difficulties about arranging times and places to meet. Then one of my phone calls hit the jackpot, and she really *was* sure. We did have a problem—we were both genuinely busy—but we still managed a date for dinner.

She was not only self-assured, she was also self-reliant. She insisted that we would have another date, but this time it would be *her* treat.

I had never been to Crossmyloof or seen an ice-hockey match. But I very much enjoyed it. During the slightly less noisy break I thought I would pull her leg for a joke, and told her I was becoming engaged on the Saturday.

Her expression didn't alter all that much, but I thought her eyes had become colder. It must have seemed very strange for a man to go out with one girl when he's going to be engaged to another the next day.

'Oh, yes,' she said. 'Congratulations!'

Suddenly I was depressed. I had an awful feeling that the joke had misfired. (How often have I felt that.)

'To Maisie,' I explained. 'You know! *The McFlannels*! Saturday night! On the radio! I get engaged to Maisie McFlannel.'

Try as I might, I couldn't get it out of my head that I had put my foot in it. But that little misunderstanding passed without any further discussion, especially when the broadcast would be the following Saturday. The press was full of the wedding of Maisie McFlannel to the Rev. David McCrepe. Congratulations, even presents, poured in to the BBC.

I hadn't known that Ethel's recent engagement to another boy had very recently been broken off. That was a coincidence, I thought. I told her that I had also recently broken up with a girlfriend. That started us talking.

It looked as if we had got each other on the rebound. Having spent practically every day together for lunch, we were engaged on 11th May the following year.

The greatest panic I experienced was early in 1948, when the old-fashioned upright telephone rang one Friday and a cultivated voice asked for me. The call was from David Stuart of Perth Theatre. He and Marjorie Dence were the co-directors of Perth Repertory, and David, whom I had met in the BBC studios, was asking me if I was free to appear with the company in a play called *Scott of Abbotsford* by W. E. Gunn which, surprise, surprise, was all

191

about Sir Walter Scott, a writer I have always found extremely difficult to read. I didn't ask what the part was or even what the salary would be. I simply said 'Yes, when?' Jim was able to handle the office on his own—there certainly wasn't very much going on at Fulton Brothers. But I was a bit shattered when David gave me my instructions. He wanted me to play the part of Scott's son-in-law, John Gibson Lockhart, and he was posting the book right away, he said, and it should reach me by first post on Saturday. Rehearsals were set for Sunday and I would need to be word-perfect for Monday night. In those days that did not trouble me. I was able to memorise lines at one reading; a mere glance, put the book down and deliver perfectly what I had just read. But alas . . . !

The dress rehearsal was to take place immediately on my arrival on the Monday at the Adam Smith Hall in Kirkcaldy—Perth Rep's second home. I was far too excited to appreciate what I was taking on, but I confirmed that I would be there. This was the old Adam Smith Hall—a vast mausoleum which was refurbished some time later, removing the enormously high stage and creating a truly delightful theatre.

David himself was playing Sir Walter Scott and the cast in-cluded Rona Anderson, a lovely girl who was Gordon Jackson's wife and who was herself a well known film actress, playing the part of Scott's daughter and the wife of Lockhart. There was also Gudrun Ure, a great character called Jimmy Roughhead who was extremely popular with the company, and a man with a delight-fully dry sense of humour who became a very well known actor and a great star. That was Donald Pleasance. I remember him as Blofeld, the baddy in the Bond films, and heaven knows how many other roles.

The rehearsal was bewildering. A thousand instructions, suggestions and a few breathy curses from Bill Bentley, the director, who was worried about the girl playing the part of Scott's granddaughter—Margaret Christie, who was a very petite lady and acted the part extremely well. She was also incredibly well endowed. I could hardly keep my mind on the script. David was certainly concerned that a little girl of twelve would have such striking bosoms. There is no doubt that she was physically very attractive, but it became necessary to wrap a thin towel over the upper part of her chest. What that did for her I have no way of knowing, but it did a great deal among the male actors.

I found digs just along from Perth Theatre for four pounds for the week, everything included. Later I sat up in the dress circle and saw the final performance of the current play on the Saturday, then spent the whole of Sunday watching Leslie French and the cast dress-rehearsing *The Servant o' Twa Maisters* for a Monday opening. The rehearsal went on and on, well into the small hours, and I was very, very happy. I revelled in the sheer 'bohemianism'. Convention went out the door. Only the play was the thing. Except when the fish suppers arrived.

Scott of Abbotsford by W. E. Gunn duly opened the following evening. I had assumed that W. E. Gunn was a man, but as it transpired, W. E. Gunn was a woman who enjoyed the same architecture.

I didn't find the play remotely interesting but it went reasonably well, except for the fact that the authoress insisted on making a speech which was rather longer than the play. I was also at a loss to know when someone might offer me money. Tuesday passed without any indication that actors occasionally received remuneration. On Wednesday evening David Stuart came down from the Elysian Heights to talk bread. During a quick dash into the quaint, old-fashioned communal dressing-room of which I was the only occupant at that moment, David seemed to recognise me from somewhere. 'Ah, Rikki. Alright? Good!' He fought with a pair of tights for a moment. 'Gosh, I say, we haven't talked money have we? Would—er—let's see now . . . what about . . . ? Oh, God I'm *off*!'

He dashed off to try and reach the stage before someone yelled loudly: 'I think I see him coming NOW . . . !'

Eventually I was paid eight pounds for my week's work, and was delighted with it. Somehow this led me to the Whatmore Players in Dundee for the same play I had done in Molly Urquhart's Rutherglen theatre, *Bunty Pulls the Strings*. It looked as if it was a lucky play for me. It was the first professional performance of my life in the theatre.

I got along with 'Whattie' very well indeed. A. R. Whatmore was a lovely man. He enjoyed the funnies as much as I did. His first question to me was: 'And what funny business have you got for me then?'

I had a whale of a time dreaming up jokes with props. Whattie sat in the stalls and chortled happily, but he was also a great teacher. I think I learned more in the ten days I was under his direction than from anyone or anything else.

While I had been away, Fulton Brothers had acquired a brand new 5cwt van, which Jim and I hoped John would make good use of. After all he was our head salesman. Neither Jim nor I had much enthusiasm for selling, but John was in his element and the agencies had increased.

I was forbidden to drive the little van for a very good reason. I couldn't drive. So I took a few lessons and got myself a provisional licence. My offer to transport Eddie Fraser and his props down to Hamilton Town Hall was greeted with displeasure by my brothers. Eddie was directing and performing in his production of *Maid of the Mountain* and was grateful for the lift. I picked him up at his house in Crosshill and off we went hoping that he knew the road to Hamilton. The little van had no passenger seat—that was an extra in those days—but Eddie seemed quite happy and totally oblivious that he had taken his life in his hands. Or rather in mine! I think it was because he didn't drive that he failed to notice my uncertainty with the gears and foot pedals. But I kept a smile on my face and chatted enthusiastically as we bumped and jerked an uneven course to the Town Hall.

It was a different matter when, having dropped him off and helped him in with his props, I had to try and find my way home again.

I didn't quite understand why it had taken so much longer to make the journey back until I found myself in Strathaven. I had no idea where I was or how I was going to get back home. I wondered if I would ever see my family again. I stopped at a garage and explained to a man in dungarees that I was a stranger to Scotland and asked if he could help me. He was good enough to draw a little map for me, and advised me to go back the way I had come.

It had taken nearly two hours to find Riddrie!

The Hamilton show proved to be the first of a series of setbacks in my friendship with Eddie. He had asked me to act as a sort of ambassador by accompanying Archie P. Lee to watch the show. I'm not sure if Archie had ever seen Eddie perform outside a broadcasting studio, but I certainly had not, and I was shattered, totally embarrassed. He was not only director and actor, but singer, dancer and choreographer. We sat with our mouths open as we watched him, his face covered with ridiculous brown 'wrinkle' lines, like a map of the London Underground, his performance a travesty. He kept his eyes firmly on the floor as if they were shut, as I think they probably were. His tongue lolling out of one corner of his mouth for some reason, he bounced around like a rag doll as the dancers pushed hither and thither. This was choreography? Then he fired off some totally unfunny lines delivered without humour.

Greater professional mortals have cringed at the prospect of having to go backstage and smilingly greet friends who have been seen in a less than worthy production, or unappealing performance. There is a technique for handling such situations, but I hadn't at that time succeeded in developing it.

195

Archie and I went backstage and greeted Eddie and other members of the cast that we knew. Everyone was very excited and packing up for the night, so the moment I was dreading didn't arrive until we were on the way home.

Someone had offered us a lift back to Glasgow and I was sandwiched between Archie and Eddie in the back of the car when Eddie asked the fateful question.

'What did you think of the show, Rikki?'

That was it. But the sixty-four dollar question had still to come.

I dissembled feverishly, praising sets, costumes, individual performances, whole scenes, anything but Eddie. I just didn't know *what* to say!

'I take it you didn't like my performance,' he said coldly.

I should have lied and congratulated him, or told him the truth. But how well I remembered him saying: 'If you want honest criticism, no matter how much it hurts, we'll give it to you straight from the shoulder!' He suspected what I felt about the show; he was very angry that I had had the audacity to consider his 'performance' as anything other than brilliant. Not that my opinion was remotely important to him. I think it had much to do with the fact that Archie Lee had been there and had seen the sort of performer Eddie was. The mixture of arrogance and pettiness was sickening.

One thing I could applaud, was that he had gone to his dentist and had his teeth attended to. Eddie and I were doing a piece for Auntie Kathleen, and the entire cast were astonished to see rows of bright, shining molars. It must have taken great courage to have every tooth in his head taken out and dentures put in the same day, especially when he was broadcasting that evening.

35

SALES TALK

THE BBC DRAMA LOUNGE at this time was something of an obstacle course for the actors. The two studios always in use were Studio 5, which was structured to produce the acoustics of an indoor scene, with the smaller Studio 4 away at the other end, which was designed for outdoor scenes.

During the broadcast the scenes would cut from 'indoors' (e.g. the house) to 'outside' (e.g. the garden). Most of us used to get a bit neurotic about such moments, scared that we might miss a cue. So we would write 'GO TO FOUR' or 'GO TO FIVE' in huge letters. It produced a typical actor's nightmare, of which there are many different versions.

In those early days of radio my personal nightmare was that I had finished a scene in Studio 5 and forgotten that I should already be running to get to Studio 4. In my dream the studios are not divided by a mere twenty-foot length of carpeted lounge. Studio 5 is in the drama lounge but Studio 4 seems to be located in a pub half a mile down Byres Road! And, of course, I have forgotten to mark my script. By the time I reach Studio 4 the scene is over, and I have to run like hell to get back to Studio 5 for the scene that follows.

The nightmare ends with my meeting Jimmy Sutherland, a well known broadcaster at the time, who offers me a lift on his motorbike as he cycles back and forth from Studio 5 in the drama lounge to Studio 4 in Byres Road. No wonder I couldn't make it.

In later years my personal nightmare was nearly always to do with the theatre. The overture over, the curtain would go up, and I would make my entrance to the sound of an exhilarating play-on from the orchestra. Only to realise that I had forgotten to prepare anything for the show. No jokes, no nothing.

Broadcasting made me nervous. I don't know why. You would think it would be easier than performing in front of two thousand people on stage, but I still find it difficult to speak into a microphone. Even leaving a message on a telephone answering machine makes me feel a right twit. And there must be thousands of people who have the same problem. It may simply be the fact that you can't see who you're talking to, and there is no response. It is the same with a radio play. Even with someone on the other side of the mike, even a little group, I still found it difficult to act with a script in my hand when I couldn't concentrate on the person I was supposed to be talking to.

Every actor in radio prepared for the broadcast in some way. Eric Wightman, who played the part of old Uncle Donald McFlannel, had a carefully planned routine that made the mind boggle. We used to have a meal in the canteen before going up to the drama lounge in preparation for going on air at ten-past-seven. Everybody went to the loo and made sure they were comfortable. We washed our hands and coughed a lot to clear our throats. When old Uncle Donald went to the loo he was in first and out last. He washed his hands and face and even shaved. He brushed his teeth, gargled with a mouthwash and consistently sniffed a menthol inhaler.

I often wondered what would happen if he forgot one of his routines.

*   *   *

Obtaining a provisional licence did nothing to help my driving skills. Even so, when John and I made a trip to London, I was allowed to take the wheel for short periods on the long journey south.

I don't remember all that much about the journey, although I recall the trouble we had to find our way about in alien thoroughfares, realising that our senses of direction had not improved since the family outing to Blackpool all those years ago.

I do remember our visit to a company of manufacturers of costume jewellery. Their directors looked us over very carefully. They were typical south-east London business people. Diamond-hard and no hobbies. I didn't feel we were any match for this crowd, but John, dear John, was never one to baulk at plonking his size eights where an angel would have required counselling. Yes, he told them expansively, I am sure we can do business. We have the connections in Scotland and you are dealing with some very beautiful stuff.

I kept quiet. These people frightened me more than I could say, especially the middle-aged women with their coiffured titian hair, cold blue eyes and heavily made-up faces. I was sure we were out of our depth.

At the end of our meeting John gave them his indecipherable three-fingered 'masonic' handshake and announced that we would look forward to receiving the samples. Of course, they said. The samples would be sent as soon as they had been invoiced and they had received our cheque.

Could they give us a lift to the airport? they asked. And John's masonic handshake waggled to a stop.

It was Bennie all over again. Visions of metal furniture floated in front of my eyes. But it was John's finest hour. He smiled at them with sublime confidence, spread out his hand with absolute confidence, and said in his haughty English.

'No, thanks awfully. But we hev the vaughan!'

We drove in turn with John becoming more and more nervous about my driving. We paused in Huntingdon for a breather and some food and drink, and asked each other where we were going to get the money for the jewellery. If we had got nothing else from the trip, at least I had discovered Huntingdon. I took a tremendous liking to the little market town the minute I set foot in the place. Oliver Cromwell was born there, and he and Pepys had attended the local grammar school during the early sixteen hundreds. Not that that influenced me in any way, but the Old Bridge Hotel did, and I determined that this was where Ethel and I would spend our honeymoon.

That occasion came sooner than expected. At one of my periodic visits to the Three Wise Men at the Ministry of Pensions, and having been asked the usual question and given the usual answer, I was informed that my mental health had obviously improved, but I was not yet the full monty. Therefore my pension would be payable for an indefinite future, but at a very much reduced rate. Something like three-and-fourpence per month, so I would receive a lump sum of £101 instead, and would thereafter have no further claim on His Majesty's Government.

On that basis the marriage was set for 2nd April 1949.

It was perhaps not the best of times to get married. Clothes rationing had only been abandoned in March, and Sir Stafford Cripps, the Labour Chancellor (nice chap, nobody liked him), had announced measures for coping with the desperate economic crisis which included cuts in sugar, sweets and tobacco rations, although he assured us that there was no question of the pound being devalued!

The pound was devalued by 30.5% in September of that year.

In spite of that I got myself organised with a 10cwt van—a second hand job as temperamental as a ballerina—and began calling haphazardly on stationers with greeting cards and cake decorations, the two best agencies we had. This disorganised approach, however, simply did not yield dividends. To our great embarrassment, John and I kept bumping into one another in the same shop, or calling on a customer who had already given an order to the other. I was also totally ignorant of the ground rules so carefully observed by commercial travellers. On one occasion I entered a stationer's shop only to find another rep showing his wares to the shopkeeper. I stood waiting, unaware that I was committing a monstrous breach of etiquette. I couldn't understand why they kept casting disapproving glances at me until the rep, when he had finished his business, approached me and, in a quiet voice close to my ear, asked: 'How long have you been on the road, son?'

'All bleedin' day,' I replied.

'Well,' he explained. 'When you see another rep with a customer, you wait *outside* the shop.'

I hated this selling business. There was no doubt that salesmen were born, I felt, and I knew I just didn't have it. I also knew that there was no way I was likely to be able to cultivate it. It was simply something that I did not want to do, but we struggled on. I found it easier, and much more enjoyable, to go further afield to the coastal towns like Largs or Prestwick, and whether it was that I met a slightly friendlier attitude among the shopkeepers there or not, I seemed to be more successful at obtaining orders. I didn't mind, in fact I enjoyed the coastal areas. They reminded me of my boyhood.

I had a great friend in Douglas Gladdle, one of our Pantheon stalwarts, himself a rep for a food and confectionery company. He delighted in bringing back stories of his travels, and told me of a visit to Prestwick. Having no car, he had gone by bus and alighted at Prestwick Cross badly in need of the public services there. The small, elderly lavatory attendant was hosing down when Douglas splashed his way forward to make the first, and most urgent, call of his day, throwing his bus ticket on the sopping wet floor as he went. The little lavatory attendant was not best pleased. He stopped squeegeeing and viewed Douglas's offending bus ticket.

'Here,' he said belligerently. 'Whit dae ye think ye're doin'? Tryin' tae make a shithouse o' the place?'

Douglas was a player in *Crest of the Wave* that year, which was my final musical for the Pantheon Club. But there was a first that year, too, which was to have a profound effect on my future life and happiness. A gentleman by the name of Tom Craston, a Giffnock man, and some friends including Alan Mackill, had banded together to form the Giffnock Theatre Players with the ambitious goal of eventually building their own community theatre.

It was a joy to work with the Giffnock Players, and it was their enthusiasm and sheer enjoyment that made it so. Among them was a tall, handsome man called William Craig-Brown. He ran a long-established family business of food and confectionery agencies, so we had something in common.

But we were to have much more in common, and our lives were to become inextricably linked in a way that neither of us for a moment suspected.

36

DON'T GIVE UP THE DAY JOB

A MAJOR SETBACK to everyone's plans was the sudden illness of our sales director and chief salesman. John had finally succumbed to years of chaotic and undisciplined living, working all day, eating and sleeping when he felt like it and working until the early hours on his new flat in Sannox Gardens, and his heart had suffered.

He, Maisie, Jim and I held a board meeting at the Hope Street office. It was clear that John was going to have to rest for quite some time, and thereafter take things very much easier than he had been doing.

We took on some extra salesmen to cover John's territory and things carried on as before, except that having to give away most of the commission to the new salesmen left us without even the slight profit we had been making.

But there was a further blow. As if to follow John's example, our dear old Dad collapsed and had to go into hospital. In his case it was years of hard work, the stress of the war years and his financial problems which had taken their toll. He, too, was going to be on the sick list for some time to come.

We had only one option. Jim would have to take over the Cumbernauld Road shop, and Maisie the Roebank Street shop. The entire family depended on these two shops and we neglected them at our peril. This left me to run the office with a rather timid young typist, and such representatives as we had on the road.

As I sat brooding in our tiny office, I began to wonder if there was any point in continuing. Our manufacturers paid us a mere ten per cent gross on all orders, and we had to pay the reps seven-and-a-half per cent. What was left would barely cover the rent of the office.

Orders were coming in for the Christmas stock. In particular, Christmas crackers, and I became hypnotised by two sets of figures. We were being left with two-and-a-half-per-cent. If I bought them as a wholesaler and sold them to the same customers, the percentages would work out at something like ten times what we naively called profit.

I bought in a stock of Christmas crackers and sent samples to the reps within the Glasgow area. I took a couple of deep breaths and awaited results. Within days I had sold the entire consignment and delivered them to the customers myself in the little 5cwt. van. The figures I calculated on that consignment alone convinced me that this was the way to go. For the moment an acting career had become secondary.

There was, however, a snag in making the change, and that was the Purchase Tax—which was very similar to VAT except that it applied to wholesale purchases only. I could still buy if I could afford to pay the wholesale price *plus* the Purchase Tax, but this made matters even more difficult. *Money*! We had no capital! I had about three hundred pounds in the Clydesdale Bank, but that was hardly enough to finance the radical change of policy I had in mind. I phoned the Clydesdale Bank manager, Mr. Kerr, whom my father had known for many years, and he agreed to my application for a small overdraft sufficient to start me off.

163 Hope Street was a very traditional, rather snooty office block, and the great cartons of Christmas Crackers deposited on the pavement at the entrance, and the man-handling of them up to

the fifth floor in the lift, caused comment—mostly from the lift man, especially the amount and variety of stationery products that were increasing every day with my enthusiasm.

The whole machinery of the business had changed, including the book-keeping. How grateful I was that I had taken the trouble (without knowing what was ahead) to study the subject earlier. Perhaps I imagined it because there was certainly no sign of complaint, but I became rather concerned about the increasing amount of stock I was buying in, and my embarrassment grew in direct proportion to the decreasing space in the office.

I gave the salesmen orders to go for the crackers, and such were the sales that I had to order a further load from the manufacturers and we sold the lot. But this time the percentages were much higher and Fulton Brothers went into profit.

Having tried out the theory with success, I decided to go for better and larger premises. I discovered premises that were to let in Brunswick Street, above a wholesale stationery warehouse with whom we would do a good deal of business. It had obviously not been in use for a very long time. There was a large open area entirely suitable for my purpose and a smaller room which would do very well for a private office, and more space immediately above, which was perfect for further storage.

I concluded the rental deal very quickly, and we were mutually happy with the arrangements.

My new warehouse had been, of all things, a balloon factory—and latex was everywhere. It was filthy, and difficult to visualise as a stationery and greeting card centre. I called in an army of cleaners who got rid of the muck and dust, and the remains of the latex. I had a joiner friend create a small office, brought in some trestle tables, a desk for the office, and I started buying every kind of greeting card I could find—birthday cards, Christmas cards, every kind of card that was available. From here on I was in the wholesale business and I was sure I would start making money.

John, whose health had improved, paid us a visit and, after a guided tour, pronounced the move as insane. I thanked him for his support and encouragement, and just to make his view explicit, he left with a final 'You're *mad*!'

Within a few months I had a typist and a couple of packers on the payroll.

Mad or not, I was doing business. The bank manager, Mr. Kerr, looked in occasionally, and by this time he was very happy to see that Fulton Brothers was developing into a fine little business. And, as always, he left me with a 'thank you for the business.'

But there was someone who was not quite so happy.

The economic strategy that was being employed in Britain at the start of the 1950s was described as a last desperate measure. It was painful, and indeed fatal, for a large number of small businesses like mine. Although Fulton Brothers was developing well, when the Chancellor's squeeze came into effect we came up against that well-known company disease known as 'cash flow syndrome'!

I was called to the head office of the Clydesdale Bank in St. Vincent Street for a meeting with a Mr. Smith in one of the upper suites.

He was a small, handsome man with steely grey eyes which I found rather menacing.

'You're overdrawn Mr. Fulton.'

'Yes, I know. But I keep paying it back with the interest as my customers pay their bills.'

'And then you go into the red again. We didn't invest in your company Mr. Fulton, and yet we seem to have more money in your business than you have.'

I had to agree, but I knew we were solvent and the cash flow would improve with just a little more time. The squeeze was affecting our retail customers just as painfully, but sales were increasing all the time.

He was unmoved.

'With the present economic climate, the government has forced us to operate a new discipline. Your overdraft is unsecured. . . .'

'I have a large stock.'

'. . . unsecured! In fact I was unaware that you had an overdraft at all until recently, or that it was so high. I can give you a week, no more.'

'You'll close me down.'

He spread his hands.

'Surely we can come to some arrangement,' I pleaded. 'It's a good little business, and will become better and better. The potential—'

'*One week, Mr. Fulton.*'

I seethed with hurt and frustration.

'You know something, Mr. Smith,' I said. 'I don't like you!'

He rose to his full height and hit the desk with his fist. '*I am the banker!*' he shouted.

He took a deep breath and pulled himself together.

'I apologise,' he said. 'I shouldn't have lost control like that. However, I have nothing more to say. The overdraft must be paid off within the week or we shall be forced to instigate proceedings.'

Well, that was that, I thought. I tried the only possible sources I knew—the president of the Pantheon Club, who was the boss of a large wallpaper concern, and an uncle of Ethel's known to be sufficiently well-heeled not to have to work, but it was not on with either and there didn't seem to be anywhere else to go.

I had two particular worries. I was absolutely confident that once I dissolved the company I could clear all outstanding debts, but the timing was tricky, and I was concerned for the few hundred pounds I already had invested in the business in the form of final wages for the staff and outstanding accounts.

The other worry was HM Customs. I had managed to obtain a Purchase Tax registration on the promise that we would begin manufacturing. This meant that I had been buying stock from manufacturers free of purchase tax which I would collect from sales. This was regarded as a Crown debt, and had to take precedence over all others. The young ginger-headed inspector who had kept a check on the books was pressing for immediate settlement.

As my customers paid their accounts and I accumulated cash, I quite deliberately hijacked the exact amount of my own savings and opened another bank account with the Bank of Scotland.

I quickly sold off the office furniture and tables (I almost cried to see my favourite desk go). But the next problem was how to get rid of the remaining stock of greeting cards—there was no time to sell it in the ordinary way. Here fortune smiled on me, or should I say 'gave me a sickly grin'. One of my warehouse staff had gone immediately to another small business much like my own and told her boss that I was looking to dispose of current stock. Her boss, a tiny little Jewish gentleman appeared and offered to buy the entire stock at my valuation, and I jumped at the chance.

Suddenly my warehouse was as empty as the day I first walked in. No desks, no chairs, no stock, no people. It was over, finished. But I had come out of it without owing a penny to anyone—*and* kept my own small savings, now safe in a friendly bank.

A very kind man, the managing director of one of our local suppliers, came to me and offered his condolences, remarking that he had always thought that the small company would do well. He offered me a job as a salesman. Salary, commission and a company car. I had never wanted to be a salesman, as I've already said, but the attraction of a company car was great, and I relished the thought of being free from the hazards and heartache. So I said 'Yes!'

It was this kindly man who put paid to my commercial ambitions, such as they were. He returned a couple of days later and told me: 'I have thought a lot about this, Mr. Fulton, and I'm withdrawing my offer of a job with us. I admire you, and I was sorry about what you've been through, but I believe that in inviting you to join our company, I may well be doing you a disservice.'

I couldn't quite see the point. I could only see my lifeline slip away. 'You see,' he said very kindly, 'the salesman's job leads nowhere. There's nowhere to go, and I think you are the sort of young man who would expect to progress in the company, possibly hoping for a seat on the board one day, but because of the structure of the company, alas, that is not possible. I wish you luck. I'm sure you will do well.'

It was the great moment of truth; almost as if everything had been driving me in one direction, and one direction only, and I understood what I had to do.

Mr. Smith, he of the Clydesdale Bank, would never know the huge favour he had done me.

I arranged an interview with Gordon Gildard, Head of BBC Programmes, for whom I had great respect, and explained the situation. I was now, I told him, a full-time professional actor with positively no interests outside of showbusiness.

'I am delighted,' he said. 'I'll make sure everyone is notified.'

37

CASTING OFF

FOR A WHILE I couldn't go near the empty warehouse. I couldn't help thinking what a waste of time it had all been. I should have made the move much sooner—it would have taken me where I truly wanted to go.

Jimmy Sutherland approached me with a view to starting up a touring company to be called The Scottish Theatre Guild. His idea was to provide an outlet for the talents of actors temporarily out of work, and there were plenty of those.

The warehouse in Brunswick Street made a wonderful headquarters. My lease wouldn't be up for a while yet, and the great empty space was perfect for rehearsals, with facilities for the inevitable coffee breaks readily available. I was grateful in a sad sort of way that the warehouse hadn't been a complete disaster, as John had thought. At least it had produced something good.

We started with that tremendously popular farce *See How They Run*. Jimmy had secured a contract with Butlin's in Ayr to provide a popular comedy at weekends, the sort of show that the holidaymakers would enjoy. Which meant we were already in business.

The next important step was to get myself an agent. I was aware of opportunities for film work around this time. I kept seeing actors like Duncan Macrae, Fulton Mackay, Roddy MacMillan, Andrew Keir and others, who were getting a lot of film work, especially from Scottish film-maker John Grierson, 'father of the documentary'. In fact I had already done a screen-test for him—sadly unsuccessfully—for a Group Three Production called *The Brave Don't Cry* featuring some very well known names including my radio mother-in-law, Meg Buchanan of *McFlannels* fame. Eddie Fraser was there, too, but we didn't seem to appeal to the casting director. (Strange how most of them are women!) 'Ah,' she said sadly tapping my nose. 'That nose. . . . Not right for films.'

I had no idea how to go about getting myself on to a good agent's books, and no idea who that good agent might be. However, I discovered that most of the well known Scots actors were in the hands of an agent called Christopher Mann in London, under the personal supervision of a redoubtable lady by the name of Helen Gunnis, whom I determined to see. Money was a problem, though, in that there wasn't much of it, so I decided to travel to London by bus.

The bus! It was the most miserable experience of my life. It was even worse than when I got my tonsils out. After sixteen very tiring hours, I arrived in London, hot, sticky and with a blinding headache. The telephone directory told me that Christopher Mann was at Marble Arch. I made my way there and telephoned from a coin box from where I could see the office windows with the name in gold lettering. Very posh, I thought.

Helen Gunnis had a voice that revealed her Scottish origins, but had been overlaid with a translatlantic drawl. The voice was not enthusiastic about taking on yet another Scottish actor, nor hopeful about the prospects.

But I wasn't prepared to let her put the phone down. After all, I suggested, it wasn't quantity that counted, it was quality! How would she feel, I asked her, if, with a hundred artistes on her books she found that the hundred-and-first turned out to be a great star, and she had turned him down.

She liked the sound of my voice, she said. It was—interesting.

I was duly flattered. It was certainly more cheering than having my nose insulted. Perhaps she could find a little time. I had better come up and see her. And this was the time.

She looked exactly as she had sounded. Very dark hair, beautifully and carefully coiffed, with make-up which had received similar care, while the heavy, expensive frames of her glasses set off the American look her voice suggested.

We got on famously. Neither of us wanted a sole-agency agreement, but my name would go on her books and I would pay commission on the jobs her office were able to find me. It was the perfect arrangement at this time, and I left to take the turn-round bus journey home with a strong feeling I had made progress.

At first sight 1952 looked like being a quieter year, but, in reality it turned into one of the most eventful. I totted up the previous year's earnings and was surprised to find that I had earned a total of just over £350 in fees from the BBC alone. An average of seven pounds a week. Not to be sneezed at in 1952. However, prospects of work did not immediately show themselves, and I became a little apprehensive. My nature being what it is, my anxiety quotient has always been in inverse proportion to my ability to make planned provision.

Suddenly the visit to Helen Gunnis in London paid off. I got a small part in *Laxdale Hall*, a quaint little film about a tiny Hebridean island that refuses to pay its road tax. I even had a line to speak! The cast included Fulton Mackay, Roddy MacMillan, Andrew Keir, Jameson Clark, Jimmy Copeland, Jimmy Gilbert, and Eric Woodburn (who became very well known as Dr. Snoddy in *Dr. Finlay's Casebook*). To give the English actors their due there was Raymond Huntley, Ronald Squire, Sebastian Shaw, Kathleen Ryan and Kynaston Reeves, who would bring out his Latin book and read it avidly during the breaks.

We all managed to squeeze into the pleasant Highland hotel at Lochcarron and had to commute daily by bus over mountainous roads to the location in and above the little coastal village of Applecross.

It was bliss. Like a paid holiday living and working in mostly fine, warm weather amid some of Scotland's most spectacular scenery.

Jimmy Gilbert, Eric Woodburn and I played the parts of three Glasgow poachers and, consequently, our scenes were nearly always together. Sometimes, if we had finished before the location bus was due to take us back, we would walk over the rugged countryside, zig-zagging down the steep single tracks, across the streams, and through the forest and fields filled with friendly insects including dragonflies as big as sparrows.

I enjoyed the company of these men enormously. Jimmy Gilbert was a very clever writer of comic songs which were often featured in the Citizens' pantos, and his talent for producing comedy was such that he eventually became Head of Light Entertainment for the BBC in London.

Eric Woodburn was a placid, easy-going man some years our senior. Very popular with his fellow actors because of his dry wit and good nature. He loved nothing better than to sit on a rock in the warm air, his pipe creating more pollution than a dozen cars, and work through the crossword, or chat philosophically about life in general.

Picture then, this placid, imperturbable man walking with us across a field on our way back to the Lochcarron Hotel, his pipe belching Balkan Sobranie, his tread measured and sure, his contribution to whatever we were discussing well worth listening to, delivered in measured tones.

Suddenly, with a strange little gasp, he threw up his arms and, breaking away from us into the centre of the field, he started leaping about and flapping his arms in the frenzied, ecstatic whirling dance of the dervish.

Jimmy and I were stunned, and for a few seconds could only

stand and stare as our friend, his pipe still clenched in his teeth, bounced and jived back and forth across the field, little whimpering sounds coming from his mouth and his eyes staring as if he had just witnessed the ultimate Satanic obscenity.

We wondered seriously if he was having an epileptic fit or, perhaps indulging in some superstitious rite every time he crossed a field.

We made to go over to him but he waved us back, gasping and shaking his head. We could only stand and watch, desperately hoping he would recover. We were miles from a hospital, or even a local medic and in the middle of a beautiful but barren area with no one in sight apart from ourselves.

Eric was singing now, or was it a chant? We had never seen him like this. We tried to make out the words that were coming from his clenched teeth but it was only the odd profanity now and then that we could distinguish. The rest sounded like some unknown African patois.

As quickly as it had begun, the dance stopped. Eric turned to face us, his eyes protruding, his hands outstretched pathetically appealing for help from his friends, his pipe pointing straight out of his mouth. Suddenly he undid his braces and whipped his trousers down to lie wrinkled around his ankles. His underpants followed, and we rushed towards him, thinking the worst.

We thought it time we really had to take some sort of action to help, no matter what he said. He was obviously seriously ill with something, but what? As we reached him, we were just in time to see and hear what his ailment was. He was now completely naked, and as he divested himself of the last of his undergarments, an enormous bee emerged angrily from Eric's long johns.

I received £20 a week for the three weeks filming, but I would happily have paid that amount for the joy of watching Eric Woodburn in that field!

Back in Glasgow, the filming over, we had news of the reopening of the newly refurbished Palace Theatre in Kilmarnock, then re-named The Exchange.

They were running a summer show with a scratch company. Whoever and whenever top line artistes were free to appear. Duncan Macrae had donated a week, as had Molly Urquhart, and I was so happy to see my old idol—George West—perform some of his classic material after years of impoverished retirement. I wish I had taken the opportunity of speaking to him and telling him what pleasure he had given me from a very young age. Such a situation happens all too often, something comes up, we forget and miss the opportunity.

Jimmy Sutherland's offer of two comedies by The Scottish Theatre Guild was readily accepted by Mr. Kurt Lewenhak, the theatre's administrator. (I'm not sure, but I don't think he was born in Paisley!) He was planning an autumn schedule of repertory and two plays from The Scottish Theatre Guild would possibly give a boost to the start of the season.

We decided to present *See How They Run* as our first offering which we could rehearse in the Brunswick warehouse. Although I had no interest in the original Butlin's arrangements, I was happy to play parts in both plays and rehearse *Tons of Money*, an elderly farce, while playing the first. We did a try-out of *See How They Run* at the Athenaeum Theatre in Buchanan Street, and somehow or other played to packed houses. I have to admit that it seemed a blatant act of deception to put my name there as the star attraction since I didn't appear until the last scene. But such is the way of marketing, and I had to confess to a little thrill of pleasure at seeing my name at the top of the bill for the very first time:

The Scottish Theatre Guild
presents

RIKKI FULTON

(The Rev. David McCrepe of the McFlannels)

in
the outstanding comedy

'SEE HOW THEY RUN'

See How They Run was a sensation. The audiences loved it, and a lot of people came to see it.

On the other hand, *Tons of Money* was not the success we had hoped. It was the third time I had performed the play, but it was the first time I had directed as well, a difficult task at the best of times, and I certainly wasn't up to it. An urgent call after the first night and Jimmy Sutherland hurried down to redirect the piece, but it was never very great. It is very possible that it was well past its sell-by date.

Long after we had gone, though, the statistics proved interesting. The two plays had played to over seventy per cent capacity. A figure which remained an unbeatable record for the rest of the Exchange's short life before it had to close down again. I stayed on and did one more play before I had to get back to Queen Margaret Drive. There were two series and a *Children's Hour* programme waiting for my attention. I was really very busy.

The news that Howard M. Lockhart, having returned from Australia, had decided to retire came as a surprise to all of us. He would remain in charge until a replacement was found. Charming man though he was, it is true that his stewardship of the Light Entertainment department was not inspired. 'Too well bred,' some said. 'Too perjink,' and that was probably right. It takes a sense of anarchy, and sometimes a touch of vulgarity, to present light entertainment, particularly comedy, and Howard would never have admitted to such qualities.

When the post was advertised, I applied. Although I now had three solid years of experience in radio and had directed a few plays, I couldn't see the BBC even granting an interview. But I thought 'what the hell.' I could see little harm in having a go.

How wrong I was!

A few days later a letter from the BBC indicated that I was to be interviewed as one of a short leet of six. This was a considerable shock, but I could hardly write and tell them I had only been kidding. So I felt obliged to go.

Everyone knew that Eddie Fraser had applied for the job, but no one, least of all Eddie, even suspected that I had! What amounted to a written examination describing the applicant's idea of an acceptable running order for a light entertainment radio show was first on the agenda, and we were shown in to the old conference room on the second floor as we arrived. Three of the four other members of the short leet were ex-BBC staff. I greeted the three applicants I knew, took a place at the other end of the huge conference table, facing the door, and got down to creating a programme.

Such is the capriciousness of fate that Eddie was the last to arrive, and as he entered our eyes met. It is difficult to describe his expression at that moment, although I remember it very well. He was enraged. I could see him trying to cope with his anger. His porridge face was an eloquent mirror of the thoughts that must have gone through his mind. 'How dare you,' I could imagine him saying. 'How dare you challenge me by even thinking of applying for such a prestigious position when you knew that I had done so. Where is your loyalty? You should have been out there lobbying everyone on my behalf, never mind sneaking off to get the job for yourself.' What he actually said was: 'What are *you* doing here?' His arrogance was showing.

My interview with the BBC board was no worse than I had expected. There was an irascible little man who was clearly of the opinion that it was a waste of time talking to someone with such a low I.Q.

'Yes, it's all very well, Mr. Fulton—you say you've done this and you've done that, but you don't particularise.'

So I rattled off a large number of musicals and plays, but I was where I thought I would be—nowhere! I hadn't applied to deliberately spite Eddie, but he never forgave me, and my season ticket for the *soirées* at Crosshill was withdrawn.

In due course it was announced that Eddie had been appointed.

I was coming from the canteen one day when I met him coming in the opposite direction along the basement corridor. He was very affable. Possibly he was in an extremely good mood because his interview had come to fruition and he was now the king of the castle.

For a moment I thought he was going to walk past me, but he stopped and turned to me.

'Rikki,' he cried. 'Just the man I wanted to see.'

How was he settling into the job, I asked him.

'Oh, fine. Excellent. Of course there are one or two problems which have to be solved rather urgently now that I'm no longer in a position to perform.'

I pricked up my ears at this, I wasn't sure why.

He looked at me very directly, his watery blue eyes twinkling.

'I mean there's the question of *It's All Yours*—I'll need someone to take my place, won't I.'

I smiled and nodded my head, and my blood pressure went up. I had an idea what he might be talking about.

There had been an exchange of producers with Howard Lockhart and an Australian producer who set up a comedy programme called *It's All Yours* and Eddie had been one of the characters.

'Well,' he said. I've given it quite a lot of thought, and I—think—I know—the young man who could fill my shoes.'

I couldn't believe it. I was really excited.

'If I tell you who it is will you keep it to yourself?'

I promised.

He looked round to make sure no one could hear the news. Then. . . .

'The young man who will take my place is—*Stanley Baxter!* Cheers, Rikki!'

Eddie's desire for vengeance had not yet subsided.

Bill Meikle asked if I would come and see about taking part in the coming annual radio pantomime, a very popular bit of fun which took place in *Children's Hour* once a year.

We went down to one of the two large studios used for shows involving the orchestra which had a control booth high above the floor of the studio. He thrust a script of the previous year's show into my hand and asked me to go in front of the microphone and read it over. When I looked up to the control booth I saw Eddie Fraser sprawled on a low-slung chair, secure, confident, the last word in relaxation, God of all he surveyed as he gave instructions to Bill Meikle that I obviously couldn't hear.

Bill came on to the speaker and said: 'Eddie would like you to try the scene on page twelve.' So I wasn't dealing with Bill Meikle, producer. He was taking his instructions from the Head of Light Entertainment. This was an audition. It was strange, there wasn't anyone in the building who didn't know what my abilities were. It was the first time since 15th January 1947 that I had been asked to audition. However, I did as I was asked; I read several passages from the script—with Bill receiving instructions from Eddie.

The *coup de grâce* took some time in coming.

'Eddie is coming down to show you how it *should* be done,' announced Bill over the talk-back. I was aware of a certain embarrassed unease when he told me what was to happen.

This petty, untalented twit was coming down from his throne into the studio to show me how it should be done. I had seen his performance in Hamilton. He was no actor, he was no director. To add a certain amount of insult to the injury already inflicted, he instructed me to read opposite him while he demonstrated the perfect delivery of the lines I had been speaking.

'There you are,' he said. 'Try it *that* way.'

I tried it that way and there followed a silent argument between Eddie and Bill in the control booth. I could see Bill nodding and Eddie shaking his head.

I walked out of the studio.

Next day a cryptic little note came from Bill saying:

'Dear Rikki, After very careful consideration I am not able to offer you the part of Jacques le Duc in *Cinderella*.'

Not long after, Bill sought a more civilised situation with the Beeb, and I imagine he was only too relieved to have the so-called Head of Light Entertainment out of his hair.

38

FESTIVAL CITY

DONALD MACLEAN was the young producer who had taken over the two radio series that had kept me busy for some months. *Andy and Sally* and *The Ferriers of Milton* were keeping me in reasonable funds.

Donald and I got along extremely well. He was a go-ahead young man, forever looking for new and interesting ways of doing things, a quality that did not find favour with the BBC establishment of the time. It seemed to me that many of the higher members of staff were too busy having *affaires* in which they indulged openly. It was more like a game of musical chairs than a highly technical, innovative production group.

Donald and I had a very strong bond brought about by our love of modern music. We often spent our breaks from rehearsals listening to some particular piece that Donald wanted me to hear.

This proved to be a providential friendship and Donald became the first person in my very short, but very important, list of kind people who had created opportunities for me.

Ethel had got herself a job with the Duncan Macrae company which was scheduled to present a couthy Scots comedy called *Bachelors Are Bold* for the Edinburgh Festival. Why didn't I contact Sadie Aitken at the Gateway Theatre, she suggested. It would obviously be to our advantage if there was a job going and we could work in Edinburgh at the same time.

I wrote at once to Sadie. She was the manager, casting and artistic director. She may even have cleaned out the lavatories for all I knew.

Sadie is a well-remembered lady, one of the great eccentrics of our generation. An aficionada of lewd jokes which in retelling she could make twice as vulgar, with a vocabulary that would have embarrassed a Billingsgate porter. Her affirmative arrived almost by return of post, and I quickly put the date in my diary.

The Gateway's Festival production was, appropriately, a play called *Festival City* by Albert Mackie who was the editor of the *Despatch*, and author of the very popular scribblings by 'MacNib' in that newspaper. It was to star Molly Urquhart, another eccentric lady, and big Archie Duncan, who was best remembered for his appearances in *Robin Hood* with Richard Greene.

Festival City had, of course, been specially written for the three week culture bash in the capital. The plot concerned a landlady (Molly Urquhart) who ran a guest house in Edinburgh where a spurious bard with the unlikely name of Aeneas Kilbarchan (Archie Duncan) boarded along with various other American and German guests.

My part was that of a young plumber who flitted cheerily through the action with various bits and pieces of plumbing and youthful philosophy. As sometimes happens my smaller part was easily the best in the play. An absolute gift.

Rehearsals were interesting, and confusing with Molly and Archie arbitrarily editing the script as the rehearsals progressed, and often bringing us to a grinding halt when one of us lesser mortals delivered a line only to be told that it had been cut.

'I don't think we need that, darling. Do you?'

Not that we had any say in the matter.

The plumber was a young, sympathetic character, full of fun

and with more than his share of laugh lines. There was also a very corny poem about plumbers which I delivered from the top of a table and which received an enormous round of applause. The reviews also came my way and the two stars were much miffed. But it would have been difficult not to have made a success of it.

Although this was only the third time I had found it necessary to avail myself of their services, I had heard countless stories about theatrical digs and the extraordinary ladies who ran them. There is one which, although possibly apocryphal, describes very well the kind of thing itinerant performers had to deal with during the 'great' days of touring.

A variety artiste had called upon a landlady well known for her love of music hall performers, and was being shown upstairs to his room. He was very tired, having travelled far to get to his next port of call, and all he wanted was to flop down in a clean, comfortable room.

The landlady insisted on showing him the sort of artistes she was used to looking after over many years, as she encouraged him to follow her. The wall of the stairway was a mass of photographs of famous performers, all signed to the landlady with overwhelming affection and extravagant claims for her cooking. As they ascended, she stopped at each photograph, putting names and personal reminiscences to the faces, current and long dead.

'That's Gracie,' she announced in a strong North-country accent. 'She always stays with me when she's in these parts. And there's darling Bob and Alf Pearson. They'd never think of going anywhere else. They've all stayed with me, as you can see. Rob Wilton, Harry Hemsley, Peter Brough and Archie, Will Fyffe. . . .'

And so it went on until, on reaching the top stair at last, the weary trouper noticed a large picture of 'The Last Supper'.

'Oh,' he remarked innocently. 'I see you've had Doctor Crock and the Crackpots here as well.'

As it transpired the lady we went to in Edinburgh could hardly be described as a typical theatrical landlady.

She was a lawyer's widow, and whether she had let out rooms because she was in need of money or company, she never said, but even to my inexperienced eye it was obvious that she was as new to the game as I was.

Her home was one of these lovely big Georgian houses in East Claremont Street, and when we called to enquire about accommodation, we were shown not only the room that was to let, but the whole house.

The most outstanding feature was her kitchen.

Like the entire establishment, it was extremely old-fashioned. With its huge inbuilt range it looked like a parody of a television set, rather than a cooker where food was currently being cooked.

The walls and ceiling were hung with long-forgotten utensils of every possible kind, and the floor was completely covered with huge iron cooking pots, pans and pails, with little narrow open trails along which it was necessary to navigate in order to reach the various essential oases like the sink or the cooker.

But our landlady was most anxious to please. She wanted to know if she was charging too much, or if there was something special that we liked to eat. I have always had a problem with vegetables. I have detested them since I was a child, apart from a few peas or even turnip, provided it is to accompany mince. Mrs. Landlady was amazed. 'Surely' she said, 'you must eat your greens. They are tremendously good for you.'

So I compromised, thinking I might just be able to sink the odd broad bean, but, apparently pleased to be able to do something special for us, she proceeded to provide an enormous heap of fat, sludge-green runner beans with every meal. Even if I had adored such awful stuff, I could never have finished half of what I consistently found on my plate. Not wishing to offend the dear lady, we took to wrapping huge quantities of them in the morning newspaper when discovery was less likely, and hiding the parcels all over the bedroom until we were able to decant them into a litter bin just outside.

Festival City continued to play happily to packed houses, although the reviews had not pleased the two stars. Molly and Archie tended to remain aloof. They took themselves very seriously and were very sensitive about their status, and quick to send notes to anyone who offended. Especially Archie, who seemed to be under the impression that he was playing Ibsen rather than a piece of topical trivia which was good fun for the moment but would probably never be heard of again.

Among other things his attitude was apparent in his mannered speech offstage, much the same as the budding young officers who used to try and straighten their regional accents. He used a quiet, cultured form of speech which occasionally produced sounds that were unintelligible. There was a men's outfitters immediately next door to the Gateway, and one day I met Archie as I was headed for the stage door. He was standing peering in at the window of the gents' outfitters with a frown of concentration on his face.

'Hello, Archie,' I greeted him. 'I think you're trying to go in the wrong door.'

He looked at me as if he had never seen me before, and was not prepared to sign autographs. Obviously there was something of great importance on his mind.

'I need a shee-et!' he said.

I begged his pardon!

'I need a shee-et. What's so-oo strange about thet?'

'Nothing,' I said. 'Nothing. It's just that I don't understand why you're set on going into this shop for . . . *you know* . . .'

'A shee-et,' he repeated patiently. 'I need a shee-et, and I'm going in here for one!'

You can see the problem. I could hear what he was saying, but

I couldn't believe he was saying what I thought he was saying, and if he wasn't saying what I thought he was saying—what *was* he saying? Although if he was saying what I thought he was saying, why in the name of God was he going into a gents' outfitters? I wondered if perhaps he hadn't noticed the word 'outfitters' and saw only the word 'GENTS' and got confused.

We got it straightened out, of course. He was very patient with me and even pointed to the garment in the window that he wanted to purchase, which was a rather snazzy striped shirt.

'Oh, a *shurt!*' I said. 'You're needing a *shurt* and you're going into this shop for it.'

'What the hell d'you *think* I've been saying?' he shouted. 'A shee-et, boy. A shee-et!'

All in all it was a happy season and the play, while not regarded as a contender for the Nobel Prize for Literature, had nevertheless done all that had been asked of it. I had enjoyed it tremendously. No impresarios had come knocking at my dressing-room door, but my standing with the management, i.e. Sadie, was high, and I began to wonder if I could persuade them to mount a rep panto for the Christmas season. I lobbied Sadie as well as the director, Gerald Primrose, and writer Albert Mackie, and, perhaps because of our success with *Festival City* they became very enthusiastic. It was agreed that Albert would write a panto/revue to which I would contribute, and Gerald, who was nervous, never having done anything of the sort before, asked me to co-direct.

I didn't bother to tell him or anybody else that I had no experience either.

Young Donald Maclean, who had only a few weeks before decided to shake the stuffy dust of the Glasgow administration from his feet, phoned me from London. He was now a music producer for the BBC in London, and had his office in the Aeolian Hall in Old Bond Street. In this capacity he had come under the authority of an Australian gentleman by the name of Jim Davidson who was a character-and-a-half, although he would have been horrified to hear himself so described.

It appeared that there had been much discussion in London about giving the Sunday lunchtime *Billy Cotton Band Show* a three month break and Joe Loss and his orchestra had won the watch. Joe Loss had been one of the top and most popular dance-bands for a generation and would remain so for a long time to come.

The problem was that Joe was not all that good with scripts. As a matter of fact he wasn't very good with words at all, and there was no way he could have presented his own show. They needed a compère, an anchor man, and Donald had persuaded Jim Davidson that I was worth considering. Donald's call was to ask if I was interested, available and prepared to come to London and discuss it. Without knowing what it would all mean, the desired qualifications, the work involved, the commitment . . .

I said: 'Yes, when?'

The meeting took place as soon as I was free to come to London and I stayed with Donald and his wife, Margaret, for the duration of the discussions. We went off to Aeolian Hall in old Bond Street to meet the Wizard of Oz.

He was a dapper man in both dress and speech. He spoke in great quotable lines, using descriptive, picturesque words and phrases he had invented himself. It was impossible for him to come to any decision there and then. I rather think he was depending on the sales pitch he had been given by Donald whose views he obviously respected.

Donald told me later that the list of desired qualities was nearly thirty items long, and included: a good flexible radio voice, solid microphone experience, scriptwriting, good personality, a strong sense of comedy, ability to play characters, ability to use different accents, etc. If I had seen that list before I went down to London, I think I would have stayed home. But Jim Davidson, perhaps having no one else in mind, decided on a single trial broadcast to go out live at lunchtime on Sunday 28th December 1952.

It was the first of a small number of opportunities which were created for me in the following few months, and which were to bring about devastating changes in my career and private life.

I was sent a running order and proceeded to write the first script, using Joe and his star singer, Rose Brennan, occasionally for a quick bit of apparently unrehearsed chat with the sole purpose of finding new ways of saying: 'and now the band is going to play . . . !'

Joe and his band were paying their annual, tremendously popular visit to Green's Playhouse Ballroom in Renfield Street, so the broadcast had to be done as an outside broadcast in the old Hillhead Burgh Halls in Byres Road which was totally without heating, and could have competed with the Union Cold Storage Company and won with ease. In that desperate cold, the boys in the orchestra, Joe and myself were huddled in overcoats, mufflers, Balaclavas and fur-lined gloves, striving to give the impression that we were in a warm, relaxed atmosphere for our huge audience throughout Britain as they sat down to their Sunday lunch. How the musicians were able to make a sound in that temperature was a mystery to me. Joe was able to maintain his body heat a little better than the rest of us because his method of directing the orchestra was very physical, his body rocking energetically back and forth and his baton swivelling elegantly between thumb and forefinger.

As our rehearsal progressed we developed the most unexpected problem. The sound engineer, an experienced and reliable member of the BBC's Scottish establishment, was deeply disturbed by the sound of a bee buzzing in time to the music, or perhaps simply like ourselves, it was trying to find some warmth. That a bee could survive in such cold seemed, of itself, worthy of scientific interest to the nation, but that it had an ear for music as well . . .

Everyone in the great high-ceilinged hall, led by Joe himself, formed a search party to seek out the baritone bee, but now there was neither sight nor sound of the creature.

The moment the rehearsal started again and the music filled the hall, our friendly Glasgow musical bee burst into his joyful buzzing song. But our intrepid sound engineer had been on the alert and had spotted the hive. After a whispered conversation, a somewhat embarrassed Donald Maclean had to inform Mr. Loss that, while it was in order to go up and down on his toes, rock energetically back and forth, and even swivel his baton elegantly between his thumb and forefinger, *would he please refrain from loudly 'ZZZZZZZZ'ing as he did so!*

Joe was astounded. In all his twenty-five years in the music business he had not realised, nor apparently had anyone else, that, when conducting an up-tempo number, he was giving an extremely accurate impersonation of a large and very busy bumble-bee!

The broadcast was a success according to an enthusiastic review by the *Evening Citizen* radio critic, and what was even better, a telephone call from Donald a couple of days later informed me that I was to be contracted for the next four of the series. I could understand that Jim Davidson wanted to make sure that the first one wasn't a fluke.

I don't remember if I had thought through the consequences of being offered the series. And that was before the harvest of the persuasive lobbying I had done earlier at the Gateway Theatre was reaped that very evening.

The Gateway's panto—*Cinderella*, at one time called a 'rep romp'—was up and running and going exceptionally well, having opened in Edinburgh on the 29th September. Packed houses and solid audience reaction spelt success for the show, and the added bonus was that it was enormous fun. Gerald Primrose, relieved that what was a completely new experience for him had not turned out to be a catastrophe, was delighted and asked me to join the company for the season which immediately followed.

It was the first time I had found myself faced with the problem of coping with two completely overlapping jobs of such a disparate nature, one of which meant commuting to London. Still, I had accepted the challenge, or to put it another way, I had eagerly grabbed the offers without thinking them through.

Hamish Turner, a good, kind, straightforward, honest man, had popped in to see the panto and then came round to the dressing-room and said to me: 'You've got it! I could make you a top class comic in three years.' My reply was rather cheeky. 'I'm sorry Mr. Turner, but that would be much too slow for me.' He was very understanding. When I explained what I was about to do, he asked if he could keep in touch, and that's exactly what he did. He used to telephone to congratulate me, to encourage me, and to build up my self-confidence. What was more important was that he had made contact with Stewart Cruikshank, who was badly in need of young comedians, but who apparently—having listened to the *Showband Shows*—was convinced that I was not Scottish. The accent, the style and delivery were deliberately put on to give a transatlantic feel to the shows, and Stewart Cruikshank's ear suggested to him that I was either Australian, Canadian, or from the mid-Atlantic. Hamish, however, kept the heat on, explaining that I could speak like a man from Bridgeton when necessary.

The first problem, however, was Ena Quade. She was the BBC Contracts Executive at the time, and renowned for dealing with artistes' fees as if the money was coming out of her personal bank account. I was offered five guineas plus travelling and subsistence for each broadcast of the Joe Loss series which, as she pointed out when I questioned it, was the top fee for a major programme. I suggested there was a difference between a programme made and transmitted for Scotland only and a network light entertainment series from London, and it should be double what she was offering.

The lady was not for negotiating. Five guineas was to be the fee—take it or leave it. In my opinion that was a very mean and shoddy contract, so I told her her offer was totally unacceptable and she could keep her five guineas and buy a toffee-apple for herself.

Thankfully, London was aghast at her cack-handedness, and told her to shut up and sign me up immediately on terms that I would accept. That settled, the next consideration was whether I had been wise to accept the offer to join the Gateway Theatre Company. But I decided that it was really a question of stamina, and I was feeling fit enough to carry out both tasks.

In the meantime, the Gateway season was to start with a very Scottish play called *Torwatletie* by Robert McLellan, all about smuggling and secret escape doors. A very funny and enjoyable play, in which I played the part of the parson.

Sadie had been talked into taking on the son of a friend in Inverness. During the dressing-room distribution she quite rightly put her long time players in the dressing-rooms they had been used to. I was quite happy with the one I had been given, and Sadie asked if I would mind if The Young Man might share. I had no problem about sharing with anybody—I wasn't going to be here all that long.

We sat back to back in front of our extremely large mirrors and started to make up. After some time, The YM asked me what sort of lighting there would be for the scene. It all sounded very professional—there are times when it is important to know about the lighting and how it might affect the make-up. I had made the parson a man who had a dark blackish-blue stubble, eyebrows that met, and a black wig that went right down his back. Then, from the Young Man:

'What d'you think? Would this be suitable?'

When I turned round to have a proper look, I found myself looking at a face which had been made in my own image. I explained that we all had to make up our own faces according to the characters we were playing. He apologised, and would try to do better.

My effort to help him led to a close friendship, at least on *his* side. Every time I came back from London and took my place in the play, I knew what would happen: I would squeeze myself through the secret door to come face to face with the YM who was standing, hands on hip, legs astride, waiting for 'his friend'. 'Did you happen to see my friend So-and-So while you were in London?' he would mince.

'No, I bloody didn't. I don't know So-and-So!'

Immediately after the final curtain of the Saturday evening performance at the Gateway, I would head to Waverley Station and board the London sleeper. I have never been able to sleep on these things, and anyway my mind was always focused on the next script. So I would arrive at King's Cross, bleary-eyed and wondering what I was doing to myself. I once calculated that I was losing three months' sleep per year. I have never managed to make it up.

Two cups of very weak sweet tea and a couple of Digestive biscuits from a cheery understanding conductor at the unearthly hour of six the next morning, however, and things seemed not quite so bad. Utilising the hour allowed by these considerate ministering angels on arrival at King's Cross, a wash and shave brought refreshment of body and spirit, and I left the train with a different outlook as I went in search of breakfast. Some of the breakfasts on offer were enough to keep you going for almost the full day, and the wonderful folk who delivered them were enough to make living worth while.

The broadcast over, Donald, Joe and I would discuss what we had just done, and what we could do to enhance the presentation.

I received my running order for the next programme and, with fond farewells, I would set off to catch the train home to Glasgow, which was where I wrote most of the script.

I had a break and came in to see the Gateway's current play. Please forgive me if I have not quoted the correct play, or its author. But the story will stand whether it is the right or wrong one. It is meant to explain the future of the Young Man, the son of Sadie's friend.

The Church of Scotland had always owned the Gateway Theatre, at least for all the time that I had known it, so there would always have been a certain concern about any play that carried unacceptable or suggestive language.

Christopher Fry had a strange, but clever way of dodging the Lord Chamberlain. No expletives were needed. He made up his own, and no one could fault him. If I'm correct, the play I watched all these years ago was *Venus Observed* in which there was a line when the young man referred to 'Captain Suckin' Redmond.' Alas, the YM, perhaps because of nervousness, came out with the actual expletive. I only wish I had had a camera and tape recorder at that moment.

The audience sat very still, their mouths open, and barely breathed, not at all sure if they had heard what they thought, especially in a Church of Scotland establishment.

The following day the Young Man was called to Sadie's office. 'You're getting your books,' she announced in her subtle way. 'However,' she continued, 'you're not getting the sack because you said f*****'. You're getting the sack because you can't f*****' act!'

233

39

AVE BANANA

THE BBC SHOWBAND, as it was in its nascent period, had a rather rough time at first. In spite of the collection of musicians of such high status, and the size of the full orchestra, the listeners seemed to find it much too expensive, since there was only music. They didn't seem to feel that the programme was worth the money involved.

The Showband was based on Cyril Stapleton's original orchestra, with added high-ranking musicians with a CV the size and length of the Aeolian itself. It was a huge orchestra, with some thirty-five musicians, plus the singing group the Stargazers, and a choir. There was a full string section, brass, reed, guitars, bass and piano. The piano was in the hands of a little Scotsman called Bill McGuffie—a brilliant pianist, even though he had lost one of his fingers (very careless!).

The orchestra had enormous class and the music it produced was angelic. Cyril himself (a violinist to trade) was about the most elegantly perfect front for such an orchestra. But still it lacked something—the populist community couldn't take to it. Anyone could switch on their radio and listen to the music, but it hadn't yet become a show. The announcers were called in to speak with their perfect speech and total lack of emotion. They sounded like an elderly cleric about to give the last rites. It was at this time that

Jim D. and Donald realised what was missing. Not only was it necessary to have a pro to lift the atmosphere, but guests, singers, comedians—everything that would make it a show. I was in heaven when I was chosen as the presenter, and to think I would have the joy of listening to the fantastic music that these wonderful men created.

Jim Davidson became really enthusiastic, and came up with the simplest title: *The Showband Show*. Also, with the approaching onslaught from television in mind, he came up with my opening announcement: 'Don't look now—listen—to *The Showband Show*!'

It was a gift.

Monday evening was the big show, with all trumpets at go, and we would have a guest singer or a well known comic. Dick Emery was a great success and was obviously set to go to the top. What I hadn't expected was his delightful singing voice. When he came into the big time, I don't suppose there was space for a song or two, which was a pity.

On Fridays the string section was eliminated and the orchestra was cut back to just the dance band, and they played only music with songs from 'the staff'. And such music! I must say I miss the big bands.

Then there was *The Saturday Show*, which was presented by Alfred Marks and me. I was the straight-man, and soon I was asked to write the script as well. To help with this, I brought in Lewis Schwarz, who had come down from Glasgow wanting to be a writer.

One thing I hadn't realised was that the Metropolitan police, detectives and all, used to have huge dinners in the Connaught Rooms. We weren't invited, but were asked to do the cabaret show later in the evening. As soon as my own show was over, a detective would arrive at the door and whisk me away to the Connaught. Stars finishing at the theatre would receive the same treatment, no time to clean up their make-up, or get out of their costumes. My first experience taught me a great deal. I discovered that by the time the cabaret had started the entire police force were seriously the worse for drink. I couldn't help wondering if all the London villains carefully chose that night to get on with their work without interruption.

I remember taking a note to make sure that I was on early. I warned newcomers that if they wanted to be heard at all, they should make sure they were on first, second or third. Beyond that, forget it!

Much the same routine took place when the Variety Club set up their Charity Concerts, generally on a Sunday. Dozens of comedians and singers would flood in prepared to do their bit. The youngest was Des O'Connor, who was just beginning his career. Gracie Fields was our star guest, and would therefore close the programme, but the organisers' method was to invite as many performers as possible in case they didn't have enough to make a show. As usual, not only did they have sufficient performers, they had a huge overflow. The rules covering such Sunday Shows were nothing if not strange. MacDonald Hobley and I compèred the show, but the rules didn't allow us to speak to each other. And props of any kind were forbidden.

As ten o'clock approached, Gracie became very restless and worried that she might find herself performing to only a handful of very tired people in the early morning. Eventually she decided she had waited long enough so insisted on going on *now*!

And it was no surprise that by the time she had finished her act, the majority of the audience had disappeared. It was rather sad when a number of performers had waited the whole evening to show what they could do, only to find themselves performing to perhaps a dozen people who had succumbed to the God Morpheus. MacDonald and I had long since decided that we would follow Gracie and go home to bed. That's a pro for you!

I had another on-and-off job. Again as presenter/compère. It was *Music Hall Time* at Shepherd's Bush, like the Glasgow Empire only on television. I was very nervous. I wasn't used to making the jokes. I had always made it a rule that I should never seek to get a laugh. I was the straight-man and it was up to the comic to get the laugh. But I was still very nervous. I couldn't eat, or think, or stop shuddering. As it happened, that dear, dear man Jack Radcliffe was on the bill with Nellie his faithful female stooge, and I remember introducing Dave King on his very first TV appearance. Perhaps he was as nervous as I was!

But Jack wasn't the one to allow me to frighten myself to death, and he forced me to go with him for something to eat; took me under his wing and talked me out of my panic. If it hadn't been for Jack I doubt if I could have coped at all. He was a truly lovely man. I was aware that I wasn't carrying it out all that well. For some reason I felt it just wasn't my scene, but after a few such programmes, I managed to settle down.

I wondered if Ethel was managing to do the same. She did try, and tried very hard. She used to say: 'I am trying to make this marriage work.' It was true, but sadly there didn't seem to be much time for marriage. It began to look as if we had a problem on our hands.

I could no longer cope with commuting, so I decided we would have to remain in London for as long as the work continued. Ethel filled a trunk, locked up our home, and came down by train in early 1953. We stayed with an aunt of Ethel's in the Wimbledon area. It was the first time I had seen a television set, with its tiny screen. The place would have been more acceptable if there had been some heating. I had never known such a cold, damp house, but it was the spur that led us to find an apartment of our own, and we landed very comfortably in Carlton Hill in St. John's Wood.

At least it was private, warm and clean, but we could not say we were living a life.

I was working flat out in London and Ethel was having a pretty dismal time. She had no friends in London and nothing that interested her. Her only job was to make food for us, particularly for Lewis Schwarz and me as we struggled to produce yet another script for *The Saturday Show*, often working all through the night. It was drudgery. She suggested that perhaps she should go home for a while, and see how we feel. It sounded like the first scene in a shaky marriage. But I carried a fair weight of stubbornness and pride and refused to allow her to go home.

It was the first serious crack in the relationship and came as a stunning surprise. Having thought about it through the years, I realised that the marriage was never going to succeed. I hadn't been ready for marriage. Indeed I should have called the whole thing off the day we stood in front of The Beresford trying to cross the street to the jeweller, especially when Ethel had gracefully offered to delay our engagement. But that wasn't done in the thirties and forties. Once you had broached the possibility of marriage, it would have been most inappropriate to change your mind. People would talk!

I had never really had a teen age. I had never really lived! Not a single wild oat had I sown. The war had seen to that.

Producer Dicky Leaman, someone who had kept his eye on me for some time, was very keen that I take over *What's My Line?*, although how I was to cope with the work I already had with even more on the way, I wasn't quite sure. For reasons not known to me, Eamonn Andrews was either taking a break, taking over a new project, or quitting for good. Whatever the reason, they had to find a new chairman. There were two candidates, and The Powers That Be decided to give each of them a chance to show their particular style. I was Dicky Leaman's choice, but the decision would have to be unanimous. The second candidate was a Canadian film actor called Ron Randell. He did very well indeed. Bright, breezy and full of fun, and on signing off, came up with a wonderful smile and wink.

It was the wink that did it—he got the job.

However, there was something else to come and that was a new quiz show called *Guess My Story*. I was already presenting *The Showband Show* on Mondays and Fridays. *The Saturday Show* and *Guess My Story* came on air to provide a rest period for *What's My Line?* Peter West was our chairman and the cast was Elizabeth Allen, Eunice Gayson, Michael Pertwee (the playwright) and me.

Guess My Story meant homework. I had to make myself aware of the more outstanding press stories. The game called on us to question members of the public who had been in the news during the previous week, and try to identify the story in which they had figured. Generally, a well-known celebrity would also be brought in, carefully disguised, for us to identify. On one occasion the guest, a highly celebrated band leader, was led in prepared to be quickly recognised, applauded and questioned as to his current plans. He appeared swathed in a ridiculous wig, beard and moustache, and answered us in a funny voice in order to preserve his anonymity.

But the disguise seriously backfired. Our probing proved fruitless. Each of us in turn tried a different tack, but affirmatives were not forthcoming. Clearly there was a limit to how long we could sit there biting our nails and getting nowhere. The programme was hurtling towards the final credits and this was the Star Guest, and we had no idea whatsoever who this person was. Peter West's friendly smile became somewhat fixed and he perspired freely. Upstairs in the control box, the director was going spare and his technical staff openly tittering. Hint upon hint came from Peter as he wiped his brow and began to peel off the mountain of hair that covered the man's face, each teasing revelation meant to be greeted with our shouts of joy and happy recognition. But we sat there staring in dumbfounded silence. Eventually Peter, with a flourish, pulled off what remained of the man's disguise revealing a man that none of us had seen in our lives before.

Peter made much of the fact that the celebrity, now glowering at us malevolently, had well and truly fooled the panel, and invited viewers to tune in the following week for another exciting half hour when we would try to drop a few more bricks. It was held as something of a gaffe that I, of all people, had not recognised him in view of the fact that for some years I had been the major presenter of the big bands, but the fact remains that I had never seen the man in my life before—with or without a beard. I can only assume that he was a famous dance-band leader who spent his career in the dance halls. Which means it could have been Louis Freeman or Lou Prager or almost anyone.

I still don't know who he was!

*　　　*　　　*

Hamish Turner was still keeping tabs on me, still listening, telling me how well things seemed to be going, and he was constantly nudging Stewart Cruikshank with a view to my joining the Happy Five Past Eight Family. Cruikshank, however, seemed to be adamant that I was either American, Canadian or Australian, and, naturally, he was only interested in Scottish comedians for the remarkably popular *Five Past Eight*.

Peter Martin was another presenter. Blond, clean-cut and very good-looking, he was in the chair for a TV quiz show starring Denis Norden and Frank Muir. The wheeze was to find people with the same name. What it was called, I do not remember.

Peter was due to take over another new radio programme which was to be called *Club Piccadilly*. It would make an excellent programme but, sadly, young Peter Martin had cancer. The bulletin issued suggested 'flu, and someone had to take over while he was convalescing. But, of course, his convalescence was not forthcoming.

Club Piccadilly was a programme which was purely for the

dance bands, and once the string section had been dismissed, an area was left where the public could come in free of charge and dance, or just listen to these brilliant players—The Showband, Eric Winston, Ted Heath, Joe Loss and so on.

All the shows that came under my control were working happily. *The Saturday Show* was still running successfully at lunch times on, need I say, Saturday. During his writing and performing stint, Bob Monkhouse had created an Irish character for me called Seumas O'Shaughnessy, whose origins were never very clear. He would appear at some point during the programme and enjoy a highly nonsensical chinwag with our maestro, Cyril Stapleton. When Bob left the show to do other things, the character remained, but I had to take over the writing of it.

As it happened, this task provided my first experience of the performer's nightmare.

My sister-in-law, Maisie, telephoned to tell me that my mother was in the Royal Infirmary undergoing a serious operation for the cancer she had dreaded for so long. It was suggested that it might be as well for me to try and get home to see her. The words 'for the last time' hung in the air, although Maisie did not say anything like that.

I have to confess I found the news overwhelming. My mother and father had stayed with us in London some months earlier, and it was obvious that my mother was seriously ill. I had tried to put that out of my mind, but the nightmares I had had as a small child had returned with a vengeance. From an early age I had been painfully aware that the people I loved were indeed mortal, and I have never come to terms with that solemn fact. Now, I was beginning to realise that I would have to. It was not the easiest thing in the world to find a break in my unbelievably busy sched-ule to take a flyer home, but I decided that if I nipped up to Glasgow on the Thursday evening and back on Friday night, my late appearance wasn't likely to dislocate the London logistics.

The first 'test' was to make myself sit down and write.

It was a strange feeling, sitting at my desk with a heavy heart and trying to think of words and lines that would, hopefully, make others laugh. Curiously, it proved to be one of my better, funnier scripts.

I stayed over Thursday night at my flat in the West End and headed for the Royal Infirmary the following morning. My mother had had her op. the day before, and was just about able to receive a visit from very close family.

Her bed was near to the ward entrance. Her eyes closed, she was a frail, emaciated little figure with a deathly white face. I thought for a moment that she was already dead, until I whispered a quiet 'hello' and her eyes opened in surprise and delight at seeing me. Such was the power I seemed to wield over this little lady that within ten minutes she was sitting up in bed enquiring about breakfast, having earlier refused all food.

But her breathless little story held a grim irony for me.

She had been, she explained, terrified of the surgeon's stated intention of performing a colostomy. To my mother, this was the ultimate obscenity; worse, even, than being eaten by a wild animal. So she had prayed to God and pleaded with Him to make the unspeakable unnecessary, and when the surgeon had visited her on his rounds that morning, her relief had been great when he explained that the colostomy would be unnecessary. What he did not tell her, of course, was that her cancer was inoperable, and that she had only a few months to live.

Nice one God!

But she had quite a few months in front of her, and slowly but surely, her face and body filled out, her lovely rose colour returned and she seemed almost like her old self. Needless to say my Dad was walking around much relieved.

They had decided that Mum should enjoy her convalescence as close to me as possible. So they came down to Eastbourne, and then on to Bournemouth where I was doing one of these holiday capers for the *Standard* newspaper that relied on holidaymakers who were prepared 'to have fun' as they call it, or show off their sartorial elegance.

The sartorially elegant ones were the ones the newspaper were after. We had a rather splendid Rolls at our disposal for the film stars who would be making the choice. I was leading with an ordinary car and in charge of the Tannoy. A bus came last and would stop on command each time a holidaymaker caught the eye of one of our stars. The holidaymaker would then be invited to enter the competition—and the bus. For ladies and their outfits only!

The chosen ones would then be taken to the Winter Gardens, and those whose style was worth showing would be invited in front of a surprisingly large audience, where they would have to tread the catwalk. I compèred that, too, and my Dad and Mum sat in special seats and watched the show.

I was rather better prepared for the public appearance this time—I had already got some idea of what the Bournemouth event would mean when I remembered a personal appearance I had made in Gravesend. But the task here was still daunting—as I drove into the town I could see the huge banner hanging across the road shouting at me: 'RIKKI FULTON WILL ENTERTAIN'. This, I thought, was a mistake—it was not my trade. I was a compère, a presenter, I was a fool—but somehow I had to do something to make the visit worthwhile. I got myself a table at the nearest coffee shop and wrote down every joke I had ever heard.

I needn't have worried. I suddenly became aware of the power of television! Shaking a good deal, I was announced and stepped outside in front of this huge audience. There was a rousing series of cheers and my first gasping word to these lovely people was: 'We-ll!' There was loud laughter and huge applause. All because they saw me on the box every Sunday.

What really shattered me was the crush that followed. I hadn't expected anything like the response from the holidaymakers. I loved it and yet I found it frightening. After choices were made and prizes handed over, I helped my Mum and Dad to head for the hotel. Both being rather small, they became lost to me for a few minutes as I stood signing autographs in my worst writing—and on sweetie-papers and cigarette packets, mostly. Not surprisingly, my Mum began to panic, so I had to call the police who were in attendance to take my Mum and Dad up to the hotel just across the road, while I disappeared again into the crowd.

Had I not experienced it before, I would never have believed the power of the box.

When I got back to work there was another surprise. I was asked to take over *Club Piccadilly* permanently. Yet another programme! This was something I could really enjoy. The BBC Showband set it off, and the other big bands like Ted Heath, Eric Winston, Joe Loss and the others had their time. I enjoyed it because I didn't have to write a script, or work with one. All I needed was the running order of the seventeen or so numbers and the rest was up to me. *Club Piccadilly* sounded just like a real night club, with the public coming in and dancing, or just sitting and listening to the wonderful music. During the breaks between numbers I used to go over and have a chat with some of our audience and they were tickled with the idea of being heard on radio. The sound of the dancers dancing created just the right atmosphere, especially when they could see many of the actors, singers and other celebrities who used to take a look in at the Paris Cinema after their shows and have a word with me. Performers were always happy to get a free plug. I chatted to them as if I had caught them in the middle of a meal just to keep up the deception. I was amused at the number of enquiries we used to get, asking how and where people could apply for membership.

My remit was wide. Sometimes it was the actual title of the next number, or I might muck up the title a bit just to try and keep the straight titles from becoming boring. This was where I put my foot in it. The cost of ad libbing can sometimes be high.

There wasn't all that much you could do with song titles, and on this occasion, I said something like 'The next number coming up is that great classic, sometimes known as Gounod's "Ave Banana", but of course its proper title is "Tutti Frutti".' I didn't think much of it either, but I didn't for a minute think it would create such a storm.

Jim Davidson phoned me much too early in the morning to tell me I was in trouble. He said 'What in the name of Christ did you think you were doing? I've just had an internal memo from His Lordship the Rev. Tatlock about your "Ave Banana" announcement. I take it it just slipped out and you're very upset about having done it.'

I was very sleepy-eyed having worked all the previous day and night. 'Eh, yes, it was very stupid, and I'm very sorry. It was just a slip of the tongue. *What did I say?*'

'How the hell do I know? I wasn't there!' It was something about Ave Maria eating a banana. I don't know. Just play it down and be penitent, remorseful, contrite! I've sent you a copy of Tatlock's memo. Read it and then write me an abject apology.'

The following was the Rev. Tatlock's memo.

Club Piccadilly—8th February 1955

To: Mr. H. Rooney Pelletier; through A.H.R.B.
[Whoever they might be!]

On Saturday night, I was so incensed that I rang up Adrian Waller [?] who was in Light Continuity at the time, and asked him to log a complaint which I would like to have investigated thoroughly. Adrian did so, but said that he would not put details but would indicate that I intended to follow it up with a memorandum.

My wife and I invariably listen to *Club Piccadilly* which we enjoy apart from the banalities and forced heartiness of Rikki Fulton. On Saturday night he plumbed the depths with the following remark: 'Our next number is really Gounod's "Ave Banana" but . . . blah, blah, blah.'

I assume that Fulton is given *carte blanche*; but when one considers the lengths to which the Corporation goes to ensure that responsible speakers, who would never put their foot in it, don't put their foot in it, it naturally makes me wonder. Can nothing be done to infuse a little good taste into this otherwise rather irresponsible person?

Richard Tatlock.

From me:

9th February 1955

Dear Mr. Davidson,

I am writing to you at once to apologise most sincerely for my unforgivable slip during *Club Piccadilly* on Saturday last. As soon as the unfortunate reference to the Gounod masterpiece had left my lips, I realised that what I had said was almost bound to cause offence to many of our listeners which is all the more unhappy in view of the pleasant, friendly atmosphere which has prevailed in the programme so far.

I have no doubt that the BBC will receive many letters of protest from our listeners, and I am afraid deservedly so, in which case I should like them to be able to state that they have received this personal and most sincere apology, not only to those whom the slip would offend, but also to the officials of the Corporation whose representative I was at the time.

I make this apology sincerely and voluntarily, notwithstanding any steps the BBC may consider necessary under the circumstances.

Yours sincerely,

Rikki Fulton.

From the Assistant Head of Variety (Music):

Club Piccadilly—Rikki Fulton.

I have looked into the matter of Rikki Fulton's unfortunate reference to Gounod's 'Ave Maria'. It appears that Donald Maclean was evidently busy arranging his additional supporting acts and was not present in the Control Cubicle when the comment was made. For this reason he did not report the matter to me as he was unaware of the incident.

Before contacting Fulton I asked V.B.M. to check with H.P.C. our contractual position. Streeton held that we are not in a position to cancel the contract as a reprimand without payment to the artist, and if the contract is cancelled, payment will have to be made. I am not sure we should adopt this course because I believe if we take Fulton off the air and pay him, all that would come out of it would be a newspaper controversy centred on a religious subject with the artist receiving a night off with pay. I have seriously reprimanded Fulton with the resultant attached apology. I gathered from his tone on the telephone he was genuinely sorry and rather astonished at what he had done. His letter supports this and I therefore recommend (if you concur) we let it go at that.

Devised, produced and directed by J. H. Davidson! Tee-hee!

It was clear that His Reverence had got nowhere and all must have been well in view of my next assignment, which was the Dance Band Festival that took place in the Albert Hall. This was where the big bands were out to show their brilliance. Some ninety minutes were to be broadcast, and the rest was for the fans alone.

It was exciting and terrifying at the same time. I was dealing with a packed Albert Hall which meant I was controlling some ten thousand plus fans. Tommy Steele made a most important début. Max Bygraves stood on my feet with his size twelves! But he was a joy to work with, and once again I had to play straight-man.

40

AN AUDIENCE WITH
STEWART CRUIKSHANK

HAMISH TURNER was still beavering away trying to convince Stewart Cruikshank that I was a Scotsman! But I seemed to be getting calls from everywhere. I got a call from Aberdeen to enquire if I would be prepared to come up from London to help present 'the great event'. Television had arrived in Aberdeen, transmitters were at the ready, and a special play had been written and was to be produced by Jimmy Crampsey, with a host of star actors. I was to cover the *Children's Hour* part of this very special occasion the next day.

The play, which had a very Highland emphasis, was to be the main item. The crew were running all over the place in their excitement. The set had been built with bricks and mortar, and it was certainly a most unusual scene.

In due course we could see Aberdeen's most important personages, including the Lord Provost wearing his best chain. His speech was interesting in that it went on and on, and I began to think that I had misunderstood. I was under the impression that the event was actually for the good folk of Aberdeenshire, and not the personal pleasure of the Lord Provost.

Eventually the pronouncement was made. Aberdeen had television and himself would take great pleasure in switching on the power. There were cheers and loud applause—and then a series of rather long pauses. Nothing happened. They tried again, and the technicians rushed to investigate what had gone wrong. Unfortunately, it seemed that there was a fault in the link. It wouldn't take a moment. . . .

The play was cancelled. Aberdeen did not have television—at least not yet!

The following day required a rush job to clear the specially created set they had set up for the play, but it was going to take a bulldozer to clear, and that wouldn't be today. It had been built to last.

I was left with the set and all the children the following afternoon. The fault had been discovered and everything was now working perfectly. So the children and I had a very happy hour. I'm not sure what the Lord Provost thought about it, but it was Auntie Kathleen's children's programme that was first heard on Aberdonian telly in 1954.

* * *

Hamish was beginning to interest Cruiky and came up with a splendid idea. The Edinburgh Festival was about to get under way, and Duncan Macrae and Andy Stewart were touring with *Gog and Magog* and would be appearing at the Palladium. Hamish arranged a late-night revue to follow the Macrae play, and I would take over at the later night time. I had to write as much material as I was capable of producing in the time.

Ethel played her part in the sketches, and Michael Howard (the famous hairy-dog story-teller) and Dawn Adams were appearing. I'm not sure what she did in the show—perhaps the comforting of Michael Howard. Dear Jimmy Copeland was with us and did a 'turn' from the *Para Handy* series. Andy Stewart took the opportunity to polish up his act which became star quality.

249

I suddenly realised that the 'Hamish Turner treatment' had already started. Firstly, there was the manager of the Howard & Wyndham King's Theatre, followed by a member of the Howard & Wyndham board, who would sometimes have the boring job of checking on a particular performer. Then, after a couple of interesting reports arrive on the guvnor's desk, he slips in to the show without anyone being aware. This is the great and wonderful Stewart Cruikshank himself. He quietly slips away again. But makes a date for a meeting in the Howard & Wyndham office in London in the company of one of the greatest directors, especially of panto, Freddie Carpenter!

We were introduced, and it looked as if we could do business. But I was disappointed to find that the business wouldn't take place until the following year. Somewhat depressed, I bought myself a new car, a red Vauxhall Velox, and we gave it its first long run travelling up to Scotland for Christmas. My Mum wasn't looking too bad, and it was fun getting round to the chums in the BBC drama lounge to hear the news.

I thought this might be an opportunity to see if the relationship with Eddie Fraser had improved. I asked him how things were going for him, and he told me all was going well. For some reason I remember he was groping in a filing cabinet while we were talking, and unable to look at me. So I dropped the bombshell.

'What would you say, Eddie, if I told you I was coming home in the near future?'

'Oh, I wouldn't advise that, Rikki,' he said. 'There's nothing for you here!'

Little did he know!

But at least I knew that nothing had changed. He was still his charming self!

I took the opportunity of making a quick visit to see George Formby, as suggested by Stewart Cruikshank. We had an interesting chat, and he was complaining that he had had to bring out some old comedy material he had used years before. That shook me a bit, too. I had been under the impression that wonderfully comic routines would be sitting waiting for me, but no. Anyway it was wonderful to have met not only George himself, but also Beryl. She told me that on one recent Royal occasion, the Queen (now the Queen Mother) had said to her: 'Now, listen Beryl, you know where we are. Don't be a stranger!'

The 24th October 1955 heralded the end of the London road. My last *Showband Show* took place in the Camden Town Studios. The boys were wonderful to me, and I knew I would miss them, having worked with them for nearly four years. But any sadness I felt was overtaken by my joyous anticipation of going home. Ethel had already gone ahead to our house in Glasgow to put it in order and I was to follow with the last of our belongings the day after my last broadcast.

I had the car packed ready to go the next day, but sleep was impossible. I tossed and turned and I realised there was little point in lying in bed. I got up and dressed, wished goodbye to London (I never liked London, and I like it even less now) and the apartment in Carlton Hill forever.

I drove through the night without a stop, and as I travelled, I couldn't help thinking of all the different and wonderful projects the BBC had put into my hands, and the people I had met and worked with. When I thought of the unbelievably famous performers who had been our guests. . . .

Matt Busby, who was one of our greatest singers. The Beverley Sisters, a fun trio. Nat King Cole, a truly magnificent performer. I could listen to him all day.

Rosemary Clooney, with whom I fell madly in love. Billy Eckstine, who later formed his own orchestra. I can hear him even now singing 'Passing Strangers' with Sarah Vaughan. Such music!

Dick Emery, a great and popular comedian—and with that

underrated singing voice. Jose Ferrer, (Jose Vincente Ferrer Y Centron) who gave Rosemary one hell of a time! Dickie Henderson. David Hughes, who went to such trouble in the make-up room to try and disguise his double chin, giving me an opening for a belter of a laugh when I was a guest on his programme *Make Mine Music*.

Benny Hill, who shared an agent with me at one time. Stubby Kaye, famous for his performance in *Guys and Dolls*, and a lovely guy to work with. Bill Kerr, who didn't much fancy the script as written by Jimmy Grafton, and I had to do a rewrite.

Frankie Lane, an introduction and interview, and that was about it! Al Martino, who was at No. 1 in the music charts at the time, but was incredibly nervous, and I sympathised.

Guy Mitchell, whom I found standing on Cyril's podium conducting a non-existent orchestra. Bob Monkhouse, the most amazing intellect I have ever known.

Spike Milligan and Peter Sellers, who couldn't do their routine for giggling. It was delightful. One day in Aeolian Hall I was introduced to Harry Secombe. He didn't shake hands, he took me in his arms and danced me round the floor. I have since met him a number of times, and apparently he enjoys the *Scotch & Wry* videos when he is resting in his Winnebago. One of the most delightful men you could hope to meet. Immediately following our tango, a strange 'creature' appeared through a slightly open door, and a voice kept saying: 'Take me to your leader!' This was Spike Milligan, just outside the door, while all we could see was his hand wearing a pair of spectacles. It must have been heaven to work with such geniuses.

Alfred Marks, with whom I seemed to have created a double act. This was in *The Saturday Show*, which I wrote with my partner Lewis Schwarz, and it went on until I left the BBC Showband to take up my new position in Scotland.

Robert Morton, with the *Bumper Fun Book*, was one of the many sad comedians who needed to be loved, and if and when the love disappeared, sadly so did they. It is amazing that so many of the people who make you laugh decide that there is no point in living if they fail to amuse.

Johnny Ray—I lent him my handkerchief. (No, I didn't!) Jon Pertwee, a very intelligent gentleman whom Kate and I met now and again in Puerto de Pollensa. A delightful man, although my contact with him was mostly chat, and not necessarily about showbusiness.

Frank Sinatra, my all-time favourite. It was the most thrilling experience of my life. Those blue eyes were really unforgettable, along with the most strikingly beautiful male hands. An absolute joy to work with.

I had made a vow to myself that when writing scripts I would never slip in a gag for myself. I was there to serve these people, and I stood by that vow. But Frank himself was a happy ad-libber, and at one point he came in with something I hadn't expected, and I automatically called the shot. In some cases the 'star' would be greatly annoyed, but Frank not only approved of the improvised routines, but enjoyed the badinage—it meant fun, laughter and it enhanced the entire programme.

My regret was that Frank Sinatra, for some reason, had lost his appeal to the public, and when I met him for the first time I almost saw him as a down-and-out. I had this stupid idea that I should take him out and buy him a new raincoat. But what a perform-ance! The audience in the Paris Cinema was loud and supportive. His reception as I introduced him was overwhelming, and al-though I knew he was having problems with his career, for that evening he was The King, and I was so proud to be with this extraordinary performer. I knew in my heart that it would all come right for him.

Dorothy Squires, showing off her new and very handsome husband, Roger Moore. But she sang as well! Frankie Vaughan, who would pop into *Club Piccadilly* for a friendly plug before he went home after his show. I could hardly say I had worked with him.

There are many I must have forgotten. After all, this old memory is doing well to bring this many wonderful performers back. But, let's face it, it was some years ago. . . .

41

THERE IS NOTHING LIKE A DAME

I WISH I COULD SAY that my first pantomime was a rousing success, but I have to confess that my performance was quite dreadful. Still, it *was* the first pantomime I had ever done, as well as the first time I had played Dame.

Jimmy Logan and I had been good friends some years previously, when I had been struggling with the ridiculous Fulton Brothers company, but it was clear that he saw me as the raw beginner, and I wasn't exactly made to feel welcome. We were appearing in *Goldilocks* at the Edinburgh King's Theatre in 1956, and there was much to put right in my performance. For one thing, having worked in London for four years in programmes that required a more sophisticated approach, I think my vision of a Scottish comedian was desperately wide of the mark. My accent had become coarse, loud and ridiculously broad. I was even annoyed that the audience had laughed when the Dame had to sell the bears. My error of judgement was that I saw the brief frontcloth scene as pathos. It was quite the wrong approach on my part. What I should have done was to play it like Old Mother Riley! What was I there for if it wasn't to make them laugh? However, I was not above learning, and improved with each performance.

I wasn't greatly enamoured of the script, but that applied to the 'book', and it was up to the performers to produce their own material.

I was very much more at ease in the *Five Past Eight* show with Alec Findlay, Kenneth McKellar (Ah! That voice! So beautiful. And his wonderful sense of humour!) and others. When I think of the cast I was privileged to work with, my memories are of the sheer pleasure of being on the same show. It is a memory I shall treasure always, especially when I can name such delightful artistes as Alistair McHarg, that delightful bear of a man; Fay Lenore who always liked to remind herself that her mother had spent a great deal of money on 'that voice'! And not forgetting Denny Davis, the very lovely young lady from South Africa who was also a member of our delightful quartet. It was a joy to listen to them as they brought us some of the great operatic songs for quartets from the well known operas in our weekly programmes. It also brought a genuine atmosphere of tremendous class.

Michael Mills was our producer, and had been with the BBC for some time. He was the producer who gave us that incredibly popular series during 1974-1979 with Michael Crawford: *Some Mothers Do 'Ave 'Em*. Lionel Blair, whose face is well known, was our brilliant choreographer.

It wasn't until I had experienced my first *Five Past Eight* show that I became aware that something had been seriously missing in the *Goldilocks* panto. It was, without doubt, the casting. The panto seemed devoid of colour compared to *Five Past Eight*. It seemed there was only Jimmy and me, the 'Sorcerer's Apprentice'. In contrast we had a very happy team working in harmony in *Five Past Eight*. We even spent a great deal of time together when we had time to spare.

Wee Alec Findlay guided many of us to a very well known landlady called Jeannie Flight, who had a habit of discussing the next meal while we were in the middle of the previous one.

'Fit am Ah gaun tae gi'e you loat fur yer tea?' she would say.

She also kept us well informed about the state of her husband's 'stoamak'.

Wee Alec was a keen golfer, and before we knew where we were at least three of us had bought a set of clubs and all the accoutrements. From then on rehearsals were secondary. The weather that year was wonderful, and the wide fairways of the Bruntsfield course made shots much easier. But how we managed to get in a full round of golf and complete our rehearsals is a mystery.

The schedule for *Five Past Eight* in Edinburgh included a visit to His Majesty's Theatre in Aberdeen—I think the run was about eight weeks.

The Glasgow, Edinburgh and Aberdeen shows had a format. There would be an opening number as the boy and girl dancers presented themselves, followed by the stars, and finally Wee Alec and I would make our entrance. The opening number finished, the tabs would come down and I would be left to warm up the audience.

I enjoyed the ad-lib chat I had with the audience in Edinburgh, especially when someone came in late. That gave me a path to some badinage with the late customers from whom I demanded a note to explain themselves. It created a warm, happy relationship between me and the audience.

My Mum and Dad were in the audience to see their youngest son achieve his life-long ambition. But my concentration wasn't at full power and I couldn't help glancing at Mum throughout the performance. It was awful to see her eyes close every few minutes. I don't know if any of the audience noticed, but I certainly did. I kept wondering how they would get her home.

If there was any comfort for me at all, it was that at least she had been there and seen it, because I was pretty sure she wouldn't see it again.

We moved to His Majesty's in Aberdeen as per schedule,

expecting the same kind of enthusiasm as in Edinburgh. A couple or two came in late and gave me the openings I was ready for, but this time the glares I received would have frightened the daylights out of Medusa herself. One of the stage hands offered to put me right about Aberdeen audiences, but I had worked that out for myself.

As far as I was concerned, I saw it as a blessing that the Aberdeen run was a good deal shorter.

There was a greenkeeper who went to the show regularly. There were two things I learned from him. One was that an Aberdonian was unable, or at least found it very difficult, to pay a compliment. The best we could expect would be: 'Quite good. Oh aye, quite good.'

Secondly he saw himself as a comic, and we learned that each time he went to a show he wrote down all the jokes he had heard in readiness for his visits to some Old Folks home or something similar, but he did show his appreciation on each occasion, saying 'Aye, aye, Ah goat a rerr loata jokes fae ye this time!'

I managed to get down to Riddrie with my movie-camera, with the idea of showing Mum and the family what the show had been like, and how we passed the time during the day. In fact we played quite a lot of golf. Again Wee Alec was leading as usual. But she was just the same as she was in the theatre—she couldn't keep her eyes open. So the movies were abandoned. She was now completely bedridden, and couldn't even turn her body to a more comfortable position.

I had to think about employing someone to look after my parents. I advertised for a live-in cook/housekeeper, and a lady whose name was Helen seemed to be just right. I think it was the way she responded to the instructions I had given her. Her understanding of what was required included the possibility that my Mum 'might need something in the middle of the night.' That was the announcement that decided it, and yet. . . .

Something kept bugging me. Helen had been slow to answer our telegram. Then she phoned in to ask if a decision had been arrived at—which meant she hadn't received the telegram. She apologised for not making contact, saying that she had been looking after a friend. We arranged to meet her at Queen Street station, but when the train came in she didn't appear, then suddenly she was there. Here she apologised again. She had been with the station master making a complaint about lost luggage.

We took her home and showed her round the house, and introduced her to my poor little mother, then had our evening meal. It was all very pleasant and jolly, and it looked as if everything would work out. We thought it was worth a try and if it didn't work out we could always try one of the other applicants.

Within a few days my Dad phoned me to say that he was very concerned about Helen. She had told him that she was just going across to Smithycroft Road and wouldn't be long. My Dad was worried that something had happened to Helen, but I was having other thoughts. I felt very foolish, but I sent for the police and told the detective the story. He asked me if I could describe the woman, but I could do better than that, I could draw a picture of her. He knew who she was at once. She had packed a couple of cases and left with all my Mum's jewellery, coats, bedsheets—everything she could find.

It seemed to me to be a truly mean act. However, she was nailed in Edinburgh and had to accept the consequences.

Meantime, I had to get back to Aberdeen's 'lovely' audience.

It was a Saturday in September 1956 when Ethel took a call during the show, but she didn't say anything until the curtain was down. I wasn't surprised. I knew the news of my Mum's death had to be imminent. I was very upset but, at the same time, I was happy—actually happy that her pain had ended. As I drove down on the Sunday it seemed that an enormous weight had been lifted from my heart. I was grateful that I had been able to get to Riddrie in time for the funeral, and I took my Dad back with me to Aberdeen.

It was for him, not my mother, that I cried.

A second blow was the burglary of our flat in Byres Road. The flat was in a powerful mess when Ethel and I got back. It was this shock that unsettled us and made us begin to think we should look for another home.

I had often passed an area in the West End of Glasgow that I liked very much. We met Ainslie Millar (who had made an attempt to breathe life into the old Empress Theatre, which became the Falcon and then the Metropole in which my good friend Jimmy Logan came a cropper). Ainslie was in property and was convinced that he had the house that Ethel and I would salivate over. It stood at the corner of Victoria Park Drive. It had the look of a large cottage, with an interesting room that would make a wonderful dining room and boasted a wall-to-wall divider that could create either a morning room or a huge room with a fireplace at each end. At first glance it was brilliant. But that was it! The other rooms were not at all exciting. Ethel loved it, but I wasn't so sure.

Ainslie gave me the keys and I kept going back to this house trying to decide if I would be happy living there. I couldn't count the number of times I stood in the hall wondering if I could make this house my home.

I even asked a friend who was a brilliant child psychiatrist, who answered the question with ease. 'Buying a house,' he said, 'is like getting married. If you have trouble making up your mind, don't do it!'

It struck me that the house had been on the 'for sale' list for some time. I made contact with the Council Planning Department, and learned that the planned opening to the Clyde Tunnel would be practically right outside the front door.

The thought of buying the house, and then being forced to accept a compulsory sale and watch it being demolished, was like a seriously bad dream. Needless to say I had a name for Ainslie Millar, and was thankful that it had occurred to me to make enquiries about this house he was sure we would love!

One Monday I read about a house only just on the market. We went to have a look, and the minute I put my head round the front door I knew I was truly at home. I tried very hard to find out what the highest offer might be so that I could top it, but because some of the partners were representing the sellers, I had to guess. The only information I could get was that the offers had gone well above the upset price. I made my offer—then later I rang them again and told them to add another fifty pounds. Apparently one of my competitors was an architect who had already made a survey and had done much the same as I had—he had made an identical offer, and then had rung back and raised it—but had added only twenty-five pounds! So on Thursday 3rd March 1960 I owned my Silverwells dream house because of a mere twenty-five pounds.

We crammed all the furniture we had in one room and left for the King's in Edinburgh for the season in the hope that decoration, rewiring, carpet-fitting and all the other requirements would be over by the time we got home.

Our very first guests were Jack and Mary Milroy, and we were enjoying ourselves mightily when every single thing that required electricity for its livelihood blew up. I can recall the awful picture of Jack (himself) Milroy starting to undo what we were convinced was only a simple blown fuse. As it happened it was the main fuse, and fortunately my call to the electricity engineers brought them to the house just in time to save Jack and me from electrocuting ourselves.

42

THE ZOMBIE WITH THE CROMBIE

MY IMMEDIATE ASSIGNMENT was to write the comedy material I needed for the shows for which I had been contracted, which
meant that I would have to write the panto material while performing *Five Past Eight* and vice versa. I used to wander up
Observatory Road, up round Horslethill and all over Hillhead.
Head down, notebook in hand, never noticing anyone, just scrib-
bling. I felt like Nigel Tranter. In the cold weather I wore a heavy
grey Crombie coat, and as a result I became known as The Zombie
with the Crombie. I think it was Archie McCulloch who christened
me, a well kent face whom I knew very well.

We had rented one of the little refurbished cottages in Cramond.
It was and is a truly lovely spot. When we came home in the
evening you could almost swear it was Paris. On other occasions
we took friends to the George Hotel for dinner and there were
times when members of the Edinburgh élite came over to the table
to have a word with us, having seen the show. One lady in
particular put her elegant foot in it slightly. When I was doing
the warm up I always had a lot of fun giving out the news from
Cramond, and I had always used a Morningside voice and accent
to get the message across. I had also been performing a rather
strange sketch in which I was playing the double parts of a man
visiting his lover in Paris and, of course, speaking in rapid French.

About which I knew nothing!

This dear lady came to our table and said: 'May Ay tell you how much may husband and Ay enjoyed your progremme toonayt. Ay just love it when you talk like the people in Morningside. It's *so* funny! As a metter of fect Ay know someone who talks just like thet! End the French sketch was very clever end very funny. May husband end Ay really enjoyed it, but then may husband end Ay were able to understand the French as well!'

*   *   *

The Dance Band Festival in London was still alive and well. A second event was being staged at the Albert Hall, and it seemed I hadn't been forgotten—or at least, not completely. Back in Glasgow, I went into town to book my flights at the British Airways office which used to be located in St. Vincent Street, only inches from where I had worked in my first job.

The lovely young girl who attended me listened carefully for my requirements. I got the impression that something had amused her, so I took a quick glance and checked my clothing. There was no problem that I could see, but the shy little private smile stayed with her, as she looked up and asked my name. 'Fulton,' I told her. 'F-U-L-T-O-N.'

'Yes,' she agreed. 'I recognised you. You're Rikki Fulton, aren't you?'

'That's right,' I replied shyly.

'I thought so,' she said. 'You're with the Pantheon Club!'

That rather took the wind out of my sails.

On the other hand, it was comforting to know that at least London still remembered me. While Wee Alec and I were moving into the Aberdeen season (I remembered I mustn't talk to late-comers) I received an unexpected call to ask if I would take over the Sunday show at The Prince of Wales. *Sunday at the London*

263

Palladium was due a rest period. I agreed happily, but I wasn't quite so happy by the time I arrived in London.

The *Five Past Eight* uniform was a full set of evening dress tails and that was what I wanted to wear for the London show.

Oh, I don't think tails would be appropriate, said the wardrobe mistress. I don't think you should say that, said Billy Marsh. I don't think you should tell that joke. I think we should wear a nice white tuxedo, said the wardrobe mistress, I wouldn't tell that joke if I were you, said Billy Marsh, it's a bit too well known. . . . And so it went on. It was mercilessly boring.

'Could you make it for us every Sunday?' Billy Marsh asked after the break.

'I'll tell you when I've decided how I feel, when the show is over,' I replied.

The director was screaming at the Floor Manager for time apparently. Could Rikki get him time. I began to dislike the whole set-up.

When the next item on the programme came up, I introduced it in something like five seconds, and as I came off the stage I paused in front of Billy Marsh and said: 'Oh, by the way Mr. Marsh, you can stick your show where it hurts most!'

Hardly polite, but succinct. I was never so glad to get out of London.

* * *

I didn't think I would meet Tommy Steele quite so soon again, but here I was in the Royal Court in Liverpool. Ethel and I had landed in rather famous digs. Mrs. Bright was Rob Wilton's landlady. He and his wife had given up the bother of keeping house, and had made their home with Mrs. Bright.

We were appearing in *Goldilocks*, the 1957/8 panto, and young Tommy was experiencing his first panto. In one way he must have been very happy when he was told that the entire eleven-week run had been completely booked out, but he had to face the gallery which was completely stacked out with university students. Why they chose to disrupt the show is not clear. Tommy had only been in the business for twelve months, he hadn't had enough time to have made enemies. The students had set up what they saw as great fun. Every time Tommy appeared they opened newspapers and covered the entire gallery with them, and then came the cat-calls. They were enjoying their childish prank without giving a thought to the rest of the audience. I was quite ready to take them on but I had to try and keep my 'barbs' in line with the panto scenario.

It was early in the panto when they started. I was pretty sure they were on reconnaissance, and, sure enough, a few performances later, their major attack had been carefully worked out. The newspapers were held up, and at a given signal, the cat-calls and so-called witticisms came fast and furious.

I had to say to the management that the production could not go on—and for the first time in my career, I experienced the curtain having to come down.

The management had no option but to offer the members of our audience their money back. There was no way that a performance could have been set up at a later date. There were no seats to be had right up to the end of the season, and Tommy and I had other commitments to deal with.

As if to compound their callous stupidity, a group—probably the hierarchy who had conceived the plan—came to my dressing-room to actually congratulate me for having stood up to them. I did point out to these young sadists that many, many people had come with their children to see Tommy Steele, but they were there not to enjoy the pantomime, more to indulge their own sadistic pleasures.

There was nothing we could do, but the Liverpool community

made clear their disapproval of how deliberately disruptive the university students had been, and, so far as I know, there have been no further problems.

*   *   *

While in Liverpool I was becoming worried, and no one worries as much as I do. I was aware that I would have to get down to preparing the material for the 1958 *Five Past Eight* in Edinburgh, and I had never been able to write away from home. I don't know why, and I still can't, unless I'm in my study among my reference books.

I sent a telegram to Howard & Wyndham's head office, telling them I had a problem. This caused a panic, and I got a reply by return that they would expect me to arrive in London around midday to discuss the matter. I explained my problem, that I was being asked to appear before the same audience in Edinburgh time and time again, and had, therefore, to produce new material constantly, and that life would be easier if I was able to use material I had already written and performed, as this would help me breathe and prepare for the next show.

The Powers were understanding and, as a result, I was rerouted from Edinburgh to the Alhambra in Glasgow, where I would share the bill with Stanley Baxter. This made life much easier.

Dance Party Roof was an STV programme for youngsters, which I compèred in much the same way as I did in London, but with much less class. It was, however, a very important pathway for the late Andy Stewart who took over from me when I had to leave to join Stanley Baxter in *Five Past Eight* at the Alhambra.

I enjoyed working with Stanley. He had employed a writer called Stan Mars who, apart from creating material, would be available for small parts in sketches. He was, in fact, a better writer than performer. Jack Radcliffe and Jimmy Logan were not exactly happy when they were sent to Edinburgh, while Stanley and I had the enormous pleasure of The Alhambra.

Stanley and I got along very well. I admired his preparation for a performance, his precision, his talent for impression, his attention to detail. We were miles apart, and Stanley had made it clear he couldn't, or didn't want to, cope with ad libs, but there was a moment when in reply to an ad lib I had made, Stanley came out with a brilliant response.

I was never quite sure if 'Francie and Josie' had been a brainwave of Stanley's or an idea from Stan Mars, but the scripts were not great, and Stan, Stanley and myself had to sit around and throw ideas and jokes around in the hope that we would have something to work with.

But that season provided the grass roots of the 'Francie and Josie' that we know, as created by myself and Jack Milroy.

Coming into the Alhambra for a rehearsal with Stanley, I found a character we knew as Mario. It was always possible to identify him, even from a distance, because of the array of cameras he had hanging around him. I got the impression that he was very excited for some reason, and so thankful that I had appeared. He started to babble that Mister Cary Grant, the film star, was coming to visit the Alhambra because at one time he had performed there. Mario wanted me to stand by and welcome this great star. I presumed my leg was being pulled and laughed it off, but as I left Mario and moved towards the stage door, I saw this incredibly handsome man appear round the corner. It was indeed Cary Grant approaching from the front of the theatre. A man who was not only wonderfully handsome, but one of the greatest actors ever, especially when it came to the throw-away.

He approached me and held out his hand, saying politely that he was very pleased to meet me. I dutifully shook his hand and responded, perhaps not in a way he would have expected!

I gazed into that God-given face and voice and said:

'Thank you very glad!'

Ad libs were my stock in trade, though I had always been terrified of doing or saying something unexpected in a television studio. It's all very well on stage, but a television studio is so tightly controlled, and the programmes were 'live' in the fifties, so an ad lib could not have been cut or changed, and even if it could it would have wrecked the director's camera-script. But on this occasion I could not avoid the simple ad lib I had let loose.

*   *   *

It was about this time that I got the longest laugh of my career. David Hughes—he of the double chin which he insisted had to be made up—was a delightful man who died much too young. I was doing one of the sketches I had performed in *Five Past Eight*. This was Rikaivitch Fultonoffski. The act took David and Rikaivitch into an argument about the brilliant inventions of their respective countries. David claimed that it was Baird who invented television in 1903 (which was rubbish), but Rikaivitch even claimed that it was his country that had 'inwented telewision in nineteen-0-fwee. In fact we even inwented nineteen-0-fwee!'

During the so-called argument, Rikaivitch says to David: 'Are you standing there *with your double chins all made up* to tell me . . . ?'

At this point Eric Robinson's huge orchestra burst into uncontrollable laughter (they were aware of David's self-consciousness about his double chin). The audience rose to the orchestra's laughter, and it became the longest laugh I have ever experienced. Not only that, but it brought me a great number of invitations to be a guest in many of the programmes like Billy Cotton, Vera Lynn, David Nixon, and then my own television show from Shepherd's Bush.

*   *   *

The 1959 *Five Past Eight* show had been reprogrammed to appear more like a London West End revue. It meant the sketches would be shorter, but there would be more of them. So I wrote accordingly. The show had been moved from the King's to the Lyceum in Edinburgh. The performers were myself, Clem Ashby and Ethel (the Comic's Labourers, as we used to call the straight men or women), then there were Edith Macarthur, Jean Bayliss, Eileen Gourlay, Peter Butterworth and Janet Brown, and Digby Wolfe who was particularly unpopular, and spent most of his time listening through the Tannoy and writing down every word performed by any of his colleagues. Eventually he was more or less run out of Britain, but did rather well in America and, I think, in Australia. But if any comedian had caught sight of him in this country, I think a contract might well have been taken out on him.

When we opened the show it seemed it was going particularly well, but Stewart Cruikshank, our boss, was unhappy. He was aware that he had made a serious error in casting. I was very happy with the reception I had received, but it was true, as Stewart Cruikshank had realised, that the Scottish audiences preferred their own favourites.

Stewart Cruikshank promised me that he would make sure the cast would be entirely Scottish the following year (1960), and give me all the support I needed.

From this seedling, there grew a double act of delightful popularity.

I was attending one of Jimmy Logan's parties after the 1959 season. We were in a rather small room which had an upright piano in it. I had been at one of those parties before and, like most pros, I preferred a chinwag to the guests having to 'do a turn'. So I sought out Jack Milroy and asked him what his next engagement was, and how he had coped with the Gaiety Theatre summer after summer, playing to the same audience. I asked him if he would be interested in joining me in the *Five Past Eight* show, and he said 'yes' without hesitation. I contacted Stewart Cruikshank immediately and that was the beginning of our long career together.

*　　　*　　　*

Ethel and I went off on a 17-day Mediterranean cruise on the *S.S. Chusan* that year. We were not expecting to meet the owner of The Barras, but here was the famous Sam McIver and his wife. We made one of our stops at Casablanca (shades of Bogart), and arranged to go ashore together to have a look at the city. We were warned to be alive to the number of pickpockets around, but Mrs. McIver was unmoved. 'Listen,' she said. 'If they waant ma diamonds they'll huv tae cut ma bliddy fingers aff!'

Leaving the ship we had a long walk towards the city. There were stalls all along the one side. The Moroccans were out in force screaming at us: 'Come and buy. Come and buy. Bargain! Bargain!' They came right across our path and Sammy's reply was simple and to the point. 'Naw,' he said determinedly, 'Ah'm no' wantin' nothin'.

A huge Moroccan called after him: 'Hey, you from Glas-gow?'

That stopped us in our tracks. Sammy was astounded, as we all were.

'Wait a minute,' he said. 'How did you know Ah wis fae Glasgow?'

The large gentleman replied. 'Aw Jesus Christ,' he said. 'Everybody come from Glas-gow!'

43

THE ADVENTURES OF FRANCIE & JOSIE

JACK MILROY AND I gelled together immediately when we first walked down to greet our audience in 1960. It was clear this *Five Past Eight* was going to be fun, and the audience immediately warmed to their new stars. *Five Past Eight* at the Alhambra in Glasgow and King's Theatre in Edinburgh had a programming plan to overcome the problem of certain members of the audience who were more interested in what the bars were offering than what was on offer on stage, and reckoned they could just manage 'that extra hauf' before they went back and unsettled the rest of the audience. So the psychology was that the opening number to begin the second act would be short, 'the stars' would appear in 'a big sketch', and the latecomers wouldn't want to miss anything—so they would return to their seats in good time.

Francie and Josie as performed by Jack and myself was certainly different, with all the ad libs flying about. It was from these unexpected lines that many of our best routines developed, provided I could remember them and polish them up.

That was how the 'Arbroath Gag' came about.

· The routine was supposed to find Francie and Josie in front of the tabs for only two or three minutes while the major scene was being put in place, but there were times when we became so engrossed in our conversation that they couldn't get us to leave the stage. These were challenges to each other on stage, hence some great material emerged. Ten minutes was nothing to us, but our producer, Michael Mills, would be tearing his hair out. The major scene would long since have been set up, but Francie and Josie were still enjoying their discussion.

One of the early sketches found Francie and Josie, having seen the burds home, seeking shelter in a haunted house. Suddenly faced with a Frankensteinian monster followed by a Mummy, Francie and Josie were terrified. Francie, hiding behind Josie's shoulder, said: 'Tell 'im the one about the Arbroath, Josie.' And, of course, came the bit where Josie, not very skilled at telling jokes, did his best with Francie prompting him—leaving the poor young dancers who played the parts of the Monster and the Mummy wondering what to do next!

This must have been one of the most popular routines we had ever accidentally created. As Johnnie Beattie remarked at the opening of the newly-refurbished Gaiety Theatre in Ayr: 'I've heard of a request for a well-known song, but I've never heard of a request for a comedy routine!'

On one occasion we held up the proceedings while we had a twelve-minute dissertation on how marmalade is made!

It was, and still is, a unique partnership. When the *Five Past Eight* season had ended we went our different ways. Jack to the Pavilion panto, and I to the Alhambra, the Edinburgh King's or even the Theatre Royal in Newcastle.

*   *   *

In 1960 Freddie Carpenter had decided on a dramatic change from the well-known fairy-tale stories.

I had found myself in the Pavilion some years before. I don't remember what panto it was, but I loved its Scottishness, the kilts, the sashes, the pipes, the dancers in full dress tartan. When I learned that a full-blown, very Scottish panto called *A Wish for Jamie* was to be the panto for 1960 at the Alhambra I was over the moon. Kenneth McKellar and I starred along with Fay Lenore, Ethel (who made a tremendous hit as the little old Fairy), and Clem Ashby. Then there was Russell Hunter as the King Frog who makes a covenant with Jamie that he will free the princess if Jamie will swap his magnificent singing voice. The play was written by a very clever young man called John Law, and a truly delightful story it was.

The panto was an astonishing hit. But the curious thing about it was during the dress rehearsal, which Stewart Cruikshank always attended. At the end of the rehearsal he got out of his seat and started to walk out. Freddie was very upset when Mr. Cruikshank turned on him. 'They'll eat you for this, Freddie,' he said. 'They'll eat you!' And he walked out.

Mr. Cruikshank had made a rare error of judgement. The public loved it!

He always brought his mother with him on an opening night, and she would sit in her box like a member of Royalty. Mr. Cruikshank always sat in the stalls in row 'F' at the aisle so that he would have room to stick his gammy leg out.

There was a standing ovation at the interval when the pipes and drums came on the stage and down into the auditorium followed by the entire cast of characters. This was mightily unusual. When the second half started, Mr. Cruikshank was in the box beside his mother and indulging his favourite hobby—watching the audience.

The box office was inundated, and Cruikshank had to steal a couple of weeks from the show that was to follow. Even then there was an enormous crush.

There was only one thing to be done, and Cruikshank did it. He decided to repeat the production with the same cast the following year. And it was just the same—the Alhambra was packed to the gunnels for 1961 as well.

Eric Maschwitz saw *A Wish for Jamie* in 1961. I was due to do three shows down in London, but he decided instead that he would approve three network Rikki Fulton shows produced in Glasgow—'among his own people' as he put it.

He asked me if there was someone special in BBC Scotland I would wish to have producing the shows. This seemed a possible opening for the healing of the relationship with Eddie Fraser. So I nominated him.

We got along all right. I thought he might be interested in the *Five Past Eight* show in Edinburgh, which he had obviously never seen, and I was explaining that Francie and Josie had become a great attraction and the Edinburgh audiences were loving them. There was a very particular Saturday in Edinburgh when the people trying to leave the theatre found it almost as impossible, as our audience were trying to get in. There was a complete jam of cars and buses and people. I was so sorry I didn't have a camera. It was a dramatic sight.

I pointed out the popularity of the 'gruesome twosome' in the Edinburgh King's, and suggested to Eddie that it would make a super comedy series.

I can still remember his answer. 'Oh,' he said. 'I don't think that would work at all.'

It was at this point I realised that he had been handing out two of the three programmes which Maschwitz had pledged to me. It was as if they were sweeties. Andy Stewart and Jimmy Logan profited by that little decision—not that they could have been aware. Eddie's attitude seemed to suggest that he would be happy to get the first one finished and done with, which would allow him to work on the programmes for Andy and Jimmy, his favourites.

Eddie had never seen Francie and Josie in action, and obviously wasn't remotely interested. But Gerry Le Grove was. He was the Head of Programmes for Scottish Television. He had asked me to do four Sunday spectaculars, but I suggested that 'spectaculars' were a little old-fashioned now. The picture I drew was of these red and blue characters—along with scripts ready and waiting—who were a great success in the theatre. I suggested that such a series might run away with us.

'Oh, please,' he cried. 'Please give me something that will run away with us!'

We were due to start rehearsals in October of that year, but Equity had decreed a strike of all things. It seemed very strange to me—in view of the threat posed by television, the theatres should be making every effort to pull people in. To keep people out was insanity.

However, it didn't last long, and by April 1962 the pros could get on with their business.

We managed to get Aberdeen taken off the schedule for *Five Past Eight*. We were convinced that it would be more profitable to come to the Glasgow King's for *Half Past Seven* and run the Alhambra *5P8* in tandem rather than suffer Aberdeen—it seemed to us that only Andy Stewart and the Alexander Brothers could bring in the punters up there.

It was worth a trial, but despite our individual popularity at the Alhambra and Pavilion theatres, Jack and I were signally failing to fill the seats of the Glasgow King's.

We found it perplexing in view of the rave notices and complete sell-outs which were the hallmarks of *A Wish for Jamie* at the Alhambra and *Five Past Eight* at the King's in Edinburgh. I was possibly taking it less philosophically than Jack, although he often hides his feelings, an example of our disparate natures offstage. So many times I stood at the long mirror in my dressing-room and stared at my made-up face and comic costume as Jack and I went through some sketch or other which had created hysteria in

275

Edinburgh, but was now dragging itself to an early unmarked grave in front of a handful of mourners.

I kept asking the reflected clown what he thought he was doing there; and worse, what he thought he could do if he followed the yearning of a heavy heart and quit. I was severely depressed.

Fortunately such depressions are limited by the extent of the run and, in the meantime, we had available to us that ancient and highly efficacious panacea so well known to our profession. At the end of a long, hard and disappointing night, Jack would come into my room and, in the dark, lonely silence of the empty theatre we would get thoroughly and determinedly pissed.

Full of whisky and brandy respectively, and coping magnificently with the heaving pavement, we would bid each other fond farewells and swear oaths of undying friendship—as well as other, greater oaths of infinite variety and invention, all aimed at the audience which had not long quit the theatre. With much giggling each would insist on seeing the other into his car, sometimes the wrong car and forgetting where the clutch was kept, only to realise that the trick was impossible even for seasoned performers like ourselves. Making do with extravagant hand-waving out of open windows and great shouts exhorting the other to take care, Jack would roar off across the river to Ralston, while I would zig-zag sedately to the West End, both of us much more philosophical about the show and life in general, convinced that, given time, the King's audience, like our Edinburgh audience, would come to love us!

It was difficult to understand why, when this wish was granted so dramatically, we were totally unprepared for it.

Jack had taken himself off for his favourite break before panto which was to sit in a London café and 'watch the world go by'. When the first episodes of *The Adventures of Francie and Josie* hit the small screen, the series was being transmitted to Scotland and Northern Ireland only. Consequently Jack was unaware of the staggeringly warm welcome it received from press and public, children, adults and the elderly.

I had reason to go to London, to see my agent and at the same time to give Jack the wonderful news. The children were doing The Walk, people had come to use 'Hullawrerr' rather than 'Hello'. Men finished their pint and hauf, and made for home to settle at the telly. Similarly, a mother had only to call that Francie and Josie were on the telly, and in seconds the streets were cleared of children. Jack couldn't believe the impact the series had made on the viewers. It perhaps had much to do with the fact that it was a series for the Scottish viewers only. We were in great demand for advertising—Jack got a tremendously good deal for his new car for example. Then we were approached by a Mr. George Lochiel Brown who was running British Relay, a TV Rental company, who asked if we would open the new shops they were planning. We said 'yes' rather quickly. Things seemed to be going our way again.

The first opening was in Airdrie. We were driven round the roads to the square in a truck, waving to anybody and everybody, and everybody waved back. They also wanted to shake our hands, and one enthusiastic member of the public was loth to let go of my hand, wanting to hang on to my pinkie for a souvenir. The shop window was smashed with the pressure of the crowds trying to get close to us. I have no idea how many British Relay shops we opened, but after Airdrie every shop window had to be protected.

An extraordinary phenomenon, we thought!

We returned to the Glasgow King's with heavy hearts, assuming we would be performing to empty seats as usual. The café just across the road from the theatre was where we met for breakfast. Coffee and a bacon roll. We were furious when, as we advanced towards the King's Theatre, we saw this enormous queue which stretched from the theatre to what was once Newton Street. I immediately sought out the manager and told him I thought it was totally unfair of him to be selling tickets for the pantomime when we had only just arrived for our season of *Half Past Seven*.

He did try to explain, but it wasn't the explanation I had expected. When he was able to get a word in he said: 'But this queue is for you and Jack! Look at the makeshift cards that say GALLERY ONLY.'

It was joyful news. It looked as if we had cracked it. And to add to our delight, we both had pantomimes on the list. Jack at the Pavilion and me at the Alhambra with a new storyline for Ken and me—*A Love for Jamie*, the sequel to *A Wish for Jamie*.

But there was more. So successful was *Half Past Seven* now, that Cruikshank asked us to do three weeks in the Alhambra, which would otherwise be dark. Unfortunately Jack took ill and I had to hold the fort. At the walk-down Ethel whispered in my ear: 'I was proud of you!'

It was a long time since she had said anything like that to me. Too late, I thought, too late! Ethel and I were now going our own ways. We even drove to the theatre in our own cars. It was well known. We had only been in our home for some three years and it was obvious that the fabric of our relationship had almost completely eroded. Ethel likened our relationship to that between a brother and sister, rather than a husband and wife. That said it all.

44

GOOSE!

A LOVE FOR JAMIE, like its predecessor, sold out, and was repeated in 1963. Kenneth McKellar and I reminisced over those four profoundly enjoyable years many times, especially some of the jokes we played on each other. On one occasion a large number of characters were doing a scene in frontcloth which would take Ken into his songs. The net curtain came down to allow the other members of the cast to exit, and just as Ken walked forward, I put a tin of liquorice humbugs in his hand. He couldn't think what to do with them, so when the time came for him to leave the stage and come down into the auditorium, he put the tin of humbugs into the musical director's hand. He quickly passed it over to one of the dancers, who passed it on to a man sitting in the front stalls, who passed it on . . . and so it went on. Eventually it found its way back where it had come from!

My own favourite was when Ken as 'Jamie' was chained to a wall in the wicked wizard's domain. Beneath him were hundreds of snakes trying to reach him, and then I appeared in a white coat and a doorkeeper's cap, followed by the entire cast in their out-door coats—I was leading them on a sightseeing tour! Ken slipped his chains off with ease and leaned down to speak to us, but I told him I was too busy to speak to him. And Ken said: 'Yes, I'm pretty tied up myself!' as he slipped back into his chains.

These shows were truly tremendous fun.

1963 was another interesting year, for a number of reasons. For one, Jack and I received the Personalities of the Year Award from Lord Goodman at a 'do' in the Trades Hall in Glasgow.

In an effort to see if we could make a new beginning, Ethel and I snatched a holiday in Torquay before we went back to another season of *Five Past Eight* at the Edinburgh King's. It was a very pleasant break; it wasn't as if we were at daggers drawn, we were hoping to rekindle a fire that had long since turned to ashes, and I think we both had doubts. But, curiously, when we were working in Edinburgh in 1964, and living in Cramond, there was an unexpected change in our relationship. Ethel had the thought that since we were in our forties we should have a complete check-up. Sadly that suggestion would prove to be prophetic. Our health was not in any real doubt—it was the marriage that was failing.

It was the best of times, it was the worst of times. Even though I had approached the end of my fourth decade with dismay and the occasional twinge of nostalgia, I would later come to remember my forties as one of the most interesting, most exciting, and most rewarding of my life—so far.

As a new, if reluctant, conscript to Middle Age, it seemed an appropriate time to take stock. The career was cracking merrily along, but I was conscious of the fact that I had reached the recommended time when a thorough check of the state of the body was more important.

Ethel and I duly made an appointment and turned up at the door of a house in Park Circus.

I have no idea why I felt so chirpy. I suppose it was because I was feeling extraordinarily well. And perhaps because if the worst came to the worst and there was something amiss, this was the day it would be discovered and dealt with.

I rang the doorbell with complete confidence.

The door was opened by a young woman in a white receptionist's coat which she wore like it was the latest design from Yves St. Laurent. She was tall, slim and beautiful. Standing slightly below her because of the front steps, I couldn't help take in the long, elegant legs. When I eventually managed to drag my eyes away from the legs, I looked up and gasped at the flame-coloured hair framing the lovely face and the unbelievable emerald-green eyes.

Everything about her screamed class!

This was one very cool, confident lady, very sure of herself and well aware of her looks. I began to wonder if I was too old to study medicine and get myself a receptionist like her.

I gave her one of my special smiles and said: 'Good morning. I'm Rikki Fulton. I hear you do a wonderful barium meal!'

She smiled a strange sort of knowing little smile and lowered her long lashes.

'Yes, we do,' she said. 'Won't you come in.'

'Thank you,' I said as Ethel and I entered the house. 'Oh, and by the way, could I have chips with mine?'

Again a flicker of that little smile.

We followed her into the house, and she showed us into our cubicles and asked each of us to take our clothes off and put on a blue gown—and tie it back to front. We were the first on the list, and I had no idea that there were several people reading magazines as they waited their turn. What they must have thought when they saw me walking up and down the corridor, my entire back torso uncovered for all to see, and doing funny walks at that!

I was first to go in and meet the radiographer. He was a large man and, with the strange red-coloured glasses, he looked like a huge bear with sunglasses on. He bade me lie on the table and just relax. Would I be good enough to turn onto my right side. Splendid. This was a dawdle. It was very dark on the other side, but I had the feeling that there was someone else there. A nurse, perhaps? The bear asked me if I would be good enough to just bend my left leg. That wasn't difficult, but my eyes popped and my hair stood on end when I realised I had been well and truly goosed. When the lights came up I could see the Ginger Lady standing there, but this time with a huge grin and a tube in her hand!

I had no idea you could eat a meal that way!

*   *   *

Still on the trail of some sort of compromise, in November Ethel and I set off on a special holiday to America. We left from Prestwick on a freezing cold morning to stay in New York at the Waverley (I think) for a few days, before going on to Los Angeles which was enjoying an Indian Summer. We saw the making of some of the television programmes. What interested me in particular was that they brought in two audiences for the shows and could put right any problems at the second sitting. I was tickled to see Ann Miller, the queen of tap and with the longest legs I have ever seen. She wasn't happy with the first take, and I was amazed to realise that she had already recorded her tap dance. I had never heard of an artiste who could mime to her own tap dance.

We had also been given tickets for the Dick Van Dyke show. It was interesting to see how the Americans did it as compared to how we did. It was even more interesting when the producer of the show asked if I would play the part of an Englishman in the next episode for them. I explained that we were on holiday, and in any case I didn't have a work permit.

We moved on to Hawaii where Ethel had relatives. We were booked into a lovely hotel called the Halakilani (that may not be the way to spell it, but that's what it sounded like). It was a wonderful thought that we would be thousands of miles from anybody we knew. The minute I approached the reception desk a girl shouted at me. 'HULLAWRERR!' she screamed delightedly. So we had a chat, but we were there, I hoped, to seek peace and quiet. They didn't have rooms, they had delightful little huts and

I couldn't believe the courtesy that seemed to come naturally to these people. I had hired a car, and I couldn't count the number of times some other driver would actually stop to let me pass. I wished fervently that we in Britain could adopt the same kind of friendly courtesy. Ever since that experience I have enjoyed helping fellow car drivers where possible. The resultant wave of thanks makes it well worth while.

Anyway, we returned from America to Prestwick and got down to the preparation of the second presentation of *A Love for Jamie*. This really was something that had never happened before. It was even considered as a possible production for the West End of London, although I'm not at all sure that the stars would have been particularly interested.

45

FRANCIE & JOSIE:
A HISTORY LESSON

DURING THE MENTAL TORTURE of creating our material for *Kings High 1990*, it occurred to me that, while most people are vaguely aware of the background details of Jack and myself as private citizens, few, if any, know anything at all of the *curricula vitae* of our alter egos, Francie and Josie; an omission I tried to put right with the following:

> Francis ('Francie') McKenzie was born unexpectedly on the second bottom stair of the third landing of a tenement in Govanhill—a building long since demolished in his honour!
>
> His precipitate birth was the result of an incorrect diagnosis of her own condition by his mother who was convinced it was wind, when a nosy neighbour called to her wittily: 'Ah see yer up the spout again, Rosemary,' as she was taking the ashes down to the midden. Mrs. McKenzie was so startled that she missed a step and proceeded in undignified fashion from the fourth to the third landing where she was assisted with Francie's unheralded début by an itinerant coalman.
>
> 'It was nothing,' the coalman said later. 'I was making a delivery anyway.'
>
> A few years later Joseph ('Josie') Tierney was found

outside the front (indeed the *only*) door of a single-ended establishment on the top landing of a tenement in Dennistoun, and taken in with twelve bottles of milk and two dozen morning rolls. The family of which he thus became a part was both Catholic and large, and did not even notice the sudden increase in their number.

In the 1930s the McKenzie family moved to Dennistoun and occupied the room-and-kitchen apartment opposite the Tierneys with whom they became firm friends, throwing wild parties, drinking Pepsi Cola with aspirin and dancing to Linguaphone records. It was here that the two boys met and became inseparable chums. It was from here also that one day a short time later, while Francie and Josie were at school, their respective families ran away together. Alone and obviously unwanted, the boys immediately sold all the furniture and left to complete their upbringing with the only relative they could turn to—Francie's Auntie Jessie, who lived adjacent to the Coocaddens Labour Exchange, a fact that was to be so advantageous later in their lives.

Their schooldays were spent at a backward school for forward children. Aunt Jessie well remembers waving them off on their first morning with their little schoolbags, their comics, their play-pieces, their fags and their shaving kits.

In due course they managed to get the School Cert (not both at once, you understand. She was most certainly not into that sort of thing).

Francie excelled at book-keeping, making book on exam results and the changing colour of the history teacher's hair. Josie, too, was a book lover. As somebody said: 'A book is a man's best friend outside of a dog. And inside of a dog it's too dark to read anyway.'

They both remember with warm nostalgia the class of 69, which was a lot of pupils even for those days, and which boasted such distinguished former pupils as Sir Alexander Fleming—(he wasn't knighted then, of course), Adolf Eichmann, Lord Lucan, and the daughter of the Chinese consul who, because of her disregard for personal freshness, was known as Hi Pong.

At the outbreak of World War Two it was suggested by their headmaster that Francie and Josie should be evacuated. This received widespread approval from the entire staff and they were duly shipped off to Dunkirk.

On completing what is laughingly referred to as their education, they went directly into positions of considerable responsibility as shop stewards for the Nyucks Association of Frustrated Flatulence Sufferers (NYAFFS) in the Coocaddens Labour Exchange, for which service they were eventually honoured to receive engraved Mickey Mouse watches which, like themselves, never worked.

Our television series ran for three years. Jack was of the opinion that we could do this for the rest of our lives, but I felt that the press were beginning to feel that we had had sufficient accolades and the time was ripe for a bit of criticism. So we pulled the plug on the television series, and if and when we were in the mood to do so, we could always set up another show.

At long last in 1965 we were starring in the *Five Past Eight* show at the Alhambra, although it was my view that it was now too late. At the same time our final television series was transmitted, and I was directing *See How They Run* at the King's Theatre with Duncan Macrae at the same time. I can't remember, but it may well have been Duncan's last performance. He died in 1967.

*   *   *

The following is a letter written to Tom Shields, famous for his Diary in the *Herald*, on an occasion when Francie and Josie were seriously disturbed (so what's new?), when their beloved Glasgow dialect had come under attack:

Sir,

We could not believe wur ears when we conceived the diary the other day in what Tom Shields appeared to disride the Glasgow patwah. After all, us Glaswegians are already impaled with the burden of wur enthic indentification because, admittedly, some of us do not metriculate wur words properly and are at times, therefour, slightly incomprehensive. For too long Scottish people in general, and Glasgow people in particular, has been subjugatit to the debilitating situation in which they are not understood by the English, or that they are told that they do not sound Scottish (from which Francie and me has often suffered), which is rich coming from people whose accents have to be seen to be believed.

It is oblivious to me that very few of wur Scottish cultyers ever gets past Beattock (and that goes fur the trains as well, by the way). A particular example is found in wur own profession. For many years our Scottish performers, even in the depth of their popularity, never got the chance to do their stuff south of Wentford because they were told that they were not understandable. Those who has made it across the border have did so only because they were prepared to use infected accents.

So what does the future hold for us? Is it to be like the well-known Bibulous stories of Moses that our great Scottish tribe has to suffer similar ante-seminal feelings for all maternity?

Only time will tell.

Yours,

Francie and Josie, Coocaddens.

46

KISS ME KATE

I HAD ALWAYS APPRECIATED Francis Essex's work with LWT.
His productions were innovative, distinctively different, and always enjoyable. When he took over as Head of Programmes for
Scottish Television it looked as if a change for Jack and me could
be on the cards. Instead of keeping the two of us together for 1966,
we were each given our own show. This was all very well, but
what kind of shows would they be?

I had a series of half-hour sit-com sketches called simply *Rikki*.
Jack had a better series of variety programmes. But both were
unmitigated disasters. So far as we can remember, Francis Essex
produced Jack's shows personally, while I was in the hands of the
Fat Boy, Brian Izzard. We were both in the hands of the Philistines.

In my own case, the scripts were rushed up from London and
we had little or no time to read them, or do rewrites when necessary—which was most of the time. The scenery was already in the
process of being built and the show was transmitted within a few
days.

The press had a field day. We were slaughtered. Jack was
appearing at the Gaiety in Ayr, and the press were doing incredible damage to the box office. He had a word with the editors and
the savage critiques calmed down. But I was still in deep water—
and drowning. In my personal opinion Izzard should have been

banned altogether. The rubbish that we were putting out would have been enough to demolish any performer's reputation, indeed the rest of his career. The late, splendid Bill Brown of STV once described Izzard as being 'totally unable to even organise a children's picnic!'

I called a halt and demanded that they take the series off. Which they did. Francis Essex was a bit miffed about some of the things I had been saying about his department. He was aggrieved and complained to me. My reply to him was that he should, perhaps, find out what the canteen were saying about *him*!

There was a certain irony about the fact that the last call for Izzard's utterly ridiculous direction came on the same Sunday in May 1966 that Ethel said goodbye. I had no idea that she had so carefully and brilliantly organised her exit from our home. A friend in London had arranged an apparently delightful apartment, and the skips and cases had already gone. Our marriage of seventeen years was definitely over.

I stood at the window and watched her as she climbed into a cab. I felt so incredibly sad. We waved to each other knowing it was the end of everything.

* * *

I spent much of the summer driving down into foreign territory and visiting some of the performers I had worked with or at least recognised. Bridlington was one of the most unbelievable areas I had ever seen. Holidaymakers were kicked out after breakfast and were not allowed to return to the boarding house until it was time for a meagre cup of tea and digestive biscuit. I noticed a woman sitting against the esplanade wall covered with warm clothes and a travelling rug, determined to make the most of her pathetic holiday come rain or shine.

It was at this time also that my father died. I was down in

London when I received news that he had been taken into hospital. I returned to Glasgow, planning to go immediately to see him, but by the time I arrived it was too late.

It was indeed a time of endings.

*   *   *

At home there was a request from, of all people, Eddie Fraser, to be Moira Anderson's guest for one of her programmes. I wrote a special comedy act which was entirely in mime, the fun being the interruptions the maestro of a large orchestra had to suffer from the audience. It wasn't possible to write down mime in the way you could write a script, so Eddie asked me to give him notes that would tell him when I would be facing the 'orchestra', or facing the 'audience' with sound effects such as the sound of walking feet, coughing etc.

When the programme was complete, we discovered he had shot it backside foremost. Eddie's plea to me was: 'It wasn't *too* bad, was it?'

He had ruined a rather good act. He wasn't much better than Izzard. If as good.

But for me it was now Wine, Women and Freedom.

Foster's were my agents for a while, but I had a severe dislike for Foster himself. This was Shylock in real life. He had a habit of writing letters and filing them with a view to using them if litigation ever took place. I had only one way to get out of his clutches and that was to say thanks but no thanks to Howard & Wyndham and accept an offer from the Alexandra Theatre in Birmingham with The Four Monarchs and Des O'Connor.

I really had a ball there. Back home I had a wonderful dear lady who had been my housekeeper since Ethel and I had first lived in the house. This was Mrs. Wares. I knew all would be well, but what would she think when she realised what was about to follow when I got home? Whatever happened, I knew she would always be very circumspect.

I had set up two channels for darts, and a table tennis area. Sir Ian Stewart was a pal of mine and Sean Connery was a pal of his. This is how Clem Ashby and I met him. Here we were, four guys either living apart, divorced or thinking about it. Much wine was taken in those days. One of our favourite challenges was to pin a fiver to the 'bull' of a dartboard, stand with our backs to the board, bend down and throw a dart at the fiver from between the legs. A bit dangerous, but worth a fiver. On one occasion Ian Stewart, Sean, Clem and Jackie Stewart came to the house after watching Francie and Josie at work in the Pavilion. We had a table tennis challenge. Jackie Stewart won the game—but then he was the only one who was sober. He was racing the following day. A positively delightful man.

Word got around about the darts and table tennis. Sometimes the 'games room' was packed with chums, who always brought a bottle, and the cigarette smoke was such that we could hardly see the dartboards. And when we opened the windows, I was sure we would have a call from the local fire station. At times I was also concerned that any young children passing by the open windows might well learn some language which would not be acceptable to their parents.

I was really enjoying my life. I could come and go as I pleased. Stay out all night if I felt like it, and had the privilege of escorting some of the most attractive ladies a man could wish for. There was a price to pay, however. When the parties, or ladies I had escorted that evening, had made for home, usually about dawn or in the early morning, I felt very lonely and depressed, and even worse when I was wakened by dear Mrs. Wares who regarded me as her third son, and could recognise a hangover when she saw one. It was often a question of lying flat on the floor and having to hang on.

Living in a fairly large house all by myself, I was naturally grateful for the chums' company, and looked forward to the next *soirée*. So I spent a lot of time on the driving range every day, putting myself in the hands of the pro and then playing eighteen holes at my own club in Balmore. I remember once standing on the twelfth tee, wondering if I would ever get around to marrying again, and what sort of girl it might be.

One day Ian, Sean and I were heading for a round on the Prestwick course. We were picking up Glen Michael, and Sean, who looked as despondent as I did, came up with the all-important question: 'Would you think of getting married again?' 'I don't think so,' I said. 'How about you?' He thought for a moment, then said: 'No, I don't think I'll get married again!'

As it happens all three of us did! Although I had no reason to expect that it was going to happen so soon and so unexpectedly.

For reasons I cannot explain, I was preparing a short summer season at His Majesty's Theatre in Aberdeen managed by young Jimmy Donald. He was a splendid golfer who played off four. We had often had a game of golf when I was in town and I had wanted to try and at least make a game of it.

The show starred Moira Anderson and Terry Hall with Lenny the Lion. I thought these wonderful performers must help me bring in the public, but nothing had changed. They asked me to open this, present that, judge something else, but they refused to buy tickets.

I remember nipping across the short distance from the theatre to get a pack of cigarettes (I smoked in those days), and the lady in the tobacconists looked at me and said: 'Wail, wail, it's a laang time since we've seen you here. And whaur ur ye the noo?'

'Just across the bloody road!' I said.

'Oh,' she said. 'Ye mean the theetar. Aye, we jist hivna managed tae get in this year.'

I swore blind I would never enter His Majesty's Theatre ever again!

I can't help remembering W. C. Fields, who also had a particular audience to which he had an aversion. I thought I might adapt his epitaph for my own, which will say simply: 'IT SURE BEATS ABERDEEN'!

I feel I owe a debt of gratitude to the Giffnock Theatre Players. Having acted in a number of plays and directed many, I came to know a very handsome gentleman by the name of Bill Craig-Brown. A witty man, he wrote a humorous column for the *Evening Citizen*, called 'Clydeside Echoes'. We became good friends and on one occasion in 1950 he invited Ethel and me to dinner. I met his wife Nita and his fourteen-year-old daughter, Kate.

Kate was determined to be an actress and went on to attend the Edinburgh College of Speech and Drama. She wrote to me quite regularly over the years and I always replied. It was August 1967 when I received a letter asking if the show at His Majesty's was fully cast. I hadn't realised she lived in Portlethen, just outside Aberdeen, so I invited her to come and have a chat.

The fourteen-year-old had become an incredibly attractive young lady. She was a newsreader and continuity announcer with Grampian, Border, Ulster, Tyne Tees and STV. We were chatting when Jimmy Donald came in to say hello. He knew Kate from her appearances on television. Most people knew her in the area, and I wanted to get to know her much, much better. I simply couldn't take my eyes off her as she sat there, very smartly and tastefully dressed, speaking to Jimmy Donald. Her voice was music to listen to, and I could have listened all day to her delightful articulation. I could hear and feel the compassion in this girl. She was obviously very talented. I was aware, too, of a quick wit and a wise head.

This was a girl in a million. The show and its pathetic audience could go hang, I now had something really important to think about.

Clem Ashby and I were invited to dinner the following evening. Her husband was a gentle, pleasant man, and I thought 'how lucky could he be?' He and Clem got along swimmingly, but I made for the kitchen. I was more interested in hearing about Kate and her life. The fact that emerged was that her marriage had been over long ago also. That was a relief.

It was also the first wonderful kiss.

We met the following morning and sat in the house I had rented, and we talked for hours on end. She told me that when she was fourteen she had seen me in a play and fallen completely in love with me. She was now thirty-one, and I was forty-three—I reckoned we had both waited long enough, so I asked her to marry me. 'I thought you'd never ask,' she said.

The summer show in His Majesty's Theatre had cost me a good deal of money. I was all for pulling the plug, but the Donalds were anxious about how the press might see it. Their benevolence was overwhelming. They would cover the wages for the cast, 'but there'll be nothing for you,' said Dick Donald with charm. I agreed wholeheartedly, and although I had a serious dislike of the kind of audiences His Majesty's attracted, I was totally convinced that I was really the one who had profited, in a way that had nothing to do with money.

When I packed up and went home Katie, who would always be the love of my life, came home too!

47

HOME FROM HOME

KATIE AND I were settling down very happily. She wasn't too taken with the decor, but liked the house. My feelings exactly. So we set about some changes. At forty-four I figured I was still fit enough to do the redecoration with the help of a chum.

For some reason Ethel had decided that it would be necessary to have three guest bedrooms. I wasn't sure if she had expected a great many friends to stay over, or was planning to run a hotel. However, Katie and I had other ideas, and by the time we had finished, we had created a totally different house.

My divorce came through on 2nd March 1968. Ethel had been more than generous. No other names were mentioned, there were no problems whatsoever and it was over very quickly.

Katie and I had our first holiday together in Mallorca. Frank Ewing, who was the executive that dealt with the television commercials, had been asked by Mercury Holidays if I would be prepared to make a commercial for them. This was at a time when actors were inclined to pooh-pooh commercials because they felt it was rather demeaning. However, Frank had told them I was very expensive, but that I might say 'yes' if I could be paid by having a holiday for two laid on at one of their best hotels. We had a delightful fortnight at the Daina hotel in Puerto de Pollensa, which was the only hotel to have a pool at that time.

There was a lovely couple there who had saved up for a long time for their holiday. The man was a bus driver, and they were both somewhat rotund. Katie and I can still laugh about this delightful couple. He was teaching his wife to swim—but didn't seem to be able to swim himself. She was plowtering around like a dolphin that had taken the wrong turning, while he kept calling to her from a safe depth: ' 'AT'S IT! 'AT'S IT! KEEP YER ERM GAWIN' LIK 'AT!'

They really were a delight, these two.

It took only the first visit to create our love for Pollensa. We bought a little apartment and enjoyed it for many years, sometimes staying for as long as five weeks if commitments permitted, and even now we insist on a three-week break in our favourite hotel.

On our return home in October I had an engagement to appear in *The Old Time Music Hall* produced by Barney Colehan. I will never forget the pain of that performance, and I hoped I would never have to suffer like that again. I remember watching Johnny Victory the night before. The audience seemed to think it was their duty to heckle in the manner of a long-gone age of raucous response.

I was petrified. I will never know how I survived my few moments on stage. I was beginning to understand where my true strengths lay. It had taken some time, but I had come to understand that there were certain areas which were not my cup of tea. Variety was one of them. Perhaps it was because of my earlier acting experience. Perhaps, then, that was truly what I was—an actor.

*　　　*　　　*

Katie and I, in love with dogs, were conscious of something missing in both our lives. Therefore Jeeves and Jonathon (our beloved twin West Highland terriers) came with us when we stayed in Eynsham while appearing in *Babes in the Wood* at Oxford with Bruce Forsyth, whom I admire greatly. He is a multi-talented man but, unhappily, he failed to bring in the theatre folk on that occasion. Perhaps he had been seen on television too many times, or perhaps the kind of audience we were dealing with was similar to Aberdeen! I have always thought that there is grave danger in being over-exposed whether in the press or by constant appearances on any presentation, especially on television.

One of our little dogs, Jonathon, managed to eat his way through the kitchen wall, and large areas of the linoleum. This posed a challenge, but when Kate, the dogs and I were leaving, I managed to make sufficient repairs—much like a jigsaw puzzle—to allow us to leave with complete innocence. Certainly, we have never heard any more about it.

Katie's divorce came through while we were at Oxford, on 25th January 1969. Now we were completely free to marry, which we did in the Martha Street registry office on 13th August that year, aided and abetted by four friends.

The 'Wedding Feast' was held at the house with Bill and Nita (Katie's father and mother), sister Doreen and her husband Tom, who produced some rather unexpected musical instruments. The dinner went very well, apart from the fact that I thought the duck was actually a small turkey which I splashed all over the walls, and I almost brought the ceiling down with the opening of the champagne which was a gift from Tom and Doreen. It was just as well that we hadn't yet made a decision about the decor for the dining room.

But it was a happy wedding feast. I liked my new in-laws greatly.

*   *   *

Further happiness came my way from my dear 'china' Jack Milroy when he asked if I would be prepared to do the panto at the Pavilion in Glasgow. I said 'yes' and got right down to ideas, but owner Eric Popplewell said 'no'. But then he wasn't exactly likely to become a member of Mensa! We decided it would be helpful to try out some material, and with the help of Ross Bowie (a well known agent and friend), we appeared on a Friday and Saturday evening at the Barrfields Pavilion in Largs. People were literally hanging from the rafters. Ross was kicking himself that he hadn't booked the Pavilion for a full week.

Eric Popplewell changed his mind (!) when he saw the crush, and suggested that a Francie and Josie panto might be a good idea.

We were asked to do the late night cabaret at The Edinburgh Palladium during the Edinburgh Festival that year. The Palladium had been a variety theatre, but had been completely refurbished to create a very pleasant night club. The man who owned it at that time was something of a fan, but neither Jack nor I can remember his name—if we ever knew it. He was as happy as we were when he found he had to send for extra seats. Francie and Josie were really getting around.

In April 1970 we arrived in Ulster for a two-week visit. One week on tour and the second week at the Grove Theatre. We had forgotten that the Francie and Josie television series had covered the North of Ireland. One of the problems was that we had presumed that a pianist would have been employed, but, alas, I had to try to do the Act as well as play the piano. However, things were not too bad and we got through this strange tour.

In Ballymoney, a priest was conducting a fête for his parishioners. Later in the evening we found ourselves in a church hall, and the audience was reminiscent of the Barrfields, literally hanging from the roof. We were very happy that the show had gone so well, and the priest was happy to be our guest at the show at the Grove, especially when he found where the gin was.

On our way to our hotel with our wives, Mary and Katie, we realised we were starving and asked the cab driver to find us a fish-and-chip shop. We got there in time to see the shop close. We chapped on the window and a girl shook her head, but a second look told her who we were, and before we could say 'salt and vinegar' she had the fryers going again and suddenly the shop was filled with women in their nightgowns, and dressing-gowns, their hair plaited, and obviously just out of bed. They were so happy to see us and we spent a good hour signing autographs on anything the ladies could find.

One very large lady folded us in her arms and said: 'D'yese know this. Y'er the greatest thing since the pill and penicillin!'

We reckoned that was as good a reference as we could have wished.

Later that year we were awarded the Light Entertainment Award for 1969.

48

ERE I FORGET . . .

1971.

Katie's birthday was on 18th May, so I took her to Paris to celebrate. We had a delightful time looking at everything. The weather was superb, and we were standing on ground that belonged to another time altogether—like the Hotel des Invalides, where we had a look down into Napoleon's vault. What interested me was that Napoleon's catafalque was one floor lower, and anyone moving round the circular walkway to look down would find themselves bowing to the great man.

A clever ploy.

Katie was very keen to see Maxim's. She had always been very interested in food, and was a splendid cook herself. She ordered pea soup and I followed suit. 'Why not, M'sieur,' said the waiter, his nose in mid-air. The price of the pea soup was more than Katie's dress cost. I ordered chicken. Katie went for grilled trout, but they didn't do it that way, they only poached the fish—but if it was going to cost what we thought it would cost, Katie insisted on having it cooked the way she wanted it. Seven waiters appeared with a huge chicken, and I only wanted a portion. I think I could guess where the remainder of the chicken was going to go.

Katie was sitting with her back to a screen when it fell on her and the zip of her dress came apart. The head waiter was mortified.

'Madame, we have a seamstress upstairs who will repair this for you.'

'Don't go!' I shouted. 'It'll cost more than the dress!' I fixed the zip, and it didn't bother us until the coffee. We had enjoyed our meal, but then the zip went again. 'Stay where you are, darling,' I said. 'I will bring your cloak. We don't want to buy the place.' I brought the cloak and put it round Katie's shoulders. The clientèle were greatly impressed as we swept out of Maxim's—and the dress fell off!

*   *   *

I studied Spanish on my own for quite a long time, then Katie 'bought' me a tutor called Emilio Blanco. By 1978 I was fluent enough to have a conversation. I tested it on Pedro who looked after the swimming pool, and what had been a dour little man who would barely say 'hola' was suddenly telling me all about his family, and what they did in the off season. Katie got fed up with having to ask me the Spanish for the things she wanted to buy from the market. So she decided to take up the beautiful language too—even going as far as taking an A-level. She became so good that I didn't have to bother even trying, and I now leave her to do the talking.

When I was doing the talking, there was a nice moment one day. Katie and I frequented Katy's Bar, and I often had a chat with Margarita, an elderly little lady who helped in the bar. A Scot went into the bar to get a couple of pints for himself and his pal. He came out slightly dazed, having watched and listened to me, and said to his chum: 'Heh, Willie, ye're no' gonnae believe this, but there's a Spaniard in there the spitten image o' Rikki Fulton!'

*   *   *

301

1977.

Katie's father died in July. It is odd that so many spouses die just a short time after the death of their mates; it turned out to be true enough when in 1978 Katie and I were on a short tour with Noël Coward's *Blithe Spirit*, appearing in Perth Theatre and the King's in Glasgow. Katie's Mum was seriously unwell, but she kept insisting that, by hook or crook, she would see the play. 'I will be there,' she kept saying.

The production had a splendid scene design, which included a rather ancient clock that stood on the mantelpiece and had no hope of ever telling the time again. Sadly, Nita died before she could see the play, but on the opening night the clock, which had not made a sound for years, suddenly came to life and chimed the time with consummate accuracy.

Nita had indeed been with us.

* * *

1978.

This was the start of *Scotch & Wry*. From a short series called *The Scotched Earth Show*, Gordon Menzies walked up the stairs and declared he wanted to produce a series. When he had spoken to my agent, they spoke to me. 'You will of course want to read the script before coming to a decision,' they said. But I didn't have to. There was something about it that I liked. I was loving it. I had never heard of a producer/director—indeed I had never met anyone—who laughed so hard, huge tears running down Gordon's face as he directed the programmes. Gordon Menzies made the rehearsals and the filming very happy and uplifting. The series won heaven knows how many awards, and ran for some fifteen years.

It was wonderful the way *Scotch & Wry* aficionados had their favourite characters, as indeed I did. It was John Byrne who had been watching the rather boring *Late Call* on STV and wrote a very funny monologue involving 'The Prodigal Son'. It was then that Gordon and I decided that we should do what they call a 'God Spot' to finish off every episode, so I had to dream up dozens of different strange clerical characters, who included the very first of our 'fellows'.

There were two ministers whose characters our viewers seemed to enjoy so much that the two became one. The young man who was trying to cope with his very first appearance on the box and became completely blootered was, in fact, Rev. David Goodchild— not, as viewers came to believe, the Rev. I. M. Jolly. Mr. Jolly was created when I saw a pathetic, mournful creature who was taking his turn on STV's *Late Call*, and I realised this guy was suffering from deep depression and unable to help anyone, not even himself.

The first time I performed him, I had no idea he was going to be so funny. One of my major problems was the little man who sat right on the front row almost within a couple of feet of Mr. Jolly's chair. He was in convulsions, and in view of the character I was trying to create, I had to keep my face straight. No easy task, I can tell you. When Mr. Jolly had been completely established and was doing the New Year sermon every year, the little man somehow managed to grab his seat in the front every time, and would start roaring with laughter long before I had opened my mouth. Many times when Mr. Jolly was being particularly mournful I found it extremely difficult to keep my straight face.

After fifteen highly successful years of *Scotch & Wry*, I thought it was time to retire. I also felt that the writing talent available was diminishing rapidly. Colin Gilbert, however, took me to lunch one day in 1993 and laid out an idea. It was very tempting. It was a very good idea. The suggestion was that Mr. Jolly would have the whole show to himself. I gave it the necessary thought, and said 'yes'. As we parted to go to our cars, I called to Colin to say 'Good luck with *Para Handy*, and if ever you're stuck for an engineer, I'll take over.'

'I'll remember that,' he said.

The part of McPhail the engineer was to be played by Russell Hunter. A fine actor who would make a splendid McPhail. He had been in a previous production made many years before. Unfortunately, Russell took ill, and I got an S.O.S. phone call from Colin saying: 'Remember when we had lunch? You said . . . !'

So that was me unretired!

Two things about that series were particularly enjoyable. We were filming around the Tarbet area and were ensconced in the Stonefield Hotel. There was a fairly large contingent of SAGA people, and one of the ladies opined that one of the actors was the only one who brought his wife.

At this point, the driver of their bus had found a rather large photograph of myself and Kate in the *Herald* magazine, and held it for all to see, explaining that this was a very well known Scottish actor.

One lady worked it out: 'The one who brings his wife is actually a vicar, but does a little acting on the side.' The lady in question wanted to know what we were filming. She seemed impressed. 'Oh I think we might want to watch that. Will there be scenery?' Greg Fisher did a positively brilliant parody of what the lady was asking. 'Will there be scenery?' 'Oh, yes,' he assured her, 'there will be scenery and sacks of it.'

The midges at that time of year were unbearable and the moment they even came within a kilometre of me, I was eaten alive. They didn't seem to be interested in Katie's blood group— 'O-Neg' was the one they were after.

We were about to film around Loch Melfort and lived in a delightful hotel, not surprisingly called The Loch Melfort Hotel. Very much to be recommended, incidentally.

If you attempted to walk through a small forest and across a large field to get to the delightful beach, and dared to face up to the co-ordinated attack of the midges and horseflies, and you carried the O-Neg blood of your ancestors, it would be greatly to your detriment. It must have been to the absolute delight of those disgusting, silent and invisible creatures. I have suffered from their savagery for many years, and have often wondered what their purpose in the world could be, other than the discomfort of anyone who has a blood group which the ghastly wee things will enjoy.

It was the lovely Claire Neilson who came up with an antidote. We had been down to London to receive an award for *Scotch & Wry*. In the course of the dinner, she told me about a spray called 'Anti-Mate' which was used to make a bitch unattractive to dogs, but could be used to make midges and other delightful insects change their minds and go to the pub instead.

Admittedly Greg Fisher did not find the pungent, citron odour to his liking, but, to my surprise, with my clothes covered in Anti-Mate, I found myself able to walk through a huge cloud of midges while remaining totally ignored. Ever after I have carried an aerosol of Anti-Mate. Even when I have to make an appearance in my back garden, it appears to be the only thing which will send these loathsome things to somebody else's garden.

But we have allies! I'm told that 'the most important service to mankind performed by bats is undoubtedly the destruction of billions of insects every night throughout the world.' So I think we should cultivate bats the way we cultivate dogs, and maybe we could even ask them to increase their output—or should I say input?

*   *   *

1980.
We had just moved into our little London flat and were thankful

when the telephone had been installed—the only option I had until then was to nip down across Edgeware Road to the telephone box with enough suitable coins.

However, we found it strange when our phone, just installed, was ringing almost non-stop. Male voices asking for someone called Marilyn during the evenings.

To begin with we were reasonably polite, and then we started shouting that 'you've got the wrong bloody number!' And then we discovered what had happened. There is a magazine that advertises 'what is going on in London', and inside there is a smaller magazine called *The Adult Guide* which advertises nothing but massage parlours. What had happened was that the publishers had mistakenly printed our phone number. So we started taking the calls and asking what the caller would be looking for—blonde, brunette, what sort of age? We were having fun. I answered the phone each time and explained that this was a membership-only establishment and the fee would be £50 which would have to be paid at the following address. If that was acceptable I would give the caller the address, which I did. What happened after that was up to him. And we often wondered how the 'clients' felt when they discovered that it was the address of the Metropolitan Police Recruiting Office.

I so much enjoyed working with George Cole at Greenwich Theatre that year, in the play *Liberty Hall*. In it I played a double part, and made up so much 'comedy business' on the hoof that it drove the director out of what he claimed was his mind. Alan Dosser was his name, and brilliantly named he was, too. I didn't like him very much. He was hoping that Michael Codron would take the play into the West End. Michael Frayn, the author, had tried a rewrite but it was obviously not going to work. But he told me that he was loving the 'business' I was making up as I went along. He told me he came into the theatre every night to see what new 'business' I had produced.

One day, just before a matinée, Dosser took me to one side and told me off for getting laughs that weren't in the script. 'This is *my* production,' he said, 'and I want it back!' So I cut out every single thing I had put in, and the scene flopped, but Dosser had got *his* production back. Michael Codron walked out, then Dosser pleaded to have the 'comedy business' put back in.

Oddly, I just couldn't remember any of it.

*   *   *

1982.

I had the dubious privilege of playing in *Cinderella* in Plymouth with Harry Worth, Mark Winter, Sam Kelly and far too many others, all of them expecting their few minutes of glory. The show was an out-and-out disaster, but out of the blue I received a call from my agent, who at that time was Richard Stone.

Michael Apted, a much-admired director, was looking for someone to play a KGB officer in a film called *Gorky Park*, which was to star William Hurt, Lee Marvin, Michael Elphick and Ian Bannen. I had been recommended to Mr. Apted by a friend and colleague of his, who had directed a film called *Dollar Bottom*, in which Robert Urquhart and I played the leading roles. (Incidentally, the film won an Oscar for Best Short Film.)

I told my agent that I was thrilled. Less thrilling was the fact that I would have to travel up to London to meet Mr. Apted. Sundays were the only days on which I had any free time, what with this dreadful panto, but Kate insisted that I should go and speak with him.

On the train she gave me a copy of the book to read. I was horrified when I found the page on which the author, Martin Cruz Smith, described my character, Pribluda—as ape-like, with very long arms. The KGB man sounded grotesque, and at this point I stopped reading.

When I was shown into Mr. Apted's office, he would not look me in the eye, but straight away asked if I had read the book. In a situation like this, the director is king, and actors are expected to be obsequious. However, the man would not make eye contact, I had given up my precious Sunday to be here, and I was being asked to play an ape. I did not feel like bowing and scraping.

In any case, I could not pretend to have read the book, so I said: 'No. Tell me about it.'

This he did, but still he did not look me in the eye. I said no more until the end of the interview, when he asked if I had any questions.

'Yes,' I replied. 'Do you want me in the film or don't you?'

It turned out he was quite keen, and he suggested that he should send me a script.

I read the script when it arrived, and called Mr. Apted to tell him that I thought Pribluda's character was underdeveloped. He amazed me by asking if he could come down to Plymouth the following day to discuss the matter. (It is almost unheard of for a director to go and see an actor!)

He was terribly hungry when he arrived, so Kate made him a meal while I explained what I meant about the character. The upshot of our conversation was that Dennis Potter, who had written the script, had to do a considerable amount of rewriting. He was clearly miffed about this. He was also seriously lacking in charm—I discovered that in conversations he would try to wind people up deliberately.

Filming began in Helsinki the following year, and Kate came with me, the only wife there except for Ian Bannen's wife, Marilyn. Kate and I stayed in the Intercontinental Hotel, and I was given three overcoats—one for wearing, one for the moment when Pribluda is shot, and a spare in case we had to retake. I also received a mink hat and a gorgeous full-length sheepskin—which to my dismay the producer took afterwards!

We worked all through the night on the first scene, as it kept snowing quite heavily, and this played havoc with the filming. I got back to the hotel at about 7 a.m., to find that Katie had had to pay £50 for a bottle of gin, so that we could keep to our routine of having what at a more reasonable hour I would have called a *night*cap.

Lee Marvin and I were given titled chairs to sit on. We got on famously, and used to watch William Hurt preparing himself for filming. He would go off into a field and perform a series of strange antics, which he described as 'putting my head together'. I asked Lee what he thought of this idea. He replied that he did not approve of putting his head together in a field. 'Just get on your mark and remember your lines.'

We had been filming my 'final' scene in a large snow-covered field, and when we returned there the next day to resume filming, all the snow had vanished. But film-makers do not lack ingenuity—the fire brigade were called, and they sprayed foam over the entire field. Luckily I got my part right first time, so there was no need for messy retakes!

Being shot is a strange experience. In order to co-ordinate the supposed impact of the bullet with falling down, I had in fact to 'shoot' myself—by pressing a button which set off a small explosion. This blew a hole in my coat from the inside outwards, but on film the effect is quite convincing.

The animals depicted in the film are sables, but there were restrictions which meant that we had to use pine martens. This was fine until the scene at the end of the film where the animals are released from their cage. Our pine martens found the cage rather comfortable, and had begun nesting, so when the cage door was opened they stayed put. Once again, film-makers' ingenuity came to the rescue, and the animals were 'encouraged' to leave.

Katie was told later by one of the promotional people that Michael Apted's keenness to have me in the film was due to the fact that he thought I had the cruelest eyes he had ever come across. Perhaps audiences did not see me in quite the same light— at a preview of the film in Edinburgh, the minute Pribluda appeared on screen the entire cinema burst out laughing, before giving a round of applause!

*   *   *

1984.

Jack and I were playing King (Jack) and Queen (me) in *Sleeping Beauty* at the King's in Edinburgh.

As he sat in the car, he was obviously in some discomfort. But like many people, we put it down to indigestion. That was a Saturday, with a matinée and an evening performance to deal with. Jack did seem to be a little better later, and all would be well, since he would have the benefit of a rest during the weekend, if you could call a single day a 'weekend rest'.

By Monday he was in trouble, and was taken into hospital. He was very fortunate to find himself in the hands of a neighbour of mine, Henry Dargie, a heart specialist whom I knew very well.

We had to find someone who would be able to take over the part at a moment's notice. Our dear friend Walter Carr took over Jack's part, and was positively brilliant. He had had no time to learn the script properly, but what he didn't know, he made up. A man after my own heart.

Jack kept asking for me, and as soon as I arrived back in Glasgow, I was at his bedside. After a brief chat he seemed to be coping so I left him to rest. Later as luck would have it, he had a visit from Greg Fisher, also on his way home. It was while he was with Jack that the major attack hit him.

Mary, Jack's wife, had also succumbed to an illness and had been taken to the Western Infirmary. But happily these two were tough enough to brave the storm. Henry Dargie saw to that. Henry told me more than once that he enjoyed the times when Jack came along for a check-up, which was not so much a check-up, as a comedy act. I have never talked to Jack when he didn't have a funny story to tell.

In February of that year, my agent was very anxious to have me seen in the West End. I was still concentrating on the panto and with so many things on my mind, I nodded my head. I would be playing second lead to David Jason whom I admired so very much which was a plus. Maybe that was why I nodded my head.

When *Sleeping Beauty* was over, Kate and I were able to give the West End offer a lot of thought. It was then we realised what it would mean. We would have to find a place to live in London, since I would have to be prepared for a run of several months. Kate and I had already been through that when I was working in Greenwich in 1980. I have never liked London, though if it had looked like a smash hit it might have tempted me, but even the title (*Look no Hans*) was truly pathetic, and when I had read through the play, I thought it even worse.

As it happened my so-called agent had already sealed a contract with Michael Codron. However, my instructions to the agency were to forget it. I was not interested! I had no faith in the play, and although there was a bit of an argument about the situation, I think Michael Codron understood, perhaps from his experience at Greenwich.

Incidentally, as I thought, the play flopped, and flopped badly.

*　　　*　　　*

1985.

Denise Coffey and I began the task of translating and adapting that delightful play *Le Bourgeois Gentilhomme* by Molière which was renamed *A Wee Touch o' Class* by Frank Dunlop, the Edinburgh Festival director. This brilliant partnership worked like a dream.

Denise translated it into English, and I did the adaptation. It proved to be an outstanding success. We had the first reading in Perth under the direction of the late, wonderful Joan Knight.

I noticed that Clem Ashby was a little shaky, but then it had been some time since he had done a play, and his first appearance was a dreadful mess. He was unable to remember any of his lines, though admittedly they were a bit difficult to cope with. I arranged that we would make a book for him which would allow him to read his lines, and with this in his hand he was happy and comfortable.

It was first performed at Perth Theatre for a couple of weeks, and then presented at the Edinburgh Festival in the Church Hill Theatre for one week. But so great was the crush for tickets, that Frank Dunlop sent us off into the Leith Theatre for the last two weeks. He then asked us to repeat the play for the full run of the 1986 Festival. Clem had had a very rough time since his contract with STV had come to an end, but I had been able to offer him *A Wee Touch o' Class* in Perth and at the 1985 Edinburgh Festival, plus another couple of weeks in Perth because of some changes in the cast before opening in Glasgow King's with *The Play*. Then came *A Wee Touch* for the whole of the 1986 Festival running into a tour including Aberdeen, Arbroath, Kirkcaldy, Perth again and ending in Kilmarnock. He also got a good part in the 1987/8 *Cinderella*— my last panto.

We finished our run of *A Wee Touch* in Glasgow, and were due to open at the Edinburgh Festival on the following Monday. Clem was very relaxed and looking forward to a happy weekend. What was so very sad was that when I said 'goodnight' to him and asked him how he was feeling, he said: 'You know, mate, I feel as if I've become a member of the human race again!'

It was the last thing he would ever say to me.

Clem lived alone in a very large, very untidy room in Cleveden Drive. His life, and he himself, came first. His requirements were food, sex and whisky. I can't explain the haunting apprehension each time I arranged to call for him, but I always relaxed when I saw him coming out of the front door. But on Monday 11th August when I rang the bell there was no response. The curtains were still shut and the lights still on.

Fortunately the lady who was presumably the housekeeper could open Clem's door, and I went in. I remember standing on the tiny staircase peering all over the room—I couldn't see him because of the disarray. When I did see him I touched him and it was pretty obvious that he was very dead. He must have fallen flat on his face, and for a moment I thought perhaps he had been assaulted, but it became obvious that he had had a heart attack, tried to grasp the small water-heating radiator and pulled it to the floor as he fell. I asked the housekeeper to call the police just to make sure. I left the rest to them.

Kate and I had to get to Edinburgh and give everyone the sad news, and in the true spirit of the performer we had to ensure that the show would go on. I cut the whole scene in which Clem had played the Professor. And I kept it that way. It was Clem's voice that was his greatest asset, and a great many women found it sexually attractive. I have no way of knowing, but I would be inclined to think that he had had one helluva Saturday night! It's not a bad way to go.

*   *   *

1987.

I had my own unexpected health problem. It was a simple straightforward, almost everyday, surgical operation just eleven days beyond my birthday. They had discovered a polyp, a small, usually benign growth. At least it wasn't life-threatening, although the loss of blood was rather worrying.

It was a strange experience in the intensive care unit. When I was awake I noticed that the lights were kept very low and all I could see was a white angel. I was anything but unhappy as I lay there with nothing whatsoever to think about or worry about.

Katie was, of course, constantly by my bedside, sometimes until the early hours. I heard her crying and I wondered what had upset her. It was a massive haemorrhage which was causing all the panic. Nevertheless I survived, and when I was eventually taken back to my room I couldn't help but remember a strange little poem I once knew:

> Oh Death, How long have I anticipated thee,
> And wondered in what form thou wouldst present thyself to me.
> And where. In thoroughfare or glade,
> And if looking on thy face would feel afraid.
> But now I lie awaiting that first touch,
> That tells me death and darkness soon approach,
> I'm ready. Stay calm, my heart. Show him not fear.
> Why bless my soul, He's been and gone. And I'm still HERE!

I was very weak, but the thing to do was clearly take a holiday close to home. We spent a week in Kinlochard and then we headed for Ayr. I could scarcely walk, but somehow I had to get myself in shape for what was going to be my last panto. This was *Cinderella*, and I was working with my dear friend Wally Carr. I had more than a performance to think about since, as usual, I had to write the script and direct the show. It was an amazing nine days we had in Ayr. Every day I walked along the beach and took in that wonderful sea air. By the time I got home and down to work I was as fit as a fiddle.

Happily, that final panto was a huge success—and needless to say, my plans for retirement didn't quite come off. There are many people in showbusiness who have found it difficult to quit, and I was no exception. I was asked to play the Lord Chamberlain in *Iolanthe*. I was astonished to see the cost of production of an opera requiring some six weeks rehearsal for a ten-day season, when our pantomimes were ready to go in two weeks. But that was no concern of mine.

And still the bug was there. I was still smitten. So one Sunday Kate and I took our friend, Billy Differ, to lunch. He was then the manager of the Glasgow King's Theatre, and I asked him what he would say if I told him that I was thinking of writing a new show for Francie and Josie. He did the most splendid pratfall. There and then we arranged dates, and once again I slaved over a hot computer and received a series of postcards from Jack Milroy Esquire, each one saying: 'Keep at it, China. Weather excellent. Wish you were here!'

*   *   *

A message from Francie and Josie (Dictatit by Josie and writ doon by Francie who owns the pincil):

And welcum to wur latest brand new final farewell concert. Forbye that we do not wish youse to be under any dissolusionment, we are taking this opperchancity to confirm that this will absolutely definitely be wur very last and final appearance.

Until the next wan.

Francie and me is delightful to pervade the King's Theatre wunct again. After all who could fail to be infectit by the almosferics of this great institushin, the origins of what go back beyond the midst of ambiguity, and which so many backward performers has used as a breeding ground for to become much loved nonentities not to say legionaires in their own lifetime like wurselves. Francie and me always obtain a thrill of pressure as we lissen for wur signature tune and hear wunct again that exstatic and tumulous welcome as the musical director raises his stick.

Of course we always get a good clap as well.

Many of youse will no dowt experience a serious knee tremble as we present wur furst exit before you for we have

perspired thegether to make a pair of spectacles of wurselves by foisting upon a highly expectorent public an
outstanding shower of incredible nonenties, all of who has
been steeped in the rancid legend of showbusiness since
early puerility right up to the age of adultery. With their
unbridled talent, truss and support, it will be wur ernestist
endevir for to present before your very eyes a production
which for sheer hypocrisy and slite-of-hand will live forever in the annuals of all maternity.

Eyes will bulge and perspiration will roll as wur residen-
tial dancers and singers cavort before youse. These dancers
is haun-picked (an we know whose haun it wis!) for their
beatitude, stamina and acute ableness for to move quick.
(Something that Francie and me has teached them personally!) These goddesses of nubileness wear costumes that
cost as much as £750 a square yard, which seems a terrible
waste of dosh seein' as how they never wear more than a
fiver's worth. We must pay tribute to wur producer, Jamie
Phillips, who sows the costumes by haun—sometimes while
the burd is in it. Also our director and corryographer (so
called because he is corry-fistet), Dougie Squires. Dougie is
a most popular and skilful opponent of The Dancin' seein'
as how he wis the winner of the Fandango Competishun at
the Drumchapel Arts Festival in 1937. Dougie has offen
been compared to Gene Kelly—mainly because he wis a
dancer as well.

Yours faithfully,
    Francie and Josie.

And that was our 'Nineteenth Final Farewell!' One of the
funniest things I remember Jack saying was when he was my
guest at the Saints and Sinners during my chairmanship. We were
gorging ourselves with *filet de boeuf en croute*. When I went over to
his table and asked how he was enjoying the meal he was enthusiastic about the dinner. 'See this, Rikki,' he said. 'It's the best
bridie Ah've ever tasted!'

And it was also my time to retire. Again!

*　　　*　　　*

One of the joys of our home is the back garden. Although we are in the heart of Glasgow's West End, the back garden is so quiet you could believe you were miles into the countryside. It is also completely enclosed and we can't be overlooked.

On a very hot day in the summer of 1982, Kate and I had stripped off and were enjoying the cool of the grass, the warmth of the sun, and each other! Suddenly the silence was shattered by the roar of a helicopter which, flying so low over us, looked as if it was going to land on the roof. *This was the Pope on his way to Bellahouston Park!* If he had looked down, he might have been very embarrassed.

It always seems to be Katie who plans the celebrations of our various anniversaries and birthdays, so on my seventieth birthday (and my third retirement at least), and as she had always wanted to visit Rome, nothing would do but that we would spend that special time in the Eternal City. We stayed at a lovely hotel right at the top of the Spanish Steps next door to where Keats had lived, and we had the holiday of a lifetime.

I had been there before, so I was able to point out a few of the sights, such as the Coliseum, the baths, El Duce's window, the Pantheon. Katie reckoned that surrounded by thousands of years of history, seventy would seem positively childlike.

Also it was an opportunity for Katie to make contact with a friend in Rome whom she hadn't seen for many years, and we spent a delightful afternoon with them, although I have to confess I hated the food. On top of that we received an invitation to lunch in the Scots College, courtesy of a close friend in Glasgow. Not that we are very religious, but it was a pleasure to see round and meet the Scots students, although I doubt if *Scotch & Wry* would be on their minds. But we were surprised to discover that we were treated to seats in the reserved area in St. Peter's Square where His Holiness the Pope gave his addresses in an amazing number of languages. We were surprised to find ourselves in the front row, incredibly close to the throne, and as the Pope appeared I could feel Katie sliding down in her seat as she hissed: 'D'you think he'll recognise us?'

Certainly the flush on two faces in the front row was not due to the Italian sun!

*   *   *

1999.

A show was produced to celebrate my fifty years with the BBC, and a tribute programme was broadcast on 15th April 1999 to celebrate my seventy-fifth birthday.

What more could a pro want? I have worked in some truly wonderful shows with some truly wonderful performers who have given me the pleasure and privilege of their friendship. On the night the tribute was transmitted, Katie had organised a party for the gang. Gregor Fisher and his wife Victoria; Colin Gilbert, the man who created the BBC Comedy Unit, was there with his wife Joanna; Jack Webster of the *Herald* and Ayliffe; Jack Milroy and Mary Lee; Philip Differ and his wife Anne; Billy Differ, who is now Cameron Mackintosh's right-hand man; Ron Bain, who has guided me through so many television productions, and who was responsible for the tribute programme, was there with his wife Jenni; Jim Preacher, who is the BBC Contracts Manager and has helped me out of a contractual hole many times, and his wife Caroline.

These were truly showbusiness people, but we also had some of our closest friends there, and the mix was superb. Katie and I were so sorry that Donald Dewar and Helen Liddell could not be with us because of the hustings, having been so kind in their delightful tribute. When the time came we all squatted on the floor and watched the programme. It was an enormously happy, enjoyable evening.

I was in bits!

*   *   *

I feel I have justified the work I have done. I found my way to the other side of the curtain and have been there now for some sixty years, and as I stroll through the long grass of my memories I can only say that it has been a long and happy life and career. And I find that, at this age, time seems to rush past as if there was some great event taking place, and all I can ask is: '*Is it that time already?*'

Finally, I would just like you to know that my greatest success in every way—I owe to Aberdeen! And that was when I married my only true love, Kate Matheson Fulton!

AWARDS

1. PERSONALITY OF THE YEAR (TRICS)—1963

2. THEATRE BEST LIGHT ENTERTAINMENT AWARD (STV)—1969

3. TELEVISION PERSONALITY OF THE YEAR (TRICS)—1979

4. TOP AWARD (TRICS): *SCOTCH & WRY*—1985

5. TOP PLATINUM ENTERTAINMENT AWARD (BBC VIDEO)—1987

6. PRESIDENT'S AWARD FOR MOST NOTABLE CONTRIBUTION
    TO BROADCASTING (TRICS)—1987

7. TOP PLATINUM PERFORMANCE AWARD (BBC):
    SCOTCH & WRY—1989

8. O.B.E.—1992

9. LIFETIME ACHIEVEMENT AWARD (BAFTA)—1993

10. DOCTOR OF LETTERS DEGREE CONFERRED BY THE UNIVERSITY
    OF STRATHCLYDE—1994

11. DOCTOR OF ARTS DEGREE CONFERRED BY THE UNIVERSITY OF
    ABERTAY, DUNDEE—1995

12. HONOURED BY BBC SCOTLAND BROADCASTING COUNCIL FOR FIFTY
    YEARS WITH THE BBC—1997

INDEX